TRENCH TALK

WORDS OF THE FIRST WORLD WAR

PETER DOYLE & JULIAN WALKER

For
Arthur Doyle (d.1962)
Frederick Walker (d. 1961)
William Black (d. 1915) and
Leonard Lightfoot (d. 1917)

First published 2012
by Spellmount, an imprint of

The History Press
The Mill, Brimscombe Port
Stroud, Gloucestershire, GL5 2QG
www.thehistorypress.co.uk

British Library Cataloguing in Publication Data.
A catalogue record for this book is available from the British Library.

ISBN 978 0 7524 7154 9

Typesetting and origination by The History Press
Printed in Great Britain
Manufacturing managed by Jellyfish Print Solutions Ltd

CONTENTS

PREFACE

The First World War – or the Great War as it was known to the people who experienced it – largely directed the course of the twentieth century. Fought on three continents, the war saw 14 million killed and 34 million wounded, countless millions displaced and the ends and beginnings of several states. Its impact shaped the world we live in today, and the language of the trenches, the common speech of the participants, continues to live in the modern consciousness.

One of the enduring myths of the First World War is that the experience of the trenches was not talked about. Yet dozens of words entered or became familiar in the English language as a direct result of the soldiers' experiences. This book examines the first- and second-hand experience of the First World War and how it changed standard English, adding words that were in both slang and standard military use, and modifying the usage and connotations of existing words and phrases. Several words became associated specifically with the propaganda or official language of the war, some were adopted as a result of operations in parts of the world far from Flanders, and some had only a short life as part of English. In contextualising and tracing the history of what these words meant to the men in the trenches the book presents the effect the war had on the English language.

Peter Doyle
Julian Walker

Acknowledgements

We are grateful to the Imperial War Museum and to the copyright holders for access to the original diaries, papers and letters of: J. Bremner, B. Britland, W. Egington, W.G. Green, C.P. Harris, R.J. Hartley, J.T. Lawton, C.P. Harris, P.S.V. Rouse, R.I. Smith, R. Stockman, J. Underwood and K.S. Wyatt. We thank Brightsolid and the British Library for permission to quote from the British Newspaper Archive. We thank Andy Robertshaw and Paul Reed for their advice, and particularly to Paul for kindly supplying the 'Somme Knuts' and 'Bing Boys' photographs; all other images are our own, apart from that of Jack Johnson, which is from the Library of Congress. We are grateful to Jo de Vries for her enthusiastic support.

INTRODUCTION

The First World War marked a change in the relationship between the British public and the military, as for the first time a large sector of the public *became* the military, specifically the army. During this period the language of the army was a melting pot of slang, officialese, jargon, invention, adoption and swearing, from all parts of the British Isles and the British Empire, from other languages (including those of enemy countries), from all classes and occupations, with some of its technical terms dating back to the Medieval period. All this was condensed, mixed, confused and mispronounced and brought back to a country whose sense of the 'correct order of things' was collapsing.

Written communication during this period was of paramount importance – in 1913 a small town could expect up to twelve postal deliveries per day, and in 1917 19,000 mailbags crossed the Channel daily. The war was discussed, reported and commented on in letters, newspapers, postcards, pastiches of field service postcards, poems, songs, sketches, trench papers, novels, official documents and diaries. But since spoken English is not the same as written English, how can we get to the actual words spoken? With the passing of time the English spoken during the war, at the front and away from it, has become progressively less accessible.

Written words are always mediated by their context; the setting down of words proposes a reader, even if the reader is the person writing. The diaries used by soldiers during the war are circumscribed by the tiny amount of space allowed (and by the official dictum that diaries were forbidden, in case they should fall into enemy hands), or when exercise books were used for journals, the blank page was likely to create the desire to 'write well', to make a meaningful comment or aspire to a literary standard. The nature of education in Edwardian England proposed a certain style of letter-writing; even letters from prisoner-of-war camps maintain a formula of information about the weather, reassurances of the health of the writer, and inducements of optimism, like the sentiments buried within the carefully constructed official phases of the field service postcard, doing away with all necessity of original thought. Junior officers, fresh out of public schools, and Other Ranks (ORs) soldiers had been brought up to carefully limit the expression of their feelings, or to adopt formulaic postures of phlegmatic reticence. 'I must get. Cheero', writes a subaltern at the end of a letter quoted in *The Scotsman* in July 1916, while John Buchan quotes one of the Grenfell brothers as saying, 'I am bound to say I felt rather done' after a raid; terms for being killed included 'getting it', 'hopping it'; 'getting 'em' was understood as 'being afraid'. Clearly death, fear and having to attack could be made less real by avoiding giving them names. Fear at the Front had to be suppressed (often by creating witty variations of the phrase 'getting the wind up'), just as much as failure had to be hidden behind the euphemisms and false reporting which the press and the official bulletins served to the home audience. Diaries were written with the knowledge that they might be looked at later by loved ones, letters were sent by soldiers knowing that they would be examined by censors, and were written to reassure those at home, memoirs were composed for specific kinds of readers – to shock or to avoid shocking, with the desire either to not awaken old traumas or to do just that. Soldiers' memories recorded by interviews might be even more circumspect, the recording process inducing its own sense of performance, and the fear that the speaker might have to justify words he could not retract; and these would be in any case edited by the filtering and altering process of recall. Novels of the war, while holding no punches in describing the destruction of the body, avoid swearing, while shame or embarrassment mean that the body's involuntary reaction to fear is not discussed. The lack of a form of words other than the clinical or the literary to express the most extreme experiences of the front and the nature of the destruction of the body meant that for the most part a silence fell over the subject.

Against this there is the wit and invention of the concert party song and the trench newspaper, the clever banter of the catchphrase exchange, the survivor's forced indifference, the occasional slips into half-remembered phrases from literature or the Bible, the savagely altered music hall song, the outpouring of verse, the 'double-speak' of the official bulletin and the unfounded optimism of press-reporting, or the all-too-rarely recorded robustness of obscenity. 'Share this amongst you', shouts the soldier with comic-book callousness, tossing a bomb into a dug-out, while another soldier on a burial party slips into lyricism as he notes 'some seeming by their looks to have died very easy, others very hard'. It is as if the destructivity of the war had to be balanced by creativity in language.

But a study of the words of the war, though benefiting from a wealth of sources, can barely touch the core of the experience – the verbal witness of the destruction of the body as it happens. It is perhaps the inexpressibility of that core that makes the language of the period 1914–1918 so fascinating. It is as if the breakdown of language to adequately describe the physicality of the killing of so many thousands of young men is compensated for by a wealth of language for everything surrounding it. Both despite and because of the inexpressible pain and destruction, the Great War became a major phenomenon of verbal culture.

There are several small differences between the English of a hundred years ago and present English: parcels to a prisoner of war (PoW) 'land' rather than 'arrive', and he wishes he 'was at home to give you a lift with the kiddies'; 'I am going on fine', or even 'pulling on fine', is used in place of 'I am getting on fine'; a soldier in good health states he is 'knocking about' but asks for money from home as he is almost 'spent up'; a gunner gets the order to 'blarge off' (fire some shells) while noting that 'there is something coming off' (going to happen); successful gunners 'make good practice'; if there had not been confusion in defending a position 'the Germans would never have got on'; something not good enough was 'not up to snuff'; in November 1918 there is a 'socialistic outbreak' in Germany; the enemy's leaders are 'shot down'; boasting was 'swank'. No doubt some of these were individual or dialect expressions, but all are part of the constant change in the language. Military terms also changed in the first two decades of the century, not only because of technical developments; in 1909 trenches had 'banquettes' and 'bonnettes' to protect them from a 'cannonade', all of these words disappearing quickly at the beginning of the war.

The throwing together of so many people in situations of such extreme novelty inevitably had an effect on how people communicated, but also served to separate those who fought from those who did not. The inventiveness of the Tommies' use of language was a source of both amusement and friction, as those away from the fighting could not hope to understand the nuances of word and phrase that served as a bond for the soldiers, sailors, airmen, and supply and nursing staff.

The First World War was the first conflict in the modern era in which a literate British civilian army read newspapers in the theatre of conflict ('to know how the war was going', as one trench newspaper put it), and the soldiers saw themselves as both readers and subject. As well as their deeds and circumstances, their language was of interest to the press, and newspapers at all levels reflected this. The *Tamworth Herald*, 15 May 1915, stated that 'Active service slang [was] made up of an inextricable tangle of Indian, French, German, military slang and any other linguistic ingredient that comes within Tommies' hearing.' A spate of letters to the *Manchester Guardian* in August and September 1917 included one pointing to the words *mush* (guardroom), *muckin* (butter), *chukkaro* (youngster) and *mallum the bat* (understand) as examples of army slang from Hindi. The press was particularly interested in the use of nicknames by troops at the front, and the use of these inside inverted commas in newspapers shows the process of novelty expressions being introduced to the public: '"Coal boxes" and "Jack Johnsons" are the picturesque names given to these shells by the British soldier', wrote the *Daily Express* on 2 October 1914. The *Daily Mirror* on 19 November 1914 wrote under the headline 'Irrepressible Humour': 'Our troops, always cheerfully ready to treat the grimmest terrors light-heartedly, have coined another name for the German shells. This particular nickname is for the particular type of shell which makes a noise like a prolonged sigh. And so "Sighing Sarah" is the new title'. And on 12 July 1915 the same newspaper reported on the use of the term 'gaspipe cavalry', a term referring to the newly formed Motor Machine Gun Corps (MMGC), equipped with motorcycles.

Reacting to newly acquired information, newspapers at the time could not be expected to know which terms were in general use, and which were limited to a small group or area, or period of time, or even an individual. 'When they [the Guards] went "over the lid" as the slang phrase is for mounting the parapet for a charge ...' (the *Exeter and Plymouth Gazette*, 7 October 1916); 'Our present billet is a big house only 600 yards from "sandbag street" or the firing line; everything has a nickname out here' (Private P. Gilbert, Duke of Cornwall's Light Infantry, quoted in *The Cornishman*, 19 August 1915); neither of these terms, however, gained general acceptance. As the press was deliberately kept away from the Front, there was no way to check material and sources; the need to inform the readers at home meant an enthusiastic reporting of whatever information could be obtained. And some of the most inventive slang went entirely unreported until it was mentioned in memoirs years after the war – F.C. Hitchcock recorded that for the Leinster Regiment, 12in shells were known as 'The Roscrea Mail' after a local express train, no doubt from their sound and speed. However, a lot of the press interest was well-informed; the *Daily Mirror*, 8 June 1916, under the headline 'Langwidge' reported that while there were 'two dialects that are beyond the comprehension of the civilian' – army and navy slang – the navy could understand army slang, but not vice versa (perhaps deliberately, given that 'soldier' was navy slang for an inferior sailor in the 'Senior Service').

Tension between the home press and its readers in the trenches arose when civilian writers encroached on the territory of offering suggestions with regard to soldiers' language, rather than just observing and documenting it. This clearly was a case of threat to ownership. On 12 April 1915 the *5th Gloucesters Gazette* newspaper ran a brief article stating: 'Our esteemed contemporary – *The Cheltenham Chronicle* – is a little disappointed with the title of our paper, and suggests the more 'frightful' title – e.g. "The Asphyxiator". Surely the "Fifth GAZ-ette" is practically the same'. Behind the forgivable pun there is a clear implication about control. At the same time there was an awareness at the front that the words used there were being noted at home. 'How insidious is Canadian slang,' wrote the editor of *Listening Post*, the paper of the 7th Canadian Infantry Battalion on 10 July 1916: 'The leader writers of even the more conservative London dailies are characterising the present Allied push as "Som(m) e Offensive"'. Behind the simple joke there is some satisfaction at the power of being imitated, although this is tempered by the put-down that follows: 'Mercy Kamerad for the Atrocity'.

That a number of words that were specific to army life became part of common English was due not so much to newspaper interest, but because a huge civilian army had grown used to them, and retained their use after demobilisation. Thus 'crummy' and 'lousy', both to do with being infested with lice, became general terms of disgust; and according to Paul Fussell, 'souvenir' ousted 'keepsake', and terms such as 'sector', 'rank and file' and 'trenchcoat' quickly extended beyond the experience of Flanders. 'Cushy' and 'bumf' are still in use, while deviant machinery still experiences a 'mad minute.'

Less well known is the way terms crossed over no-man's-land. Germans and British used the same terms for the German stick-grenade – a potato-masher – both sides had a shell called a 'Black Maria', and both sides called an aeroplane a 'Taube'. The Germans had their own versions of French which developed in similar and divergent ways from the English adaptations, and the adoption into English of a few terms, like 'cashimbo', would seem to indicate the possibility of conversations about language between soldier and prisoner. Experiences common to European armies at the time – poor food and the logistics of transport – provide, not surprisingly, similar terms for poor quality butter or margarine: 'axlegrease' and '*wagenschmiere*' (wagongrease). The extended 'alternative abbreviations' of English, such as Rob All My Comrades (RAMC, Royal Army Medical Corps) or Rotten Fiddling About (RFA, Royal Field Artillery), had counterparts in the German '*Fährt Alles Kaput*' (Everything goes kaput) for FAK (*Freiwilliges Automobil Korps*, the Volunteer Automobile Corps), or '*Mord-gesellschaft Klub*' (Murder Company Club) for MGK (*Maschinen-Gewehr Kompagnie* or Machine-gun Company).

The commonality of language indicates a similarity of experience which goes some way to explain the rarely documented incidences of fraternisation, the more frequent 'live-and-let-live' situations, including shooting at attackers' legs rather than torsos, and the outrage at the killing of wounded soldiers by a retreating enemy. Even English and German officialese had corresponding terms, such as 'according to plan' and '*plängemass*', both of which were used euphemistically to gloss over the confusion of retreat. The separation of Germans into a distinct 'race', expressed at home, was heard less at the front, where attitudes towards the enemy included respect for humane behaviour towards wounded soldiers.

Alongside the traditional British incompetence with foreign languages, schoolboy French was found to be especially useless; C.W. Langley found himself with little opportunity to talk about '*La plume de ma tant*'. In this situation an inspired Franglais took over, with such terms as 'narpoo', 'hissy' and 'sanfaryan'. Puns were aimed at German self-assurance: a notice hung on the barbed wire with the words *Gott Mitt Uns* ('God with us', the motto on German belt-buckles) provoked the scribbled reply 'Don't Swank! We've got mittens too!' (in *Battery Flashes*, C.W. Langley, 1916).

On 31 March 1915 *The Times* ran a short article beginning: 'The French language is being enriched by a number of words which are coming into current use by way of the trenches. The soldiers bring them into vogue, and the public gets to know them from the letters which are published in the newspapers and joyfully adopts them.' The list included *poilu*, *boche* and *marmite* (a saucepan, adapted to mean a 'heavy shell'). The *Manchester Guardian*, 9 March 1918, reported on some German army slang, not giving the German terms, but stating that the identity tag was known as 'ticket to Heaven', the bayonet as 'cheese knife', and the rifle as 'betrothed'. In March 1919, with hostilities ended, *The Times* felt able to turn a patronisingly appreciative eye on German trench slang, noting that 'one interesting feature is … that all of it is indigenous – Teutonic to the last syllable; it is characteristic of the race that it should be so.'

While many words entered mainstream English via the exposure of enlisted and conscripted men to the language of the Regular Army, other terms faded; from Hindi the words 'pukka' and 'chit' survived demobilisation, while 'barrow wallah' and 'choter wallah' (big and small man or thing, respectively) did not. French military terms, such as 'personnel' and 'matériel', soon lost their inverted commas, while the 'moral' of the troops was definitively replaced by 'morale'.

On occasion newspapers went into details regarding the variants of troops' slang. On 17 August 1915 the *Daily Mirror* ran an article on Lord Kitchener: 'The new armies adore him and there is not a soldier in the ranks who does not speak of him as "Kitch" or "Our Kitchy". The synonym "K of K" is unknown to Army speech'. 'Old K of K' was exactly the term used by C.W. Langley in *Battery Flashes* in 1916. Civilians attempted to join in: *Our Kitch* was a song composed by Mrs Frances Browne ('of Pearments House, Balcombe, Surrey'). The *Daily Mirror* helpfully pointed out in its report that 'Our Kitch' was 'Tommy's nickname for Lord Kitchener'; this has not been found in soldiers' diaries – 'Lord K' was more likely. There were naturally divergent views on these points: the *Manchester Courier and Lancashire General Advertiser*, 28 August 1915, stated that 'the man in the street has never, so far as I know, had a nickname for Lord Kitchener, though he invariably spoke of Lord Roberts as "Bobs"'.

Given that the press was deliberately kept away from the frontline, or only given access to sanitised or safe areas, it was inevitable that the public's need to know, especially the need to know why their men were going and not coming back, would drive the embellishment of what few facts were obtainable, with most of these coming from letters or reports from wounded soldiers. Soldiers at the front often did not recognise the public's view of the war derived from newspapers' reporting: the *Morning Rire*, the trench newspaper of the 2nd Irish Guards, carried an article in its second issue entitled 'What We Learnt in London':

That all the trenches are concreted.
That most of the dug-outs have pianos.
That there are *no* Hun snipers.
That all the publishers want to take 2nd Lieutenant Lynch into
    partnership.

The last entry here perhaps alludes to the role of literature in the culture of the war (assuming Lynch was an aspiring writer), a subject that
has been extensively studied, with Paul Fussell's *The Great War and
Modern Memory* (1975) providing a dominant framework for understanding the war through its poetry and prose which has lasted for
two generations.

  With the extraordinary outpouring of work by Sassoon, Graves,
Owen, Thomas, Sorley, Gurney, Rosenberg, Brooke and others,
and with the involvement of major novelists including Buchan,
Chesterton, Conan Doyle, Belloc, Galsworthy, Wells, and Bennett in
the propaganda campaign, it is inevitable that the conflict should have
come to be seen as a 'literary war'. Certainly the 'new armies' comprised large numbers of literate middle-class men, many educated in
grammar schools, so that reading among frontline troops was for the
first time a common and acceptable activity. Buchan's fast-moving
(both in terms of plot and location) Richard Hannay novels were
particularly popular with the troops; *Newnes' Trench Library*, clearly
aimed at soldiers, published works by William Le Queux, H. de Vere
Stacpoole and Edgar Wallace; and Rudyard Kipling was a national
hero. Soldiers were no strangers to writing: the Expeditionary Force
Canteens and the huts of the Church Army, YMCA and other charitable organisations offered notebooks, pens, ink and pencils. But
theirs was also a world without radio or sound movies, so that public
entertainment was still largely based on the performed word. Some
1,500 concert party groups operated in the rest areas, new song lyrics
were sent from Britain to the 'gaffs' (temporary theatres – though the
word also meant a 'raid'), making up alternative lyrics was a common
pastime, and trench papers were happy to publish poems and lyrics
ranging from the sentimental to the robust. As well as readers, the
soldiers were performers and makers too, and repeated references
in trench papers indicate the importance of concert party perfor-
mances. The *5th Gloucesters Gazette* in September 1915 reported on
a performance at 'the Empire', Plugstreet (Ploegsteert, Belgium); Item
No.9, '"When Little Willie Comes" – Kay and Kayenne's performance

went off without a jamb, and many of the audience were seen to wipe the tears from their eyes with 4 by 2.' Between stints of guard duty at Steenwerck on 15 September 1918, Private (Pte) Fred Walker wrote to his best girl Ada: 'With regard to the songs there is no need to hurry with them as we shall not be able to have any concerts until we get in somewhat different surroundings to these.'

Certainly there was no shortage of invention among the troops. Australian use of language was noted for its robust cycnicism, German for its gallows humour, while British trench newspapers such as *The Wipers Times* are still genuinely witty, funny and inventive – the *5th Gloucesters Gazette*, 5 May 1915, contains a brief notice for a 'House property – airy Chateau in Northern France ... suitable to Strike Leader or Conchologist desirous of studying shells of every variety'. This conveys the resentment towards those seen as obstructing the war effort in a play on the word 'conch/conscientious objector'. The third issue of *The Morning Rire*, the paper of the 2nd Irish Guards, offered advertisements for 'Brigardine – look like a brigadier for two pence'.

The satirical adapting of military terms was often tolerated by the authorities, aware that an amount of slack which allowed the soldier to 'grouse' (complain) was good for morale. Answer and reply at a meeting between groups of marching soldiers (one side singing 'Bugger' and the other side singing 'The Worcestershires' to the tune of *Colonel Bogie*, quoted by Brophy) echoed the challenge and response of the sentry; trench papers readily printed alphabets and explanations of abbreviations mocking various parts of the army.

During the last year of the war the various specialised slangs in use at the front merged, and this was particularly the case as the slang of ORs was taken up by junior officers and nursing staff. 'The mixings of the classes is more potent than the mixing of the nations', wrote Eric Partridge in *Words, Words, Words* (1931); gradually the quotation marks that had appeared round 'coal boxes' or 'Jack Johnsons' had been abandoned as these terms became commonly recognised, but perhaps there was a conscious or subconscious association with the troops in adopting some of their terms. Helen Z. Smith in her semiautobiographical novel *Not So Quiet ...* (1930) notes how her posh mother had picked up soldiers' terms in leafy Wimbledon: '"What will Mrs Evans-Mawnington say ... to my daughter taking a cushy job in England?" How well up in war-slang is Mother'. And in August 1918 the *Manchester Guardian*, reporting on how Robert Harcourt's 'Report on the Luxury Tax', presented in Parliament, had included the

expressions 'a tidy bit of money in it', 'be a sport about it', 'all that twad-
dle', 'wangle it', 'wads of it' and 'we should hate not to have said it first',
commented that it was 'remarkable for the amount of slang – or at
least that experimental and tentative English which borders on slang.'
Eric Partridge noticed change happening similarly in French, where
urban slang was being taken up by soldiers from the countryside. In
all three armies, he observed, the influence of the Regular Army on
slang was less than that of the civilian city. A writer to *The Times* in
January 1915 proposed that 'the majority of colloquialisms used by
soldiers have a Cockney origin'. All slangs harked back to civilian life,
Partridge proposed, and all 'tended to materialise the spiritual and
brutalise the material'.

During the course of the war some new slang replaced old army
slang – Franglais became more common in France and Belgium than
Anglicised Hindi or Arabic, and words derived from earlier conflicts
were lost as the experiences were overlaid: 'being Stellenbosched'
was replaced by 'dégommé' – being relieved of one's command –
which quickly developed into 'coming ungummed', or eventually
'coming unstuck'. But the ultimate test was the sound and feel of the
words, ensuring the survival of the earlier 'wallah', 'pukka', 'cushy',
'bint' and 'buckshee', as well as the newer 'napoo', 'sanfaryan' and
'Bombardier Fritz'.

There was by the end of the war a sense that something had been
created, that the English language had been changed and spread, and
that this should be noted. *The Cheltenham Looker-On*, 7 September
1917, stated that 'children in Belgium and France live in an atmo-
sphere of Tommy's slang ... Their parents use it. Their big French or
Belgian brothers on leave make use of some of the phrases.' And the
Derby Daily Telegraph, 23 October 1917, implied that respect should
be given to trench language as part of the nation's debt to its servicemen and women: 'Some of the expressions cited may strike the reader
as extravagant and even foolish, but the collector who proposes to
print a "War Vocabulary" must not be fastidious. He must deal with
Mr Atkins' phrases, comic and otherwise, just as he finds them.'

A WAR OF WORDS

Isolationist, and dependant upon its navy for defence, Britain had been aloof from European politics for decades. Though close links with Germany had been mooted in the early years of King Edward VII's reign, the King himself rejected the idea of a triple alliance of the three major European nations, turning instead to France with the *Entente Cordiale* of 1904. Although Kaiser Wilhelm II was a cousin of King George V, there was little in the way of family warmth expressed in his direction; instead, the British press was generally antagonistic towards Germany, depicting stereotypical representations of swaggering, sabre-rattling, Prussian militarists – stereotypes that became strongly entrenched. Suspicious of German intentions, the British Government took exception to the Kaiser's desire to build an effective navy, and pre-war there was much scare-mongering over possible German invasion plans and antagonism directed across the North Sea by the new British tabloid press. William Le Queux's fictional tale, *The Invasion of 1910* (1906), serialised in the *Daily Mail*, set the tone for a 'war of words', of propaganda and counter-propaganda intended to discredit the enemy and to sponsor recruitment.

The invasion of Belgium in August 1914, in contravention of the Treaty of London (1839) guaranteeing Belgian borders, led to an upsurge in condemnation of Germany, though before the war few people would have had knowledge of what became known as 'Plucky Little Belgium'. The invasion resulted in a focused propaganda campaign that ultimately saw the British Government sponsor an inquiry into 'Alleged German Outrages' in Belgium, under a former Ambassador to the United States, James Bryce. The Bryce Report would concentrate on the 'attrocities', and would help fuel further antagonism towards the Germans, which was intensified by the sinking of the ocean liner *Lusitania* in 1915.

Britain had long held on to its position as the only major European power not to depend upon conscription for its armed forces. The onset of war drew men to the colours, which peaked in August 1914, after the setbacks suffered by the British Expeditionary Force (BEF) at

Mons. Highly charged recruiting posters issued by the Parliamentary Recruiting Committee, and the actions of some women in handing out white feathers to those at home led to the pressure on the workforce.

SERBIA

The country where the first shots of the war were fired underwent a name change, as 'Servia' was felt to have negative connotations of servility, inappropriate for an ally. *The Times* used 'Servia' in August and September 1914, introducing 'Serbia' on 21 September; this soon became the dominant form in *The Times*, with 'Servia' occurring only eleven times in 1915 and five times in 1916.

PRUSSIA

In British eyes 'Prussia' came to mean the effective, soulless militarism that threatened to destroy European culture. The 'junkers' class, the old nobility of Prussia and eastern Germany, was particularly blamed for dominating military and international policy in the region, notably after the success of the war with Austria in 1865–66, while Prussian internal policy from this time included universal conscription and rigorous training of the army. The Franco-Prussian War of 1870–71 had left a lasting distrust and fear of what quickly came to be known as 'Prussian militarism' throughout Europe, but especially in France.

Thus 'Prussian' by 1914 was placed to take on all that was feared and abhorred in the German military. For the *Daily Express* 'Atrocity was part of "the war as the Prussian wages it"' (22 August 1914); the Kaiser was 'the Prussian drill-sergeant' (24 July 1915); and the German Army was supposed to have a 'Prussian Guard', consisting of 'giants' (31 August 1914). 'Prussian militarism', compared to Britain's 'basic peaceful decency', was supposedly the cause of the war; as late as November 1915 the *Depot Review* was stating in 'An Open Letter to the Kaiser' that 'It is the glory of Britain that she was not prepared for the war. It is the glory of Britain that she is preparing for war.'

There was, however, an awareness that 'Prussia' did not mean the same as 'Germany'; a German living in London was quoted in the *Daily Mirror*, 12 January 1915, as saying 'South Germany is not Prussianised. South Germany will always hate Prussia'.

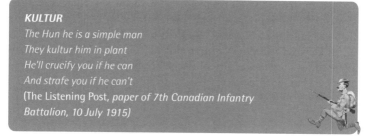

> I suddenly thought of Prussian Guardsmen, burly and brutal, and
> bursting bombs, and hand-to-hand struggles with cold steel.
> (Charles Edmonds (Lieutenant C. E. Carrington),
> A Subaltern's War, 1929)

KULTUR

'*Kultur*' was a concept of German, and particularly Prussian, supremacy in arts, customs, conventions, laws and other high ideals of western civilisation. Central to these ideals were the reliance upon discipline, obedience and military power, with an autocratic head – the Kaiser, Emperor of Germany and King of Prussia. With the influence of Prussian *Kultur* being felt in the opening campaigns of the war, it was not surprising that the Allied propagandists quickly siezed upon the idea, and depicted half-crazed, jack-booted madmen striding across Europe, all 'For Kultur'.

> **KULTUR**
> The Hun he is a simple man
> They kultur him in plant
> He'll crucify you if he can
> And strafe you if he can't
> (The Listening Post, paper of 7th Canadian Infantry
> Battalion, 10 July 1915)

'*Fur Kultur*': propaganda 'iron crosses' issued in Britain, and listing the names of Belgian cities featured in atrocity stories.

> K is for Kultur, Kronprinz also Kaiser, whose fatuous schemes
> have made every Bosche wiser.
> (C.M. Truman and J. Leslie, The Ypres Alphabet, c.1915)

> There are whole ranges of 'Minor Horrors of War'...The minor poets, the
> pamphlets of the professors, the people who write to the papers about
> 'Kultur'... the half hysterical ladies who offer white feathers to youths
> whose hearts are breaking because medical officer after medical
> officer has refused them the desire of their young lives to
> serve their county.
> (A.E. Shipley, The Minor Horrors of War, 1915)

STRAFE

To 'strafe', from the German for 'punish', was a much-repeated slogan throughout the war, and an example of a German phrase that was quickly assimilated into British speech, usually tinged with irony. Derived from the German slogan 'Gott Strafe England', it was adapted for a variety of situations. A 'strafe' in the frontline was an attack or bombardment; elsewhere 'to strafe' was to argue, chastise or generally punish.

'GOTT STRAFE ENGLAND!'
[God punish England!] German propaganda slogan, used on postage stamps, pin badges, even coal briquettes.

WANTED, Etc.
The name of a good maker-up of a 'Bucking-up' Pill to be taken before 'Strafe' time.

The Trench Times (Trench newspaper), May 1916

'*Gott Strafe England*' German propaganda postage stamps: the *Gott* pictured is clearly Nordic.

WE WILL BE HAPPY ONCE AGAIN NEVER MIND

Dear Auntie,
I write you just a few lines to say i'm still alive and well although we are having it very stiff for fritzi straffs us every morning for we are in a very dangerious plaice... but I was one of the lucky ones to escape. On Sunday he was quite busy as he straffed us both left and right but he did not kill so many he knocked the houses about. Some day we will be advancing to Blighty for leave has started again and I hope it the same as on this card the sun shining and the sea calm.
I remain yours Sincerely C.L. Landon

(Message on a silk postcard from a soldier, 4 April 1917)

'Der Tag'

Much in evidence in the early part of the war was the phrase 'Der Tag' – The Day, which was taken to mean the moment when Germany could finally get to grips with Britain following the Kaiser's build up of his armed forces.

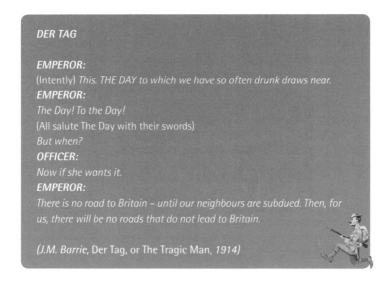

> **DER TAG**
>
> **EMPEROR:**
> (Intently) *This. THE DAY to which we have so often drunk draws near.*
> **EMPEROR:**
> *The Day! To the Day!*
> *(All salute The Day with their swords)*
> *But when?*
> **OFFICER:**
> *Now if she wants it.*
> **EMPEROR:**
> *There is no road to Britain – until our neighbours are subdued. Then, for us, there will be no roads that do not lead to Britain.*
>
> *(J.M. Barrie, Der Tag, or The Tragic Man, 1914)*

'Scrap of Paper'

The 'Scrap of Paper' was the Treaty of London that guaranteed the sovereignty of Belgium in 1839, and to which Prussia, Britain, France and other nations had put their signatures. The German disregard for this treaty was to be a cause célèbre that was used tirelessly in propaganda and recruitment posters in Britain during the early part of the war. The origin of the phrase relates to an interview between Sir E. Goschen, British Ambassador to Germany, and the German Chancellor, von Bethmann-Hollweg, in 1914: 'I found the Chancellor very agitated. His Excellency at once began a harangue, which lasted for about twenty minutes. He said that the steps taken by His Majesty's Government was terrible to a degree; just for a word – 'neutrality,' a word which in war time had so often been disregarded – just for a scrap of paper Great Britain was going to make war on a kindred nation who desired nothing better than to be friends with her.' The term 'Scrap of Paper' also became known as 'The Broken Pledge', and was widely used in propaganda.

THE KAISER: 'BIG WILLIE'

The German Kaiser, Wilhelm II, was widely blamed for the war and his posturing was mercilessly lampooned and parodied in the press. Belgian attitudes towards the Kaiser were typified by the actions of a group of refugees in Ilford, East London; they rounded off their Christmas in 1914 with a performance described to the *Ilford Guardian* as 'Making the funeral with the Kaiser from Germany'. The *Daily Express*, who had called the Kaiser 'The Mad Dog of Europe' on 4 August 1914, no doubt took some satisfaction in being able to report 'the Mad Dog Is Muzzled At Last' on 11 November 1918. In line with the customary distinction between trench language and the terms used by the home press, British soldiers hardly ever referred to him as anything but 'the kaiser'.

THE SAD EXPERIENCES OF BIG AND LITTLE WILLIE DURING THE FIRST 6 MONTHS of the GREAT WAR AS PORTRAYED BY W.K. HASELDEN IN THE DAILY MIRROR

THE FINE ART SOCIETY. LONDON 148, NEW BOND ST. CHATTO & WINDUS, III, ST MARTIN'S LANE 1/- NETT

'Big and Little Willie': the Kaiser and his son were lampooned mercilessly.

The difficulty that George V and Willhelm II were first cousins was neatly circumvented by the King, who said to F.D. Roosevelt on 29 July 1918, 'You know I have a number of relations in Germany, but I can tell you frankly that in all my life I have never seen a German gentleman.' The relationship beween the Kaiser and his son was the topic of much ridicule. Newspaper cartoons regularly referred to 'Big Willie' (the Kaiser) and 'Little Willie' (Crown Prince Willhelm), who was Commander of the German Fourth Army, and were merciless in portraying them as fools. In October, 'Littlest Willie' began to appear in cartoons – this was another Prince Willhelm, who was twelve years old by this stage. On 8 June 1916, the *Daily Mirror* reported that in America there was a nickname for the Kaiser – Hunzollern, a play on the Imperial family name of Hohenzollern.

Atrocity

In the early days of the war, anti-German feeling was stirred up by the stories of atrocities in Belgium, the extent of which is still debated. German soldiers believed there was a guerilla campaign against them, the Bryce Report on 'Alleged German Outrages' commissioned by the British Government has been largely discredited, and Belgian refugees were encouraged to talk about atrocities by the British press, eager for stories. But there is no question that there were summary shooting of civilians, that non-combatants Edith Cavell and Charles Fryatt were executed by the German authorities, and the university city of Louvain was largely destroyed. These and other events were to add to the patriotic fervour whipped up by the popular press – in September 1915 the *Daily Express* vilified Jerome K. Jerome and Kier Hardie for not believing atrocity stories. The word 'atrocity' had been around for some time; Ottoman suppression of uprisings in Bulgaria in the mid-1870s had been described as 'the Bulgarian atrocities'. The word 'atrocity' is one of the most sensitive verbal legacies of the war.

Horrors and Atrocities of the Great War

Including the Tragic Destruction of the *Lusitania*

A New Kind of Warfare
–Comprising–

The Desolation of Belgium, the Sacking of Louvain, the Shelling of Defenseless Cities, the Wanton Destruction of Cathedrals and Works of Art, the Horrors of Bomb Dropping

–vividly portraying–

The Grim Awfulness of this Greatest of all Wars Fought on Land and Sea, in the Air and Under the Waves, Leaving in its Wake a Dreadful Trail of Famine and Pestilence

Logan Marshall, Horrors and Atrocities of the Great War, *1915, US book*

'FRIGHTFULNESS'

On 27 August 1914 the American Ambassador to Belgium described the damage caused in Louvain by the invading German Army as 'perhaps the classic instance of *Schrecklichkeit* ... but it was not the worst.' The term *Schrecklichkeit*, translated as 'frightfulness' was, according to the lexicographer Ernest Weekley, 'officially applied to the intimidation of a neutral civilian population by outrage, massacre, and the destruction of historic buildings and artistic treasures'. 'Frightfulness' came to cover atrocities, any new weapons ('The Hun, with his terrible devices of frightfulness' noted by F.C. Hitchcock in his 1936 book *Stand To, A Diary of the Trenches*), as well as Germany's pursuance of the war (the *Daily Express* in December 1914 referred to 'pillage, arson, rape, butchery, treachery, and all the rest of German "frightfulness"'), and the 'inhuman hate [which] appears to possess these Prussian invaders whom terror drives' (*New York Times*, 1914). It embraced stories such as the report of a whale found stranded on the Belgian coast with a mine attached to its tail (the *Manchester Guardian*, March 1915). The effect of 'frightfulness' was 'ghastliness'; the loss of the *Lusitania* was an example of ghastliness according to the *Manchester Guardian*, 10 May 1915, as was 'the smell from dead bodies lying round' (*Stand To,* F.C. Hitchcock, 1937).

CHEERFULNESS

Frightfulness could be countered, however. In a cartoon, the *Daily Express* in January 1915 contrasted 'frightfulness' with 'fraternity' following the Christmas truces; 'fraternity' was violently stopped by 'Willie' (the Kaiser), with a caption stating: 'The Prussian lesson of war-frightfulness must be enforced by the Willie upon the fraternizing heads of the soldiers'. 'Frightfulness' had its uses in showing the value of its British opposite: in an advertisement for Sunlight Soap in July 1915, 'The Nation takes its cue from the Navy. Cheerfulness is uplifting. Frightfulness is a millstone round the neck. Cheerfulness will overcome Frightfulness. Cheerfulness at Sea – Cheerfulness on Land – Cheerfulness in trenches – Cheerfulness in Factory – Cheerfulness at War – Cheerfulness at WORK.'

SPECTACLES AND THE GERMAN SOLDIER

The German soldier was the target of much ridicule in the press. Some were shown as thuggish with protruding lower jaws and brush-like hair, others as weaklings with glasses. In *Battery Flashes* (1916) C.W. Langley imagines shooting a German soldier and hearing 'the tinkle of glass as his spectacles caved in!' The headline to a column in the *Daily Express*, 15 May 1916, is 'Through German Spectacles', rather than 'Through German Eyes', while as late as March 1918 the *Manchester Guardian* was saying 'there is a tendency, too, in this country to picture the German soldier as a fat stubbly individual with earnest spectacles …'.

HATE

The word 'hate' took on a specific meaning in 1914, which changed as it was taken up at the Front. Public opinion in both Britain and Germany was affronted by the actions of the enemy's governments: Britons were outraged at Germany's violation of Belgian neutrality, particularly when stories of atrocities arrived with Belgian refugees, while Germans were outraged at Britain's intervention. Reporting a mass meeting at Brighton in late August 1914, the *New York Times* quoted Herbert Samuel MP: 'Germany has violated the neutrality of Belgium saying "What care we for a scrap of paper – what care we for our pledged word when it no longer suits us to honour it?"' On the other hand, the *Irish Times* on 10 October 1914 carried a letter from an American of Irish descent, which stated: 'I have talked with many German-born – now American citizens – and their hatred of England is almost on the border of insanity'. In this environment the German Ernst Lissauer wrote the poem *Hassgesang gegen England* ('Hatred Against England', usually translated as 'The Hymn of Hate').

This text, with lines such as: 'We love as one, we hate as one, we have one foe and one alone – ENGLAND!', indicated a singularity of enmity, which curiously was not directed at the countries which Germany was actually invading: 'French and Russian, they matter not, a blow for a blow and a shot for a shot!'

A letter to the *New York Times*, 15 October 1914, pointed out that the German playwright Gerhart Hauptmann had declared that 'Germany has and has had no hatred against France, and that war was forced upon Germany as a measure of defense.' 'Who was it,' he asked, 'that did conspire to bring about this war? Who even whistled for the Mongolian, for the Jap, that he should come to bite viciously and in cowardly wise at Europe's heels? It is with great pain and bitterness that I pronounce the word "England"'.

The 'Chant of Hate', as it was known in America, sparked off a rivalry in the *New York Times*, blaming Germany for atrocities, England for the suppression of Ireland, and against war on the behalf of mothers. This 'hate', satirised by *Punch* in a cartoon which showed a German family sitting in their parlour concentrating on their 'minute of hate', was not perpetuated universally in Germany throughout the war. *The Scotsman* in August 1915 reported on stories from the German press: 'The *Berliner Tageblatt* quotes with approval from the *Kolnische Volkszeitung* a clergyman's letter deploring Lissauer's *Song of Hate*, and urging its removal from all books destined for schoolchildren'.

By this time, 'hate' was being used at the front for the practice of firing at each other above the parapet in the early morning – in order to remind each other of their existence – which was referred to as 'the usual morning hate', while it could also apply to any sharp artillery bombardment. *The Scotsman* quoted soldiers commenting on: 'the missiles of the German Hymn of Hate' in January 1917, and 'the enemy guns keep up a daily hate' in July 1918. This was extended to the officer commanding snipers being called 'Lord of the Hate Squad' in *Stand To* by F.C. Hitchcock; *The Scotsman*'s headline in August 1917 'Hun Hates Hun', which referred to a case where German aeroplanes bombed a hospital where German prisoners were being treated; and another instance where a German officer smashed his desk and bed with an axe before abandoning a command dugout 'as the final manifestation of hate'.

> *Thus did the mightiest War of Wars begin,*
> *The Old Earth swill'd in Blood, and War,*
> *and Sin,*
> *The best, and worst, in man was bared to*
> *Sight,*
> *And 'Hymns of Hate' were raised to God*
> *to win.*
> ('T.I.N. Opener', Rubaiyát of a Machonochie Ration, *1919)*

'WOMEN OF BRITAIN SAY GO!'

Men in civilian garb were assaulted on all sides by messages compelling them to join the nation's armed forces. Posters, postcards, newspapers – even popular songs – were deployed to maintain the recruitment drives of 1914–15, and supply the armies at the front with sufficient men. Images of women were used extensively: as the victims of war in Belgium, depicted on posters and in political cartoons; as the personification of nationhood, such as Britannia and Marianne; and in the role of sweethearts and mothers imploring their loved ones to join the fight. The Parliamentary Recruiting Committee poster by E.V. Kealey, 'Women of Britain say Go!', depicts two women and a child observing soldiers marching away. Another powerful use of images of women was in the 1914 Paul Ruben's 'women's recruiting' song, which also deployed the phrase 'Your King and Country Need You', with its verse 'Oh! We don't want to lose you, but we think you ought to go', a song which promised 'We shall cheer you, thank you, kiss you, when you come back again'. The same song was subject to merciless parody by the troops, the same lines being reworked as 'Oh! We hate you; and I'll boo you and hiss you if you sing it again!'

THE KING'S SHILLING

The King's Shilling was issued to a recruit on his enlistment into the army. The tradition of receiving a shilling as a signing on bounty began in the early eighteenth century. On joining, symbolically, each recruit was given his first day's pay – a shilling – the daily rate of the average Tommy until 1917. The issue of the King's Shilling, and the repeat of the oath of allegiance to the crown, would bind the Great War recruit to service for 'the duration'. As Pte Frederick Hodges of the Bedfordshire Regiment would later remember: 'we swore to defend with our lives King George V, and his heirs'. The full oath was: 'I …swear by Almighty God, that I will be faithful and bear true Allegiance to His Majesty King George the Fifth, His Heirs and Successors, and that I will, as in duty bound, honestly and faithfully defend His Majesty, His Heirs, and Successors, in Person, Crown and dignity against all enemies, and will observe and obey all orders of His Majesty, His Heirs and Successors, and of the Generals and Officers set over me. So help me God.'

'Your Country Needs You!' A variant of Alfred Leete's famous Kitchener recruiting poster.

'Your Country Needs You'

The Parliamentary Recruiting Committee was an all-party group that employed the local infrastructure of the political parties to distribute posters and circulars to those areas most likely to produce recruits. Typically, recruiting posters played on the individual's sense of duty and wider responsibilities. Historical figures and heroes were widely used to portray this message, as were the image and words of Lord Kitchener himself. Most famous is the image by Alfred Leete of the head and pointing finger of the Field Marshall, first published as a cover of the magazine *London Opinion* in September 1914 and used subsequently in a variety of posters with the slogan 'Your Country Needs You'; words that had been used by *The Daily Mirror* as a headline on 28 August 1914. This slogan was reused in many other posters. Other posters assaulted the conscience of the average man: 'Are You in This?', 'Daddy, what did you do in the Great War?' and 'Be Honest with Yourself'. The Parliamentary Recruiting Committee ceased its work on the advent of conscription in 1916, having produced over 6 million posters.

Duration

Referring specifically to the 'duration of the war', the term was used when recruiting volunteers during the early years of the war, with posters and official literature refering to the period of enlistment as 'three years or the duration of the war'. 'Duration' became an indeterminate period; for Brophy and Partridge (*Soldiers Songs and Slang*, 1931), 'roll on duration' was a phrase indicative of the soldier's resignation to his lot.

> *VICAR* (his mind full of recruiting posters): 'Wilt thou take this woman to thy wedded wife – for three years or the duration of the war?'
> (Punch, *2 December, 1914*)

MEDICAL CATEGORIES

A1–3: Fit for General Service
B1–3: Fit for Service Overseas
C1–3: Fit for Home Service only

(Whereas A1 had meant 'first rate' since its use for naval ships on the Lloyds Register in the eighteenth century, according to Fraser and Gibbon (1925), C3 was to become established as signifying general unfitness for purpose.)

> *Dear Nellie, I hope that this finds you 'A1' as it leaves me at present. From your affec. Bro. Alf*
> *(Postcard from a soldier in France, 21 June 1916)*

'CATEGORY MAN'

A 'category man' was a man deemed unfit for service overseas – usually of C3 category. Throughout the latter part of his recently published diary (*Tommy's War*), Thomas Livingstone of Glasgow, a 'category man' who had attested under the Derby Scheme of 1915, expressed his view that C3 men would be called to serve at some time. In fact, he escaped service – even with the Vounteer Training Corps (VTC).

WHITE FEATHER

Being given the white feather by a lady was a fear of many men not found in uniform. The white flag was the universal emblem of surrender, and the white feather was appropriated to evoke an image of cowardice. It was listed in Francis Grose's *Dictionary of the Vulgar Tongue* (1785): '*White feather* – he has a white feather: he is a coward: an allusion to a game cock, where having a white feather is a proof he is not of the true game breed.' Early in the war 'female vigilantes' took it upon themselves to issue such feathers to any man not in uniform – including in some cases wounded, off-duty, or on leave soldiers. The use of the white feather as a symbol of cowardice has a long history, dating back at least a century before the Great War. With the founding of the Order of the White Feather by Admiral Charles Fitzgerald and author Mary Ward in 1914, women were encouraged to present the feather to men who were deemed to be cowards.

Attested under the Derby Scheme; recruitment form of Private Frederick Walker, a 'Derby Man'.

'COMBING OUT'

The act of 'combing out' (otherwise known as 'the comb') derives from personal grooming, with tangles removed through the act of moving the comb through long hair. Pre-war the term was used in a literary sense, often applied in allusion to the act of sorting, or separating out. It was in this sense that the term was applied, often in a derisory way, to the act of searching out medically fit men for service in the armed forces. As the war progressed, so the pressure built to examine all workplaces for otherwise fit men who might be 'combed out' from 'cushy' jobs and put into uniform. From an advert in the *5th Gloucesters Gazette* in September 1918: 'We are now agitating for the immediate comb out from the army of all men between the ages of 60 and 90.'

STARRED MEN

Following the National Registration Act of 1915, which required citizens to register their name, date of birth, address and occupation, 'starring' was a means of identifying those men whose occupations were recognisably of value to the nation, to be deployed on the Home Front in manufacturing, agriculture and the like. 'Starred men' were therefore deemed to be exempt from military service, their status identified by a star placed against their names on the appropriate paperwork.

> *Certain trades have been taken and men belonging to them have been starred on the different forms, and they are forbidden ground for the recruiting officer. There may [also] be starred men who may enlist.*
> *(Lord Derby, Director-General of Recruiting,* An Appeal to the People, *19 October 1915)*

'DERBY MEN'

National Registration in 1915 had identified that there were at least 3.4 million men who were technically able to join the forces, but by the autumn of 1915 the numbers actually joining was falling at an alarming rate, not sufficient to fulfil the requirement of 35,000 men per week envisaged by Kitchener. In considering the issue, Lord Derby as Director-General of Recruiting was to draw up a scheme that was to bear his name. This entailed the voluntary registration, or attestation (a legal undertaking to join the colours when called to them), of all men between 18 and 40, with men of the same age and marital status being grouped together in forty-six consecutive groups.

Attested men were to serve one day in the colours – receiving their shilling – before transferring to a reserve until called up, entitled to wear an armband: khaki for the army, dark blue for the navy. Lord Derby invited all eligible men to attest by 15 December 1915; over 2 million of the 3.4 million men available for military service failed to attest. The experiment was a failure; the Military Service Act of January 1916 announced the introduction of conscription, the first of five such acts during the war.

'BADGING' AND 'DEBADGING'

The fear of receiving a feather was effective and led to the need for some way of distinguishing men on war service, from others in civilian dress. The first official badge was issued by the Admiralty in 1914, followed, in early 1915, by the Ministry of Munitions. Marked 'On War Service' the issue of these badges was strictly controlled by the 'Committee on War Service Badges' for those deemed to be employed 'on the production of any commodity directly required for the fulfillment of any contract with the Ministry of Munitions, the War Office, or the Admiralty'. As the war progressed, there were moves by the government to 'debadge' workers who could justifiably serve in the armed forces.

I want to add another instruction on the subject of badges. There are badges and badges. There are badges to which I would not pay the slightest attention ... the man who can produce to a canvasser a war badge issued by the Government has a sufficient answer to the request that he should serve his country ...
(Lord Derby, Director-General of Recruiting, An Appeal to the People, *19 October 1915*)

CONSCIENTIOUS OBJECTOR

Conscientious objectors – COs or 'conchies' – were those who objected to military service due to their deep-held beliefs that war was wrong. Mostly deriving from religious observance, for some, particularly the pacifist Quakers, war was morally wrong, and the act of taking part in any form was to condone an evil. Widely misunderstood (and often abused), with the introduction of the Military Service Acts conscientious objectors had to sit before tribunals to determine their cases individually. The press had little time for conscientious objectors, and they were not viewed sympathetically by the general public. *The Daily Express* described them as 'no-conscription cranks', 'pasty faces', 'peace cranks', and in a report on a near riot when 'COs' had been attacked in London, described one as 'a be-spectacled crank', perhaps subconsciously linked to the idea of Germans wearing spectacles.

THE DUMP SONG

We all know of certain people far too slack to fight the Huns
Who will one day face the music, tho' they dare not face the guns;
Men who hid in secret places when the bugles called to fight,
Or conscientiously objected that killing Germans wasn't right.
There's another well-known person – don't speak his name out loud –
Who when it comes to fighting is really much too proud!
There's the man who claims exemption, stays at home and steals our jobs,
There's the fraudulent contractor who the British soldier robs,
Dump, Dump
We'll put them on the Dump,
For cowards and swindlers it's just the place is Dump!

(Imshi Igri, *AOC Concert Party Programme, EEF, Christmas 1916)*

Men in Khaki

The BEF of 1914 consisted of six divisions (each division comprising four brigades; each brigade, four battalions of 1,000 men each), the first four of them taking part in the Retreat from Mons in 1914, the other two being present in France by September 1914. The British Army was destined to grow in size to seventy-five Infantry Divisions, sixty-five of which would serve overseas as an effective fighting force, distributed between the various corps and armies engaged on all fronts. Of these, twelve were regulars, one raised from Royal Naval reservists, thirty 'New Army' divisions, raised originally from volunteers during Kitchener's direct appeal to the public in 1914–15, and the remainder Territorials.

The volunteer spirit of 1914 declined as the war progressed; although still vibrant in 1915, by 1916 the army was facing a shortfall in manpower. With casualties increasing, it was inevitable that conscription would be required if losses were to be sustained. The Military Service Act of January 1916 introduced conscription for all men between the ages of 18 and 41 being liable to call-up, single men first, followed by married men in March 1916. Conscripts were to serve in all divisions by the end of the war, whether originally 'Regular', 'New Army' or 'Territorial'. Of the 7.5 million men of the right age available during the war, a third volunteered in 1914–15, a third were medically unfit or exempt from service, and a third were conscripted.

As a citizen army, the British Army of the First World War saw men of all classes and levels of education serving together. There were skilled tradesmen, labourers, students, teachers and men of the commercial classes. All had a level of education much in excess of the armies of previous wars: literate – or at least semi-literate – the men of 1914–18 were used to reading, and with an excellent postal service to and from the frontline they became used to writing home. Men of all classes served as private soldiers, and although many sought commissions, others were content to serve as members of the 'Poor Bloody Infantry'.

'KITCHENER'S MOB'

When Field Marshal Earl Kitchener of Khartoum took over as Secretary of State for War in August 1914, he was quick to understand that this war would be costly in manpower. Kitchener made a direct appeal to the public, his sights set on expanding the army by 500,000 men, with separate appeals, in tranches of 100,000, to be numbered successively K1, K2 and so on. The 'First Hundred Thousand', or K1, were recruited within days of the appeal. Kitchener issued four further appeals through the late summer and early autumn of 1914, the final 100,000, K5, being sanctioned by the government in October. Officially termed the 'New Army', Kitchener's men went by many names.

> 'KITCHENER'S MOB' they were called in the early days of August, 1914, when London hoardings were clamorous with the first calls for volunteers. The seasoned regulars of the first British expeditionary force said it patronizingly, the great British public hopefully, the world at large doubtfully.
> (James Norman Hall, Kitchener's Mob, 1916)

> Who are the boys that fighting's for,
> Who are the lads to win the war,
> It's good old Kitchener's Army.
> And every man of them's très bon,
> They never lost a trench since Mons
> Because they never saw one.
> (Soldiers' song, as reported by Patrick MacGill, Soldier Songs, 1916)

'NUTS' AND 'KNUTS'

'I'm Gilbert the Filbert, the Colonel of the knuts', went the song in 1915, by which time the 'knuts' were on their way out, their raffish superiority going down in the carnage of the Somme in 1916. The 'knuts' or 'nuts' were the flamboyant toffs and aristocrats of the years just prior to the outbreak of war. In January 1915, Rifleman Britland wrote to his family in Mossley, ' we have a chap here who is training to be an officer ... he is Lord Ponsonby's son, so you can see I am amongst the knuts.' For Eric Partridge, the 'knuts' were the VIPs crossing over to France. In *Not So Quiet: Stepdaughters of War*, the author, Helen Z. Smith, meets a 2nd Lieutenant who is 'rather a nut'. While a 'knut' meant a dandy or a gad-about, like many perjorative terms, it was re-used with some sense of irony; and it was adopted for the often educated soldiers of Kitchener's Army, with the judicious use of a hyphen as 'K-nut.'

> *U is our uniform if it's correct you will not look much of a knut I expect.*
> (Joyce Denys, Hampden Gordon & M.C. Tindall, Our Hospital ABC, *1917)*

'Somme Knuts', soldiers in France, *c.* 1916.

'TERRIER'

The Territorial Force came into being in 1908; consisting of part-time 'Saturday Night Soldiers', the 'Terriers' as they became known were intended only for home service. With the war emergency came the need to serve overseas, and the vast majority signed a pledge – the Imperial Service Commitment – to serve in frontline roles.

LANCASHIRE TERRITORIALS IN EGYPT

The Germans in high places have been considerably disillusioned already — they would have been still more disillusioned...as to the calibre of our Terriers, had any of them been in the streets of Cairo yesterday.

The Manchester Guardian, *3 December 1914*

'FRED KARNO'S ARMY'

Fred Karno (Frederick John Westcott) was a British theatrical impresario famous for his travelling troupes of comedians and comic actors; among the successful comedians he exported to the USA were Charles Chaplin and Stan Laurel. His troupe consisted of a range of comedians and odd-ball characters and it was not surprising that Kitchener's men specifically, and the army in general, would adopt the term to describe themselves.

We are Fred Karno's army,
Fred Karno's infantry;
We cannot fight, we cannot shoot,
So what damn good are we?
But when we get to Berlin
The Kaiser he will say
Hoch, hoch, mein Gott
Vot a bloody fine lot
Fred Karno's infantry.
(2nd Lt F.T. Nettleingham, Tommy's Tunes, 1917)

'THE BING BOYS'

'The Bing Boys' referred to a popular London theatre revue *The Bing Boys Are Here*, which ran from 16 August 1916 for two years, and featured George Robey and Violet Lorraine singing 'If You Were the Only Boy in the World'. The name 'Bing Boys' (alternatively, 'Byng Boys') was adopted by the men of General Julian Byng's Third Army, who were instrumental in stemming the tide of the last German offensive in the West, in April–May 1918.

> The Third Army was commanded by General Byng, familiarly known to the old soldiers as 'Bungo'. It was inevitable that we should call ourselves the Byng Boys (At the Alhambra Theatre in London, and on tour in the provinces, many of us had seen Andre Charlot's 'Bing Boys'...)
> (Pte Frederick Hodges, 10th Battalion, Lancashire Fusiliers, Men of 18 in 1918, *1988*)

'The Bing Boys', young soldiers in Britain, 1917.

'Bantam'

The idea of the 'Bantam' soldier came about through the efforts of the MP for Birkenhead, Alfred Bigland, in 1914. In common with many local dignitaries, Bigland set about raising a battalion of men, 1,000 strong, that would serve with the Cheshire Regiment, part of Kitchener's Army. Following Kitchener's call for men in 1914, recruitment had been strong. But with a minimum height of 5ft 3in, there were some men who were excluded. According to legend – described by Bigland himself in his memoirs – the idea was born of a demand by three Durham miners, who had come to Birkenhead in October 1914 in order to answer the MP's call for volunteers. The miners were shorter than 5ft 2in and so were excluded by the recruiting sergeant; one of them offered to fight any man in the room. Bigland saw the possibilities, and later offered the War Office the chance of taking a battalion of medically fit but under-height men, between 5ft and 5ft 3in, but having a chest expansion size that was an inch larger than the norm – in order to exclude any men that might be physically weak. From this was created the 15th and 16th Battalion Cheshire Regiment, two service battalions of under-height men. They formed into a complete division in April 1915: the 35th, with men from across northern England. A second division, the 40th was also raised, but there was difficulty in gaining the required number of men.

Bigland wrote to the *Birkenhead News* on 18 November 1914, outlining his plan: 'We are ready to receive the names of men who are willing to join what it has been decided to call the "Bantam Battalion".'The Bantams were born, the name derived from short, pugnacious miniature cockbirds and from the Javan seaport of Bantam; it was also applied to boxers of 118lb maximum weight from 1884 – the allusion of strength and aggression provided by both would suit the new 'breed' of soldier. The experiment had mixed success, however; shorter men were obviously suited to trench warfare, but some had physiques that were less than those of the preferred miner. The Bantam Cock was to feature in the insignia of the 40th Division, even though ultimately, with conscription, taller men were recruited, effectively 'de-bantamising' the formation.

'**Bantam**' – Men under the standard army height of 5ft 3 in. They are in a separate organisation called 'The Bantam Battalion', and though undersized have the opinion that they can lick the whole German Army. (Arthur Guy Empey, *Over The Top*, 1917)

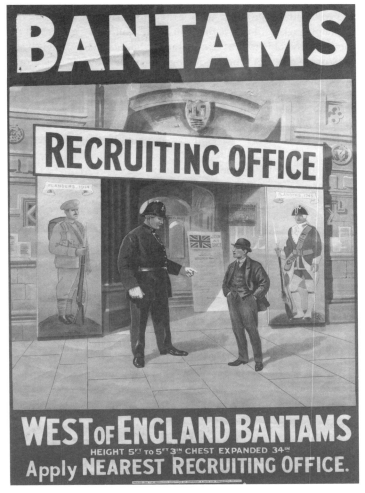

'Bantams': a rather patronising (and unrealistic) depiction of a potential Bantam recruit on a poster, *c.* 1915.

'OLD CONTEMPTIBLE'

This phrase was adopted by the men of the original BEF – consisting of six divisions of regular troops – who landed in France in August 1914. The term was derived from an Imperial order issued by Kaiser Wilhelm II on 9 August: 'It is my Royal and Imperial command that you concentrate your energies, for the immediate present, upon one single purpose, and that is that you address all your skill and all the valour of my soldiers to exterminate first the treacherous English and walk over General French's contemptible little army.' (Army Order, Kaiser Wilhelm II, 19 August 1914. Headquarters, Aix-la-Chappelle). In fact, 'contemptible' was the word used to translate the German *verächtlich*, which had a military provenance, spotted by Partridge, in the seventeenth-century Sir Thomas Browne's *Religio Medici*: 'This makes me naturally love a souldier, and honour those tattered and contemptible regiments that will dye at the command of a sergeant.' Corporal (Cpl) J. Bremner of the Royal Garrison Artillery (RGA) wrote in his diary on 27 January 1915: 'he [the Kaiser] is trying ... to break through Britain's contemptible little army but he shall get a prod and a very good one at that.' 'Old Contemptible' was first used in a review of Col A.M. Murray's book *The Fortnightly History of the War* which appeared in *The Observer* on 31 December 1916. For Bruce Bairnsfather, his character 'Old Bill' was an 'old sweat', 'out since Mons'. Post-war, the 'Old Contemptibles' was an ex-servicemen's organisation, whose membership was closely controlled.

OUR 'CONTEMPTIBLE ARMY'.
LAUGHTER IN PARIS.

A roar of laughter is the reception given here to the publication of the Kaiser's order to 'Walk over Sir John French's contemptible little army.'

The Daily Telegraph, *August 1914*

'PBI'

'Poor Bloody Infantry' – the lot of the infantryman – seems to date from the war itself. The implication of the term was that the infantry were at the end of the line of consideration – behind the cavalry, artillery, engineers and other specialist troops. They were certainly the most poorly paid. 'P.B.' – for 'Poor Bloody' – was used in other inventive ways, too.

The Song of a P.B.C.O.*

Ten of the P.B.I. went to hold the line,
R.E. wanted a fatigue, and so then there
were nine.
Nine of the P.B.I. in the hand of Fate,
Pioneers demanded one, and then there
Were eight.
Eight of the P.B.I. sitting in the wet,
Tunnellers adopted one, and then there
Were 'sept'.
Seven of the P.B.I. one whose name was Wicks
The M.G.C. demanded him, and then
There were six.
Six of the P.B.I. clustered in the hive,
One joined the 'Snipers', and then
There were five.
Five of the P.B.I. lay them down to snore.
Someone had to go to school, and so
There were four.
Four of the P.B.I., a dixey full of tea,
Then 'Tock Emmas' wanted help, that
Left three.
Three of the P.B.I. wondering what to do,
The 'Ack Pip Emma' came along, and
That left two.
Two of the P.B.I. left to strafe the Hun,
One went to give a hand to 'roads,' so
That left one.
One of the gallant P.B.I. and a Lewis gun,
But no-one at the gum-boot store, and
Here my story's done.

Of ten gallant P.B.I. there's not one left, and so
The line is held both day and night by
The P.B.C.O.

(*Poor Bloody Commanding Officer)
The B.E.F. Times, No. 3, Vol. 2, 1 November 1917

'FOOT-SLOGGER'

There were various imaginative references to marching – and to those
soldiers destined to march. 'Foot-slogger' – 'Foot slogging over Belgian
ways' was noted in the article 'The Route March', in the *5th Gloucesters
Gazette*, 5 May 1915 – was originally 'foot-wabler' or foot-wobbler' in
Grose's *The Vulgar Tongue* (1785), a term of contempt for the infantryman
much used by the cavalry. Related names were 'gravel-grinder' and 'mud-
crusher'. There were similar terms in French and German, German terms
being partiularly graphic – *Dreckfresser* (mud-glutton), *Kilometerfresser*
(kilometre-glutton), *Fusslatscher* (foot-shuffler), *Lakenpatscher* (mud-
crusher). According to Partridge, only the Germans were resigned to the
term *Kanonenfutter*, 'cannon-fodder'.

SOMETHING TO HANG THINGS ON

The soldier's total equipment of webbing, pack, steel helmet, rifle and
ammunition, etc., might easily come to half his own body weight, and
even more if he was carrying a Lewis gun or trench stores. Small
wonder that the infantryman considered his role similar to that of a
pack animal. In *The Brazier*, the paper of the 16th Battalion, Canadian
Expeditionary Force (CEF), 20 December 1916, a soldier wrote:
'When I joined the Army first they issued me with everything a soldier needs … and about fifty other things besides …They hung things
all over me. Rifle, bayonet, pack, haversack, smoke-helmet …'. The
word 'trays' used by soldiers to describe themselves carried the same
implication. 'Grabby' was a term that had survived in the army since
the Crimean War, although its origin is unknown. The word 'swad', in
use in English for about 500 years, developed into 'swad' or 'swad-gill',
meaning a soldier, during the eighteenth century, but did not give way
to 'squaddie' until after the war.

"I love the life, but Oh you Kit!"

'Oh you kit!' Postcard reflecting the concept of the soldier as 'something to hang things on'.

'KILTIES'

The frequent use of the word 'kilties' in *The Brazier*, the magazine of the Canadian Scottish (16th Battalion, CEF), indicates that Scottish soldiers were happy to call themselves by this name. The Revd Andrew Clark, in Essex, also used the word, maybe having picked it up via his daughter, who was a medical student in Dundee at the time. The use of the word for a Highland soldier dates from the mid-nineteenth century. Popular accounts have it that the Germans referred to their kilted oponents as 'devils in skirts' and 'women from hell'. An anecdote in *March to Armistice* by C. Howarth of the Argyll and Sutherland Highlanders suggests that this may have been German soldiers teasing Flemish peasants that the British Army was having to recruit women.

R.E.S

The usual designation for the Corps of Royal Engineers, who were responsible for all aspects of engineering in trench warfare, from trench construction to signalling – though signal soldiers were also called 'iddy-umpties,' 'tic-tacs' or 'buzzers' in reference to their use of morse code; semaphore signallers were called 'flag-waggers'.

> The Signal Sections of the Royal Engineers [are] tersely described by the rank and file as 'the Buzzers' or 'the Iddy-umpties.'
> (Ian Hay, Carrying on After the First Hundred Thousand, *1918*)

SAPPER

The commonest name for military engineers in the British Army –
members of the Royal Engineers – was a Sapper, someone who digs
'saps' (trenches and short tunnels). The name was in turn derived
from the Italian for a spade, *zappa*, and first recorded in the sixteenth
century and used in describing the high art of military engineering.

SOME DISPARAGING INTERPRETATIONS:
NON-FIGHTING TROOPS

APC (Army Pay Corps): Army's Perfect Cuthberts, Aunt Pollie's Chicks
ASC (Army Service Corps): Army Safety Corps, Ally Sloper's Cavalry
(also known as the London Thieving Corps, from their previous
initials of LTC, and several other disparaging terms). Other names
are: All Slackers' Corps, 'Always Sleep Comfortably', as well as 'Jam-
Stealers', alluding to the soldiers' perception that strawberry jam
rations were kept back, while 'plum and apple' varieties were issued.
AOC (Army Ordnance Corps): All Old Crocks, Angels of Christ
AVC (Army Veterinary Corps): All Very Cushy
MT (ASC Motor Transport): Mostly Tinkers
RAMC (Royal Army Medical Corps): Rob All My Comrades; Run Away
Mother's Coming, or the variant, Run Away Matron's Coming (also
known as The Body Snatchers, the Poultice Wallopers and the Linseed
Lancers). A more unusual version is CMAR – Can't Manage A Rifle

*AOC – Ordnance is ancient English for cannon. In consequence, this
unit is rarely found within sound of the guns. Though frequently
found 'in the dumps'* they are on the whole a cheerful crew.
(From* An ABC to the Army, The Salient, *Christmas 1915)*

* 'The Dumps' was the slang term for an ammunition dump or supply, located
at a theoretically safe distance behind the lines.

SOME REGIMENTAL INTERPRETATIONS:

DCLI (Duke of Cornwall's Light Infantry): Dear Cornwall's Little Idiots

GG (Grenadier Guards): God's Gifts

KOSB (King's Own Scottish Borderers): Karno's Own Schoolboys

KOYLI (King's Own Yorkshire Light Infantry): Keen on Young Ladies' Eyes

KRR (King's Royal Rifle Corps): Karno's Real Ragamuffins

LNLR (Loyal North Lancashire Regiment): Leave Nothing Loose

LRB (London Rifle Brigade): London's Real Bloods, Lively Ragtime Boys

MGC (Machine Gun Corps): Mother Goose's Children

PPCLI (Princess Patricia's Canadian Light Infantry): Proud Papa's Chewers Like Ices

QVR (Queen Victoria's Rifles): Queer Vicious Rookies

RE (Royal Engineers): Real Experts

RF (Royal Fusiliers): Real Fighters

RFC (Royal Flying Corps): Royal Flirting Corps

RNAS (Royal Naval Air Service): Rather Naughty After Sunset, Really Not A Sailor

RNVR (Royal Naval Volunteer Reserve): Really Not Very Respectable

RWK (Royal West Kents): Rather Wet Kisses

WCY (Westmorland & Cumberland Yeomanry): Lavatory Lancers

2nd Lt F.T. Nettleingham, *More Tommy's Tunes*, 1918

'REDCAPS'

The Corps of Military Police, before they were 'redcaps', were 'jacks' (or even 'nits'); if their suspect was 'rumbled' (found out) they would 'run' him (arrest him), and he might be 'limbered', from 'limbo' (prison), or even 'lagged' (put in leg-irons).

'SANITARY MAN'

The 'sanitary man' or 'SM' was usually a private detailed to deal with all aspects of latrine duties while in the trenches. These included the emptying of slop buckets, the burial of human wastes and the spreading of chloride of lime as a means of disinfecting trenches, particularly where corpses had been hurriedly built into parapets. Sanitary inspectors, commissions and engineers had existed since the mid-nineteenth century, and in largely static trench warfare the importance of the role in the trenches could not be underestimated. 'Sanitary men' were usually supervised by 'Sanitary Corporals'.

SCENE II – The Bosom of the Sanitary Man's Family – a Suburban Dining Room.
THE TIME – After tea.
THE OCCASION– The Sanitary Man's Leave.

The Sanitary Man and his Mother are seated at opposite sides of the fire. He has been home just one hour, and the incoherencies of the maternal greetings have died down.
The S. Man's Mother (after the universal questions: *When will the war end?* and *What do you think about the Cabinet?* And after the inevitable maternal questions: *Do you have enough to eat?* And *Have you plenty of bed clothes?*). And tell me dear, what exactly are you doing?
The S. Man (weightily). *Well, you see, I'm on the Health Staff.*
The S. Man's Mother (breathlessly). *Yes!*
The S. Man. *I am largely responsible for the cleanliness of the man's quarters. Of course, it is difficult, what with the mud, and blood, and --*
The S. Man's Mother. *Archibald!*
(Artists' Rifles Journal, No. 7, Vol. 1, *March 1917*)

'LANCE-JACK'

The most junior non-commissioned officer (NCO), the lance corporal, was distinguished by his single sleeve chevron; the term was in use in the Regular Army prior to the war. For Australians, the lance corporal was the 'dog's leg', after his single rank chevron.

THE LANCEJACK. These noisy, ubiquitous birds flutter everywhere, their shrill treble voices raised in frantic protest at the misdoings of the Oldsweat and the Duration Wallah. The Lancejack is vain out of all proportion to its personal beauty. Its plumage is of a plain negative hue relieved only by a single V-shaped stripe on each wing.
(*Natural History in the B.S.F.* [British Salonica Force], The B.S.F. Library, Vol. 1, 1919)

'THE CROWN'

Sergeant majors, the most senior 'Non-Coms' (NCOs) in the army, were distinguished by insignia worn on their lower sleeves. Company sergeant majors (CSM) wore only a simple, but tellingly effective, crown. Achieving the rank of CSM from the level of ordinary sergeant meant 'putting a crown' up in place of the three chevrons; 'the crown' was used to describe him. The more exalted regimental sergeant major (RSM) wore the royal arms on his sleeves.

'LOOT'

The junior officer or subaltern; those officers below the rank of captain. In some regiments, subalterns were poorly treated by their superior officers – Robert Graves in *Goodbye to All That* (1929) famously records his frosty treatment in the officers' mess of the Welsh Regiment, where he was described as a 'wart' – in keeping with the sixteenth-century origin of 'subalterne' as an inferior thing. A 'Loot' was the obvious way of referring to the rank of lieutenant (even though British pronunciation was 'lef-tenant' rather than the American 'loo-tenant'), with variants being 'Second Loot' or 'One-pip Loot' for the most junior rank of second lieutenant; other terms being 'lone star' and 'junior sub.' Subalterns suffered a disproportionately high number of casualties during the war.

THE LOOT. THIS gay, brightly-plumaged bird is very common in the Balkans. It is joyous and irresponsible by nature … uttering its drawling cry of *Cheerioltop*.
(*Natural History in The B.S.F.*, The B.S.F. Library, Vol. 1, 1919)

'WASH OUT'

Aspiring officers who failed their commissions and were sent back to their regiments were 'washed out', while a failed raid was also a 'wash-out'. By 1915 the term was being used to signify any kind of failure, from a complete set of misses in target practice to a day when fog made flying impossible.

'BLOKE'

What seems now such a common word was rather more class-identified in 1914. A batman might refer to his officer as his 'bloke', while C.W. Langley (*Battery Flashes*) refers to the 'quarter-bloke' – the quartermaster-sergeant, and in naval slang by 1914 'the Bloke' was the captain. First documented in London in the mid-nineteenth century, it was quickly taken into use in Australia. *The Brazier*, magazine of the 16th Battalion, CEF, comments: 'What curious expressions these Australians have. Fancy calling a man a "bloke" or a "cove" instead of saying "gink" as a guy naturally would!!!!'. 'Gink' being then a quite strong deprecatory term, this makes some sense of a story the Revd Andrew Clark tells about a camp concert in Essex in 1916: 'Mrs Sargeant also took great exception to an expression in Miss Bannerman's song – "I've been to the pictures" – viz. "my bloke and I". Mrs S. was strongly of opinion that soldiers' ears should not be wounded by such expressions.'

THE QUARTERBLOKE. The Quarterbloke is an object of universal respect and trust, not untinged with a certain awe. May his gleaming untarnished escutcheon – a housewife *couchant*, two rum jars *rampant* on a field of mosquito netting, with the proud motto of *Sox et Fray Bentos* – be always foremost on the field of value.
(*Natural History in The B.S.F.*, The B.S.F. Library, Vol. 1, 1919)

TEMPORARY GENTLEMAN

With the development of the new citizen army there was a crying need for competent officers. The choice was between returning retired men – known as 'dug-outs' – to the service, or promoting civilian men to become junior officers or subalterns. Early in the war men recruited from university, or ex-public schoolboys were granted a commission on the basis of status before being given training. Though a few, like Siegfried Sassoon, joined the Regular Army through the Special Reserve of Officers, for the most part the newly minted officers were granted commissions for the 'Duration of the War' only, these documents being marked, prominently in red ink, 'Temporary'. As the war progressed, a more merit-based approach was taken to officer recruitment, and 'rankers' – men promoted to officer from the ranks – became more common. They too would have temporary status; all were dubbed 'Temporary Gentlemen', or TGs, a term that was used as a badge of honour – but also as a sneer. At the end of the war officers were demobilised with little assistance and few benefits; their loss of status was keenly felt, a plight explored in the 1919 play *The Temporary Gentleman*.

'Sir, I am commanded by the Army Council to inform you that in consequence of the demobilization of the Army, a notification will be published in the 'London Gazette' at an early date, to the effect that you relinquish your commission on completion of service. You will retain the rank of 2nd Lieutenant.'
(Letter to 2nd Lt K.S. Wyatt, 23rd Middlesex Regiment, 1918)

A lot of fun has been poked at the Temporary Gentleman, but the fellows who came from shops and offices, with little education and less tradition, did their job somehow and did it well.
(Pte Alfred M. Burrage, Artists' Rifles, War is War, 1930)

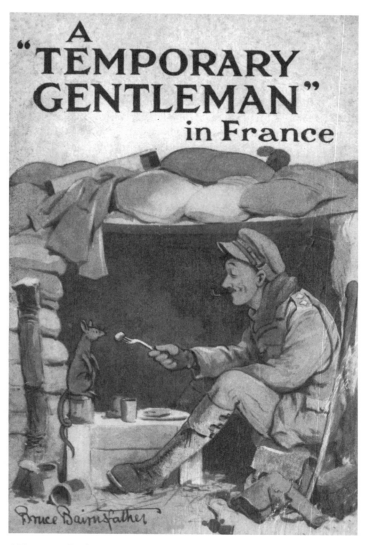

A Temporary Gentleman in France, 1916 by Captain A.J. Dawson.

TOMMY ATKINS

'Tommy Atkins' – the time-honoured name for the British soldier, a shorthand for the average man in uniform – dates back to Wellington's day, when, in an equally momentous war, an appropriate average name was needed for the model enlistment forms. The name appears in the 1815 *War Office Orders and Regulations*, and in the 1837 *King's Regulations & Orders for the Army*, where *Form No. 2* gives as an example: 'Thomas Atkins, Serjeant, Born in the Parish of St Mary in or near the Town of Portsmouth, in the County of Hants, by Trade a Labourer'. In 1864 the *Standing Orders for the Royal Regiment of Artillery* gives 'Thomas Atkins. Enlisted on the 9th April, 1857'. The earliest documented use outside the army is from 7 July 1883, when the *Illustrated London News* referred to 'Private Tommy Atkins, returning from Indian service'. According to Eric Partridge's unnamed 'eminent authority on military history', there was an actual Thomas Atkins, who died in action in Holland in 1794, whose commanding officer was one Arthur Wellesley, then a junior officer: 'He was a member of the 33rd Regiment of Foot which is now the 1st Battalion of the Duke of Wellington's Regiment (West Riding). He stood six foot three and is possibly the source of *every inch a soldier*'. Another story proposed that a sentry who stayed at his post, fatally, during the siege of Lucknow was called Tommy Atkins, and his bravery was commemorated in the phrase 'doing a regular Tommy Atkins'.

'Tommy' became immortalised in the first of Rudyard Kipling's *Barrack Room Ballads* (1892), with its bitter message of double standards applied to soldiers in war and peace:

> O it's Tommy this, an' Tommy that, an' "Tommy, go away";
> But it's "Thank you, Mister Atkins," when the band begins to play,
> The band begins to play, my boys, the band begins to play,
> O it's "Thank you, Mr. Atkins," when the band begins to play.

The name Tommy Atkins stuck and was used universally throughout the Great War as an affectionate moniker for the man in the trenches. Some correspondence to *The Times* in 1914 indicates that not everyone felt well-disposed towards the name. 'An Ensign of 1848' wrote on 23 October: 'May I ... suggest that the time has now come ... to put a period to the use of the nickname "Tommies"? ... To hear these British soldiers referred to in depreciatory patronage as "Tommies" by those who stay at home ... is unseemly and exasperating.' Three days later, another reader wrote that if you were to ask 'a company of Garrison Artillery what they think of the name and of the verses in which it was first enshrined the reply was startling and anything but complimentary to the author of the verses.' The language of this conversation and the forum in which it appeared suggests that few Tommies would have been likely to engage in this particular discussion, but Partridge states that British soldiers did not like the name. It is possible that this was a matter of opinion which differed between individuals, regiments, platoons, and any groupings of soldiers. Certainly there are clear indications of its being used by soldiers: the trench paper *The Salient* for Christmas 1915 advertises *The Buzzer*, the paper of the 49th (West Riding) Division, as 'written by Tommies for Tommies'.

There were other names for the British soldier that reflected his regional origins: Scots were usually 'Jock' and Welshmen were 'Taff'. However, despite these variations, Tommy was still a name applied to all British soldiers; even Allies could be included – *Battery Flashes* includes a reference to 'French Tommies'.

For Germans, it was to have even wider applicability: Canadians, Newfoundlanders, Australians, New Zealanders and South Africans were undoubtedly lumped together under the universal appellation of 'Tommy'.

Six months after the Armistice, *The Daily Mirror* extended the name to former enemies, distinguishing the 'German "Tommy"' from his Prussian officers.

12

Short Form of Will.

(See instruction 4 on page 1).

If a soldier on active service, or under orders for active service, wishes to make a short will, he may do so on the opposite page. It must be entirely in his own handwriting and must be signed by him and dated. The full names and addresses of the persons whom he desires to benefit, and the sum of money or the articles of property which he desires to leave to them, must be clearly stated. The mere entry of the name of an intended legatee on the opposite page without any mention of what the legatee is to receive is of no legal value.

The following is a specimen of a will leaving all to one person :—

In the event of my death I give the whole of my property and effects to my mother, Mrs. Mary Atkins, 999. High Street, Aldershot.

(Signature) THOMAS ATKINS,
Private, No. 1793.

Date 5th August, 1914

Gloucester Fusrs.

The following is a specimen of a will leaving legacies to more than one person :—

In the event of my death I give £10 to my friend, Miss Rose Smith, of No. 1, High Street, London, and I give £5 to my sister, Miss Sarah Atkins, 999, High Street, Aldershot, and I give the remaining part of my property to my mother Mrs Mary Atkins, 999, High Street, Aldershot.

(Signature) THOMAS ATKINS,
Private, No. 1793.

Date 5th August 1914

Gloucester Fusrs.

'Thomas Atkins'; the typical name for the British soldier printed on a specimen page in a Great War *Soldiers Service and Pay Book*. Tommy's Mother was Mary Atkins, his sister, Sarah Atkins.

M.O.

The Medical Officer, variously seen as patching soldiers up to send them back into the frontline or saving men's lives, was also known as 'the leech', 'the butcher' or 'the croaker'. 'Croak' had long been a slang word for 'die', so the association in the word 'croaker' was not optimistic. 'Leech' has a curious history; there were possibly two very similar forms of the word, one meaning a doctor, and the other meaning the blood-sucking invertebrate, both being documented from about the year 900. It appears likely that the association of leeches with early medicine led to the assumption that the words were connected. 'Leech' as 'doctor' died out in the nineteenth century, but its ironic use seems to have been retained in the army.

THE EMMO. THE Emmo is one of the most interesting birds of the Balkans. He belongs to the celebrated order 'Castoroilsky Numbernineovitch,' having been originally discovered by the celebrated Russian ornithologist Iodinesky.
(*Natural History in The B.S.F.*, The B.S.F. Library, Vol. 1, 1919)

'THE OLD MAN'

A name generally reserved for the senior officer in a battalion, usually a colonel or lieutenant colonel, the most senior 'field ranks'. Winston Churchill served as 'The Old Man' of the 6th Battalion, Royal Scots Fusiliers, in the Ypres Salient, in 1915.

The Old Man came round first evening, to see how we were getting on. He is a jolly good sort, and quite capable of keeping up our end, as well as his own, with the powers that be.
(Pte H.S. Clapham, Honourable Artillery Company,
13 February 1915, Mud and Khaki, 1930)

DEAR TOMMY,

YOU ARE QUITE WELCOME TO WHAT WE ARE LEAVING. WHEN WE STOP WE SHALL STOP, AND STOP YOU IN A MANNER YOU WONT APPRECIATE.

FRITZ

'Dear Tommy' propaganda leaflet left behind by the Germans, *c.* 1918.

'BRASS HATS' AND 'RED TABS'

The gulf between the 'gilded staff officer' (or 'staff wallah') and the men in the trenches was often commented upon in post-war literature. Most books refer to the quality and cleanliness of their uniforms and boots, which set these men apart. Many accounts express hostility to these men, though many of them were brave, decorated soldiers in their own right, not given to unnecessary 'showsoldiering' in visits to the front. Most slang terms refer to uniform embellishments worn by staff captains and generals, in particular the red and gilt gorget patches – known as 'tabs' – that were worn on the uniform collars, and the red cap band. The term 'brass hat' dates back at least to the nineteenth century; its origin lies in the gilded embellishments worn upon the peak of generals' service caps, as well as the red cap band worn by all staff officers.

I have only seen Staff Officers twice in places where there was trouble. One, I think, was in the support line through an unfortunate accident which no doubt he regretted; but the other, an old man, I am bound to confess was a hero and almost made me respect the Brass Hats.
(Pte Alfred M. Burrage, Artists' Rifles, War is War, 1930)

ENEMIES AND ALLIES

Turkish soldiers were referred to as 'Jacko', 'Jacky', 'Johnny Turk' or simply 'Abdul', while Austrians, if encountered, qualified for 'Fritz'. 'Johnny Bulgar' was the enemy faced in Salonica. The Portuguese were widely known as 'Pork and Beans', but also as 'Pork and Cheese' and 'Tony'. 'Sammy' was used for American soldiers, who called themselves 'guys'. Italians were referred to as 'Macaroni.'

POILU

The term *poilu* was used widely for the French soldier both among the French, and occasionally by her British and American allies – French soldiers themselves preferred *les hommes* or *les bonhommes*, according to Brophy and Partridge. Meaning 'hairy', *poilu* is supposed to have originated in a story by Honoré de Balzac, *Le Medecin de Campagne* (1834), in which a group of French soldiers are required for a deed demanding particular courage. Only forty soldiers in one regiment are deemed to be *assez poilu*, 'hairy enough'. An alternative was suggested by Herbert Ward, whose 1916 book *Mr Poilu* proposed that *poilu* was a colloquial word meaning 'pluck'. *Poilu* was familiarised as *piou-piou*, possibly imitating the sound of a bullet.

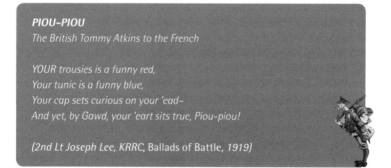

PIOU–PIOU
The British Tommy Atkins to the French

YOUR trousies is a funny red,
Your tunic is a funny blue,
Your cap sets curious on your 'ead–
And yet, by Gawd, your 'eart sits true, Piou-piou!

(2nd Lt Joseph Lee, KRRC, Ballads of Battle, 1919)

FROM HUN TO JERRY

While in the nineteenth century the word 'Hun' was applied humorously to any historical Central European living outside the *Pax Romana* during the first millennium, by 1900 it was being associated clearly with Prussian militarism. Reports of the ruthlessness of the German Army in China in 1900 refer to the use of the 'Hun' by the German Emperor as a symbolic ideal of military force, and thus the word was in place to be applied in 1914, especially in association with concepts such as 'atrocities' and 'frightfulness'. 'Who's afraid of a few dashed Huns?' shouted Francis Grenfell, just before his death in 1915 during the Second Battle of Ypres.

'The Hun' and 'the Boche' (or 'Bosche') stayed in use throughout the war, though Fraser and Gibbons claimed that only the RFC used 'Hun' regularly; there were also occasional curiosities such as 'Germ-Hun' (*Depot Review No. 5*, 1915). 'The boche' or 'boches' (or 'bosch/bosches'), with or without a capital B, was a French word which arrived through contact with French forces in 1914, and is said to have derived from French slang *caboche*, meaning 'rascal' or 'German', or from *Alboche*, a variant on *Alleman*. A writer in the *Western Daily Press*, 15 October 1915, claimed that *les Alboches* developed into *les sales Boches* ('the dirty Boches'), which provided the word 'Boches'.

Early usage in 1914 newspapers used inverted commas, indicating the word's novelty. 'Boche' could be used in a variety of ways, including as an indicator of place: a report of a football match in the *Cinque Ports Gazette*, May 1916, includes, 'We lost the toss and they defended the Bosche end'. The German counterpart to 'Boche', something that would express contempt for the French, was confusingly 'Welsche'. Albert Dauzat, the French philologist, writing from research made in 1918–19, claimed *'la guerre actuelle est la lutte des Welsches contre les Boches'* – a fight between Welsches and Boches.

The British also used 'Alleyman' adopted from the French *Allemagne*. Lieutenant Colonel E.W. Hermon, who was killed at Arras in 1917, recorded the cross-cultural use of the term in a letter home to his wife in October 1915: 'You were awfully amused how the language is being corrupted by contact with Thomas Atkins. All the locals now say "Allyman" & "No bonne"'.

If Alleyman and all its variants were to have a relatively short life-span, Fritz was first used by the *Daily Express* in January 1915 and continued throughout the war. From 1917 it was the only term used by diarist Corporal F.R. Ingrey, while the variation 'Fritzies' was a popular term among American soldiers according to R.H. Kiernan (*Little Brother goes Soldiering*, 1930). 'I can tell you Fritz has made a mess of everywhere round here', wrote Private Fred Walker to his best girl in September 1918. According to Brophy and Partridge, 'Boche' was not used by ORs, and the terms 'Fritz' or 'Jerry' would have been more common.

By 1916 the term 'Jerry' was in general use. Though the *Daily Express* had quoted the word on 3 March 1916, on 12 September 1916 it was clearly necessary to explain it further: '"Jerries" – that is the "official" Irish designation of the enemy'. By 1918 it was used frequently, as in 'Jerry had a machine-gun on us' (*Little Brother goes Soldiering*, R.H. Kiernan, 1930). The term carried more familiarity and weariness than hate; in Kipling's *A Madonna of the Trenches* (1923), portraying something of the reality of being shelled, the enemy is referred to as 'Jerry' rather than 'the Boche'.

In the period 1916–1918, the term 'German' was common. *Battery Flashes* by 'Wagger' (C.W. Langley), 1916, reports the use of 'Germings' for Germans, while the diary of Lieutenant A.B. Scott uses 'Hun' in 1916, 'Boches' and 'Huns' until spring 1918, but 'Germans' from summer 1918. Interestingly, the Germans had their own versions of these, but for specific branches of the armed forces: Ernst or Ernest for artillerymen, Fritz or Otto for infantryman, and Franz for an airman. Among American soldiers the term 'Heinie', from Heinz (Heinrich), was common. The helmet finally adopted by the German infantry reinforced the use of the term 'squareheads', which had been in use to describe German soldiers since at least 1906. *The Manchester Guardian*, 9 October 1914, in a discussion on German national characteristics, stated: 'It is the shortness of the German head that gets him the nickname "squarehead" in England and America and "*Têtecarrée*" in France. Germans themselves, by the way, say that it is the Austrian Germans who are the "squareheads"'. But the correspondent dismissed the generalisation as unhelpful.

On occasions, slang or colloquial terms were clearly not appropriate. On 25 December 1918, Private Fred Walker wrote in his diary: 'On a Burial Party at Etaples Cemetery, 17 British, 1 American, 2 German'.

At Home

Britain was booming in the pre-war period; yet the majority of the population, 80 per cent according to some estimates, were 'working-class', with a middle class of around 15 per cent. The wage for a skilled worker in an industrial job was about £75 per year – a figure way below the income tax level of £160 per year, unattainable earnings for most. Contemporary estimates suggest that 16 per cent of the population lived in poverty.

One of the most far-reaching impacts of the war was the introduction of the Defence of the Realm Act – universally known as DORA. First passed as law on 8 August, it was to control the British public in ways never seen before, affecting the lives of ordinary people, restricting their movements, their social habits and their working lives. DORA laid down strict rules regarding communication with or assisting the enemy, spreading rumours or false reports likely to hinder the military or to spread disaffection. Aspects of DORA still affect us today, in licensing laws and daylight saving.

The Great War was a conflict like no other, and for the first time the public of Britain would be under grave threat from land, sea and air. The German naval commander Admiral Hipper planned raids on the British coast in 1914. Though the first of these, at Great Yarmouth on 3 November 1914, was a failure, a more ambitious raid targeted Scarborough and Hartlepool a month later. Eighty-six civilians and seven soldiers were killed, while 438 were injured. The raids were propaganda gifts for the British – 'Remember Scarborough' now replaced 'Remember Belgium' on recruiting posters.

The assault on Britain was not limited to bombardment from ships, however, and the next phase would be the use of airships – Zeppelins. The first aerial attacks were approved by the Kaiser in January 1915, night air raids intended to target military installations in the Thames estuary. The raids soon escalated and London was admitted as a target in February. Air raids, from both Zeppelin airships and bomber aircraft, continued to be a part of Home Front life into 1918.

The Munitions of War Act of August 1915 brought all munitions manufacturers under the control of the Ministry of Munitions, and by 1918 it managed 250 government factories directly, and supervised 20,000 more. New sources of labour were required, and the government turned to the unions in order to implement what would be termed 'dilution' of the skilled workforce – the use of unskilled male labour, and women.

Prior to conscription, men had been encouraged to register as 'War Munitions Volunteers', a status that exempted them from military service – but with an increasing number of men being 'combed out' of war work in order to take their place in the frontline, women were called to the munitions factories as 'munitionettes' or as 'Tommy's sisters', and an estimated female workforce of 800,000 women was employed in all aspects of munitions work. Many more women would serve in the Armed Forces, or on the land.

Food was to become a major issue during the war; with Britain so hopelessly dependent on imports (up to 60 per cent of its food stocks), it was vulnerable to attacks on its supply system. At the outbreak of war, concerns over shortages among the middle and upper classes led to widespread hoarding. That other unholy act, 'profiteering' was also a major pre-occupation of the newspapers, and the opportunity to make money from decreased supply was perhaps too much to miss for some retailers. Both actions were loudly condemned in the press, yet rationing was not enacted until 1917. Imperial Germany was intent on starving Britain into submission, U-boats targeting any ship – neutral included – that might represent a lifeline for Britain in terms of food supply. Around 300,000 tons of shipping was sunk per month; in April 1917 alone, a record 550,000 tons of shipping was lost. This level of destruction meant that some foodstuffs were in short supply. It also led to a backlash against those shops bearing Germanic names – with riots and looting prevalent in 1915.

Rumour

Awareness that the 'official truths' were a weapon of war meant that rumour was a major part of communication at the Front, at home, and between the two. C.W. Langley wrote in November 1914: 'Only two salient facts remain certain and incontrovertible: There is a war on somewhere, but no one knows exactly where; and a force estimated at between 20,000 and 15,000 Russians in khaki passed through England on a Sunday night in August on the way to the left wing of that war if there is a left wing.' (The Russian-troop-movement-through-England rumour was particularly strong in September and October 1914, when descriptions of 'Russians stamping snow off their boots on railway platforms' abounded.)

Certainly, in the first year of the war there were frequent rumours of major Russian victories, reinforced later by frequent drops of propaganda leaflets over German lines announcing that hundreds of thousands of prisoners had been captured by Russian forces. The change in general attitude can be seen in the pessimistic and widely believed rumour in 1917 that Germany had established a 'Corpse Exploitation Factory' to extract fat from bodies retrieved from the battlefields; but on 8 November 1918 the Revd Andrew Clark was reporting rumours in Chelmsford that the German Army was about to surrender.

Rumours of atrocity in Belgium spread through both Britain and the German forces invading Belgium, Captain Walter Bloem reading in a newspaper in 1914 of 'priests, armed, at the head of marauding bands of Belgian civilians'. The rumour craze gave rise to lurid stories of bayonetted babies, mutilated nuns, and, famously, the 'crucified Canadian soldier', an atrocity alleged to have happened in Belgium.

Similarly, regular remarks in Revd Andrew Clark's diary indicate that the possibility of invasion was frequently thought about and discussed; on 15 February 1915 he reported that the Emergency Committee for the Chelmsford Petty Sessional Division had 'repeated meetings and the result of its deliberations as regards flight of residents into Hertfordshire [from Essex] had been printed.' Invasion rumours continued through the war.

DORA

One of the most far-reaching impacts of the war was the introduction of the Defence of the Realm Act – universally known as DORA. First passed as law on 8 August 1914, DORA was revised and extended many times during the war, exercising stronger and stronger controls that gave the government greater and greater means of imposing the needs of total war on the population. Though originally drafted as a means of protecting sensitive installations and public works from possible sabotage, its extension would see DORA controlling the movements of ordinary people, and restricting their social habits and working lives. Under the Act civilians could be tried by courts martial, arrested by the military and treated as if subject to military law – though this was later amended. DORA laid down strict rules prescribing any communication with the enemy, spreading rumours or false reports likely to hinder the military, or to spreading disaffection. DORA gave provisions for the control of a great many other, largely unconnected, aspects of life; through DORA came lighting restrictions, first applied in London on 11 September 1914, and the introduction of British summertime, intended to extend the daylight hours for farmers.

Travel pass for a civilian worker in a naval dockyard, issued under DORA (Defence of the Realm Act, 1914).

Disloyal Talk

On 17 May 1916 the following headline appeared in *The Times*: '£100 FINE FOR DISLOYAL TALK'. William Hawkins, a correspondent clerk employed by the Great Western Railway was fined this amount, with the alternative of three months in prison for 'having made false statements calculated to prejudice recruiting'. The defendant 'denied having made any of the statements attributed to him', and claimed that he applied from his employers for permission to attest, but 'domestic affairs prevented him from doing so'. He had apparently 'once made the absurd remark "We shall one day see the Germans marching up the Mile End Road", and he also once said, "I suppose I shall have to head a deputation if the Germans come over here", but that was mere chaff in reply to some bantering remarks. He urged that what he had said humorously had been taken seriously.' The appeal by William Hawkins (known to his colleagues as 'Von Hawkins') was refused despite his having persuaded others to attest, and he was given only two weeks to pay the fine, roughly equivalent to his annual salary.

'You Could Hear It From Blackheath'

The Revd Andrew Clarke regularly noted in his diary the sounds of Zeppelins and later aeroplanes on bombing missions as they approached London via the Essex coast. In April 1916, a Zeppelin is described as 'roaring like a railway train somewhere nearby', while another the following night was targeted by anti-aircraft (AA) guns, Clark noting 'the rattle of their reports'. Aeroplanes are noted as making a 'drumming' noise. On 1 July he noted the guns at what was later reported as the first day of the Battle of the Somme; while the guns could be heard at Blackheath, in the south-east of London, in his rectory near Chelmsford the Revd Clark also stated the noise 'making house quiver at times and shaking the window sashes.' He was told that the 'concussions' heard were the sounds of bombing in Flanders, 'the low tide before midnight and before noon rendering them very distinct.'

AIR RAID

With the development of aircraft in the pre-war period, and with the rapid growth of military air-power during the war, direct attacks on both military personnel and civilian targets were possible. The first such raid was made by the Germans against Antwerp, on the night of 24 August 1914, and was quickly followed up by the other nations. Such activity became 'air raids' or 'air-raids' in the press, with *The Times* of 24 September 1914 headlining a British attack on military targets in Germany. The first aerial attack on Britain, by Zeppelins, was made against the east coast of England on 19 January 1915. The usual warning at the front that an enemy aeroplane was approaching was 'Jerry up' or 'Jerry over'. According to a report published in the *Daily Mirror* on 31 January 1918, during an air raid on an airfield 'the sheds and hangars were well staddled', presumably with bombs.

AIR-RAID JOYS

It's an ill wind that blows no one good, and even air-raids have their useful, not to say, humorous side. Next door neighbours in London are actually beginning to speak to each other. Anyone who knows London for the past twenty years will feel sure that nothing but an air-raid, or the Day of Judgment, could have achieved that.

Soho Monthly Paper, St Anne's & Soho Westminster, *March 1918*

Air Raid Shelter

With air raids came 'air-raid shelters', or just 'raid shelters'. Though some citizens took the war into their hands (there is a listed, privately built concrete shelter in Cleethorpes that dates from 1917), most were to take shelter from raids in basements of large buildings, and the London Underground.

```
Landlords of basement houses are looking more
cheerful! In future advertisements of really
desirable tenements will offer, 'Good deep basement';
or better still, as a London theatre already attracts
patrons, 'built entirely underground'. In one London
Raid Shelter the basement of a world-famous museum
the lordly custodians disdain to shout 'All Clear',
but murmur discreetly, 'Normal Conditions,' when
danger is over.
```

Soho Monthly Paper, St Anne's & Soho Westminster, *March 1918*

'Specials'

In the face of threats by aerial assault – as well as the periodic spy scares and anti-German riots – the government turned to an Act passed in 1831, allowing the raising of Special Constables – generally known by the term 'Specials'. Unpaid volunteers, the Special Constables at first wore only civilian clothes augmented by a duty armband and decorated truncheon; but from 1916 they were issued with a uniform. Their roles were varied: guarding vulnerable points (including reservoirs, at danger of being poisoned), patrolling the streets, giving warnings of air raids (and announcing their end), and assisting the public in these raids.

'FLAG DAY'

Though the original 'flag day' was the anniversary of the adoption of the US national flag, the 'Stars and Stripes', on 14 June 1777, during the First World War the term became associated with the giving of small paper flags on pins in return for charitable donations. Charities proliferated, with many people giving their time to collecting monies for the diverse causes that clamoured for attention. There were 'flag days' for the 'Belgian Relief Fund'; for 'hut funds' to provide recreation huts for soldiers; for wounded soldiers and sailors; for the poor refugees of embattled nations; and hundreds of other minor causes.

'Flags' issued on 'Flag days': in this case for wounded soldiers in 'Blighty Blue', *c.* 1915.

'Tank Bank'

Many novel approaches were used in promoting war savings, none more so than the 'Tank Banks' which toured Britain in 1917–18 to raise money and support from the sale of War Bonds and War Savings Certificates. With the war's end, those boroughs that had raised the most money received a full-sized tank from the War Savings Committee, usually displayed in parks and squares. Of the 264 presented, the last survivor stands in Ashford, Kent.

The 'Tank Bank': tanks toured Britain as part of a war savings campaign in 1917.

Hostility to Germans

An enterprising Essex grocer decided to call 'German sausage', 'Dunmow sausage' in September 1914. There was a tide of hostility growing towards Germans and German products, and an outbreak of rioting in East London in 1915 following the sinking of the *Lusitania* led to the wrecking of German-owned businesses; the most well-known name change of the war was that of the royal family, from 'Saxe-Coburg-Gotha' to 'Windsor' in 1917, though a former Coldstream Guardsman reported to the Revd Andrew Clark that in the army there remained a residue of feeling against the King 'solely because of his German ancestry'. Dachshunds had a bad time in the war, at least in cartoons, but the term 'sausage-dog' post-dates the war by several years.

On 13 December 1915, the *Manchester Guardian* reported a speech given by Dr Henry Coward to the Incorporated Society of Musicians, in which he said: 'It is high time to awake, and one step, at least, is to ban all German music written during the time of Bismarck's period of "blood and iron".' Ford Madox Ford's 1914 *When Blood Is Their Argument* opens with an assault on the German language and German art, education and scholarship, again with 1870, the beginning of Bismarck's institution of the ideal of 'blood and iron', as the start of the evil. Even in March 1919 *The Times* was writing patronizingly of the German language: '"Stink", like many another sturdy Saxon word[s], has fallen into something like disfavour in our modern polished speech, but the Boche knows little of such squeamishness and the word forms part of many a German Army term of quite kindly regard ... if you do it in the proper spirit, you may call your dearest friend a swine in the vaterland's idiom, and run but little risk of damage to his feelings.'

> *I PROMISE IN MEMORY OF THOSE WHO HAVE DIED FOR ME NEVER TO TRADE WITH GERMANY OR A GERMAN AS LONG AS I LIVE.*
> *(Commercially produced watch-fob, c. 1915)*

If der W. A. A. C.
haf gone by, den I kan kom out.

A 1918 postcard depicting a German soldier in a typically negative light: the WAAC was the Women's Auxiliary Army Corps.

'BLIGHTY BLUE'

While in 'Blighty', soldiers sent to hospital, and convalescing, were ordered out of their familiar khaki and into 'Hospital' or 'Blighty blues', a simple suit of blue clothes worn with a distinctive red tie and khaki 'Service Dress Cap' (or other headdress appropriate to the regiment or nationality of the soldier). Cheaply produced, in general 'hospital blues' provided a poor fit, but was the badge of honour of a returned soldier with a 'Blighty one'.

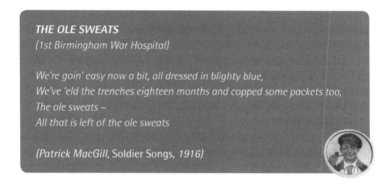

THE OLE SWEATS
(1st Birmingham War Hospital)

We're goin' easy now a bit, all dressed in blighty blue,
We've 'eld the trenches eighteen months and copped some packets too,
The ole sweats –
All that is left of the ole sweats

(Patrick MacGill, Soldier Songs, *1916)*

IN THE CLINK

Offences against military law brought one of the most fruitful movements of language, as the overstressed soldier found himself coming into contact with the slang of the criminal underworld. While C.B. – the standard military sentence – was the usual way to refer to 'confined to barracks', most terms to do with crime and punishment displayed the 'controlled communication' that is a necessary attribute of talk between criminals, some dating back centuries. Eric Partridge's researches revealed that many of the apparently straightforward terms in use during the war (particularly in Kitchener's Army) had originated in criminal slang. 'Chum' and 'cully' were seventeenth-century terms for 'accomplice' and 'companion' respectively ('chum' had degenerated from its earlier use as 'student' at Oxford or Cambridge), while 'pal' was an eighteenth-century term for 'accomplice', deriving from Romany. A 'mob' or 'push' was a nineteenth-century gang of pickpockets, while even 'doing your bit' was as an underworld expression for serving your sentence.

Military prisons

Cage, dating from the fifteenth century. The 'cage' was specifically for Prisoners of War. A cartoon in *Listening Post*, December 1917, shows a British soldier and a German prisoner standing in front of a sign with the words 'To the Cage'.

Clink, first documented in the early sixteenth century. Grose suggested this comes from the clinking of prisoners' chains, but an old verb 'to clink' meant to fasten. The Clink was an area of Southwark outside the authority of the City of London (the Liberty of the Clink), where one could be free from arrest for various misdemeanours, and was thus a favourite place for criminals.

Chokey, from Hindi, 'chauki', meaning a 'lock up'.

Dardanelles, used by PoWs in Germany.

Hulk; The *Cinque Ports Gazette*, May 1916, carried an official report of a battalion's activities, which included guarding 'about 1500 German prisoners, interned at Olympia, which we did until they were removed to hulks at Southend.'

Hutch, mush and moosh – guardroom or detention barracks.

Jankers, probably from the Navy, meant primarily punishment cells, then defaulters' punishment, then 'the defaulters' themselves. 'The jankers king' was the provost sergeant.

Jug is documented from the eighteenth century. Possibly this came from the Latin *jugum* meaning 'yoke', and had been used for centuries in Scotland.

Opera-house and **glass-house**, both pre-war terms.

Paddy Doyle, from a Regular Army word for 'defaulter'.

Quod is from the quadrangle of Newgate Prison, and appears in the *Dictionary of the Canting Crew* (1700).

Spud-hole, a cool dark storage space.

Of these 'jug' was the most serious in 1914–18.

Mostly from Partridge: *Words, Words, Words*, 1931

The 'jankers' or defaulters' squad was always rather large; but the 'jankers men' were offenders against minor points in discipline. Their crimes were untidy appearance on parade, inattention in the ranks, tardiness at roll-call ... The punishment meted out varied according to the seriousness of the offense, and the past conduct of the offender. It usually consisted of from one to ten days, 'C.B.' – confined to barracks.
(James Norman Hall, *Royal Fusiliers,* Kitchener's Mob, *1916*)

WAR MUNITIONS VOLUNTEERS

Skilled workers were required to help feed the guns, and just as in the steelworks of Sheffield, and the shipyards of the Mersey, Clyde, Tyne and Lagan, men were required to help manufacture munitions. The patriotism of the day tempted many to join the forces, but maintaining the level of skilled workers was no mean task. The drive for this was the need to maintain the flow and quality of munitions, a factor that was to come into sharp focus during the shell shortage scandals of May 1915, which led to inadequate artillery preparation before battle, and the prevalence of 'duds' (unexploded shells). However, the situation improved with the appointment of David Lloyd George as Minister for Munitions in July 1915. The introduction of the Military Service Act in January 1916 encouraged skilled men to register as 'War Munitions Volunteers', a status that exempted them from military service – at least in the short term. Over 2.5 million men worked in munitions factories during the war.

'MUNITIONETTES' AND 'CANARIES'

Women also would find their place in the Royal Ordnance Factories and a diversity of other munitions factories as 'munitionettes', with an estimated 80 per cent of shells being produced by a female workforce of nearly a million in the latter stages of the war. The term 'munitionette' may relate to the earlier 'Suffragette', and with many of the latter suspending their activities to support the war effort it is possible that they ended up in the factories. The term was by no means the only one; the phrase 'Tommy's Sister' was also used. While men and women were issued with their own distinctive 'On War Service' badges, some women were marked as war-workers through the yellowing of their skin – toxic-jaundice from TNT poisoning – earning them the nickname 'canaries'. Many died from the condition.

'Sister Susie'

The term 'Sister Susie' was sometimes used for those women involved in war work; not necessarily one of the many thousands who were engaged on the land, in the factories or on public transport, but perhaps involved in the act of 'canteening', serving drinks and refreshments to soldiers at railway stations (or in factories), or more likely involved in the provision and packing of 'soldiers' comforts'. The term derives from the tongue-twisting song by Herman Darewski and R.P. Weston, which was also made into a short film in March 1915. 'Susie's Only Shirt' was also an interpretation for the distress signal 'SOS'.

> Sister Susie's sewing shirts for soldiers,
> Such skill at sewing shirts our shy young sister Susie shows!
> Some soldiers send epistles, say they'd rather sleep in thistles
> Than the saucy soft short shirts for soldiers sister Susie sews.
> (Chorus, Sister Susie's Sewing Shirts for Soldiers, Herman
> Darewski & R.P. Weston, 1914)

Women's military services

FANY – First Aid Nursing Yeomanry. Women serving at home and overseas assisting the RAMC as ambulance drivers. Nicknamed 'The Fannies'.
VAD – Voluntary Aid Detachments. Women serving at home and overseas in hospitals, as auxiliary nurses, and in a wide variety of roles. Known as 'VADs' or Very Artful Devils.
WAAC – Women's Auxiliary Army Corps. Formed in 1917, it comprised women serving in a variety of military ancillary roles, both at home and overseas. The corps became QMAAC in 1918 after Queen

Mary became commandant-in-chief. Known as WACs or WAACs, it was sometimes interpreted as 'Women Always After Charlie's Socks'.

WFC – Women's Forage Corps. Raised in 1917 to serve with the Army Service Corps in gathering forage for the considerable numbers of horses in military service.

WL – Women's Legion. Quasi-military organisation supplying women for home service in a variety of ancillary and horticultural roles.

WLA – Women's Land Army. One of several organisations that recruited women to serve on the land. Others were the WNLSC (Woman's National Land Service Corps, formed by the Board of Agriculture in 1916) and the WDRC (Women's Defence Relief Corps).

WRAF – Women's Royal Air Force. Formed in 1918 using draughts from the WAAC, the WRAF women worked in a variety of ancillary roles. Known as 'Wrafs' (or even, alluding to the flightless birds, 'the penguins').

WRNS – Women's Royal Naval Service. Formed in 1918, the WRNS worked in a variety of naval ancillary roles. Known as the 'Wrens', interpreted as 'Wear Royal Navy Serge'.

'GORGEOUS WRECKS'

The Volunteer Training Corps (VTC) was the 'Dad's Army' of the Great War. Comprising a variety of over-age and unfit men, the VTC nevertheless grew to a formidable force by the end of the war. The VTC provided both a means of training underage would-be soldiers, and of keeping guard on vulnerable points. The men wore a distinctive armband with the letters 'GR' – 'Georgius Rex', the origin of at least one of its wartime nicknames.

> The old men who came into the club were nearly all in the Volunteers (or 'Georgeous Wrecks') or else serving as special constables. I must say I admired the latter.
> (Pte Alfred M. Burrage, Artists' Rifles, War is War, 1930)

IN THE TRENCHES

The trench was the focal location of the war. Simply, the trenches of the Great War were linear excavations of variable depth mostly open to the sky, and their purpose was to provide protection to the frontline troops from small arms fire and artillery. For the most part, trenches were 6–8ft deep, although this was the ideal as in some cases it was impossible to dig more than a foot or so before reaching water-saturated ground, especially in the Ypres Salient with its underlying foundation of water-repelling clay. Here, instead, the trenches were built-up with sandbags rather than dug down.

Most trenches were 'floored' with wooden duckboards (or 'bath-mats'), which were built up to allow drainage beneath. Trench sides (known as slopes) were supported or revetted with whatever was available, sometimes wattle, often corrugated sheeting and expanded metal ('xpm'), and even with chicken wire. Timber was used universally to hold these materials in place, and layers of bonded sandbags strengthened the whole. Sandbags were to become an important part of trench life, filling gaps in the line, creating a parapet or ultimately being built upwards as breastworks.

Fire trenches were usually arranged in successive parallel rows, with the frontline, support line and reserve line all connected by the communication trenches ('CTs'), which were the main thoroughfares of trench warfare. The purpose of 'CTs' was to link the forward or fire trenches, and to allow men, munitions and supplies to travel up to the line – as well as allowing wounded soldiers to come out of the line. In well-established trench systems, the frontline consisted of a fire trench and ancillary support trench with deeper dug-outs providing accommodation for the troops. Trench signboards were fixed to allow newcomers to a particular stretch to get oriented, and trenches were named or numbered – a complex system recorded on equally complex trench maps.

Between the frontlines of the opposing trenches was 'no-man's-land', a strip of contested ground that varied in width from a few feet to tens of yards, with the forward trenches on both sides protected by belts of barbed wire. Wiring parties on both sides would enter no-man's-land under the cover of darkness: a great many barbed-wire cutters were patented during the war.

No-man's-land was generally only crossed when soldiers went 'over the top' – when they climbed out over the parapet to face the enemy. Looking over the parapet in daylight was most unwise; putting one's head above the trench was virtually suicidal, and head injuries were common in tall soldiers and the curious. Snipers would have weapons fixed in position, targeted at dips in the parapet, at latrines and crossing points, and at loop hole plates. For the most part, no-man's-land was observed by day through 'trench periscopes' set up for the purpose.

THE WESTERN FRONT

The *Daily Express* first used the expression 'the western front' in September 1914 – 'the transfer of German troops from the western-front to the eastern', but later in the same article wrote 'the army was fighting against in the Allies in the western war area'. Three days later, on 19 September, the correspondent wrote: 'A great battle on the western front is expected soon.' *The Times* in September 1914 pre-ferred 'the Western front', which later was replaced by 'the western front'; *The Times* did not use the form 'the Western Front' generally until after the war, by which time it had become clearly defined as a place and an event. Though the *Daily Express* continued to use lower-case letters as late as 1924, the increasing use of upper-case letters reflected the growing image of the Western Front as a place, time period, set of events, people, history and myth.

IM WESTERN NICHTS NEUE

All Quiet on the Western Front was a celebrated and controversial bestselling novel in Germany and across the world. First published as *Im Western Nichts Neue* ('nothing new in the west') in 1928, it was soon translated into English and sold some 2.5 million copies world-wide – followed up by an Oscar-winning Hollywood film a year later. This term had actually been used in Arthur Empey's 1917 book *Over the Top*. It is associated with the stalemate of the war in the trenches, and the often repeated comment that, while the newspapers reported on major offensives, the randomness of death in the trenches on any given day was a continual drain on manpower.

> In the official communique our trench raid was described as follows: 'All quiet on the Western Front, excepting in the neighbourhood of Gommecourt Wood, where one of our raiding parties penetrated into the German lines.'
> (Arthur Guy Empey, Over the Top, 1917)

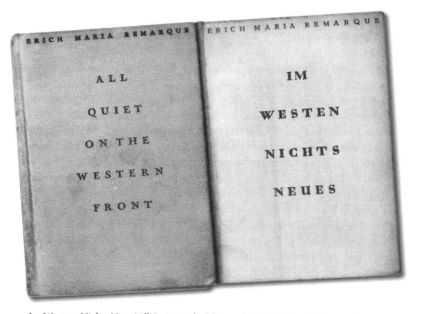

Im Western Nichts Neue/*All Quiet on the Western Front*, Eric Maria-Remarque's bestseller published in 1928–29; the English phrase had been used much earlier.

'SOMEWHERE IN FRANCE'

With censorship of letters and cards practised at 'the front', soldiers were encouraged to maintain some form of secrecy in their communications home. Photographers operated in the rear areas, and soldier groups were often shown with a card saying 'Somewhere in France'; this phrase and the less common 'Somewhere in Flanders' were soon used as catch-alls for anywhere on the Western Front.

> *Somewhere in France. God bless us and keep us all while we are parted till we meet again.*
>
> *(Pte J. Moore, Sherwood Foresters, killed in action, Villers-Bretonneaux, 24 April 1918)*

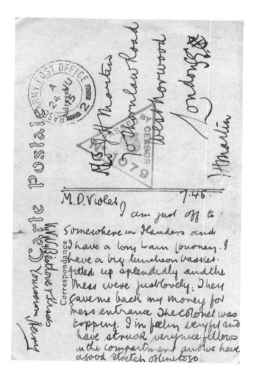

'Somewhere in Flanders': postcard sent home by an officer, June 1915.

'BULL RING'

The 'bull ring' was the training ground for the British military base of Etaples, and the main starting point for soldiers on their way to the front; similar grounds (also 'bull rings') existed throughout the BEF area. The term probably alludes either to British bull-baiting rings or the 'Bull Ring' at Birmingham which had long been a centre for political and religious haranguing. It was perhaps re-used in this sense for the ground where instructors (known as 'canaries' from their yellow coloured 'brassards' or armbands) 'baited' the troops.

The following day was spent in preparation for another journey to a place called 'Etaples' and pronounced 'Etaps'. Our stay here was about sixteen days and I may say that it was here we had our first experience of the famous 'Bull Ring' which has been the subject of discussion in past issues of 'John Bull' and 'Daily Mail'.
(Diary entry, Pte John T. Lawton, 5th King's Liverpool Regiment, 1915)

ON THE BULL RING.

'The Bull Ring'; the most famous of these training grounds was at the British base near Étaples, in France.

'OMMS AND CHEVOOS'

The term 'omms and chevoos' refers to the simple covered railway trucks used to transfer the ordinary soldier across France. These had sliding doors, and were largely devoid of comforts of any kind – which explains their frequent appearance in soldiers' diaries. The term derives from the notification painted on the sides of such trucks, advertising their suitablity for 'Hommes 40, Chevaux 8'. Travel by this means was extraordinarily slow.

Got across safely on Monday night after spending a day at XXXXXX. Am now in a deserted village some distance behind firing line expecting to move into trenches soon. Jack.
(Censored postcard from unidentified British soldier, 26th Division, 22 September 1915)

'UP THE LINE' OR 'AT THE FRONT'

The movement of troops from the rear areas to the frontline was mostly expressed as 'up the line', or, in some cases, 'up the jigger'. The term was also used in the form 'news from the Front' in the newspapers of the day. Both 'up the line' and 'at the Front' were acceptable shorthands for serving soldiers writing from 'somewhere in France', who wished to escape the attentions of the military censor.

Dear Kitty,
I have been up the line and have come down to the base for rest. I received your letter the day I went up the line. Yours truly, Percy.
(Letter home from Pte Percy Edwards, 17th Battalion, Royal Welsh Fusiliers, 10 September 1918. (Pte Edwards died of wounds nineteen days later))

'IN THE TRENCHES'

'In the trenches' was almost universally applied as 'the place where soldiers served' during the First World War, and was frequently alluded to in letters and in the press at the time. The phrase became a shorthand for the frontline, and in most cases was used to describe life on the Western Front – though the terms 'in the trenches at Gallipoli' or 'in the trenches at Salonica' would also be used to express the soldier's presence in the frontline. Postcards sent from the rear areas by soldiers sometimes bore the legend 'from the trenches'; little else was needed for the soldier himself to write.

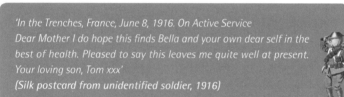

Dear friend, I hope you are very well in the trenches – little huns don't bombard you. From your little friend.
(French pen-pal postcard to Pte Charles Frederick Willis, 6th London Regiment, 1916 **(In the Trenches, France, June 8, 1916.** *On Active Service))*

'In the Trenches, France, June 8, 1916. On Active Service
Dear Mother I do hope this finds Bella and your own dear self in the best of health. Pleased to say this leaves me quite well at present. Your loving son, Tom xxx'
(Silk postcard from unidentified soldier, 1916)

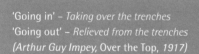

'Going in' – *Taking over the trenches*
'Going out' – *Relieved from the trenches*
(Arthur Guy Impey, Over the Top, *1917)*

'The Front'; *Daily Mail* bird's-eye map of the Western Front, *c*. 1916.

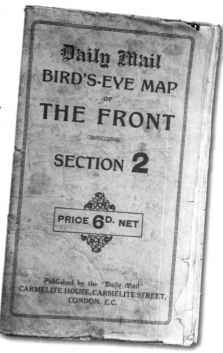

TRENCH

The word 'trench' has a history that stretches back to at least the sixteenth century, when it was applied to the works created in siege warfare. One quote from Edward Hall (*The vnion* [union] *of the two noble and illustrate famelies of Lancaster* [and] *Yorke*, 1548) could be applied to the war on the Western Front some 360 years later: 'They without made mynes, cast trenches and shot gunnes dayley'. The function of trenches varied; in the main there were two consistent types: fire trenches, which formed the frontlines, and communication trenches (CTs), which joined them. Fire trenches (i.e. fighting trenches) were divided into a regular pattern of fire bays and traverses, which meant that no soldier could walk in a straight line for long. This was intended to limit the effects of shellfire, or the possibility of rifle and machine-gun fire along the length of a trench (known as 'enfilade fire'). The architecture of trench warfare became increasingly more complex as the war progressed, and the prefix 'trench' was added to everything: trench stores, trench boots, trench cap, trench foot, trench fever and trench boards.

'Trench' – A ditch full of water, rats, and soldiers. During his visit to France, Tommy uses these ditches as residences. Now and again he sticks his head 'over the top' to take a look at the surrounding scenery. If he is lucky, he lives to tell his mates what he saw.
(Arthur Guy Empey, *Over The Top*, 1917)

ARMY TERMS AND THEIR DERIVATION

TRENCH — So called from the trenchant remarks from those inhabiting them.

The BEF Times *No. 1, Vol. 2, 15 August 1917*

> *The fire trench was built in much the same manner as those we had made during our training in England. In pattern it was something like a tesselated border. For the space of five yards it ran straight, then it turned at right angles around a traverse of solid earth six feet square, then straight again for another five yards, then wround another traverse, and so throughout the length of the line. Each five-yard segment, which is called a 'bay', offered firing room for five men.*
> *(James Norman Hall,* Kitchener's Mob, *1916)*

'**Communication trench**' – A zigzag ditch leading from the rear to the frontline trench, through which reinforcements, reliefs, ammunition, and rations are brought up. Its real use is to teach Tommy how to swear and how to wade through mud up to his knees.

'**Fire trench**' – The Frontline trench. Another name for hell.

(Arthur Guy Empey, *Over The Top*, 1917)

> *Communication trenches must be wide enough to allow rapid movement of the men and should admit of easy egress.*
> *(Major A.R. Richardson, University of London Officers Training Corps,* Trench Warfare, *1915)*

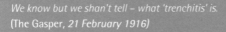

> *We know but we shan't tell – what 'trenchitis' is.*
> *(The Gasper, 21 February 1916)*

'Trenchitis' – A combination of 'fedupness' and homesickness, experienced by Tommy in the trenches, especially when he receives a letter from a friend in Blighty who is making a fortune working in a munitions plant.

(Arthur Guy Empey, *Over the Top*, 1917)

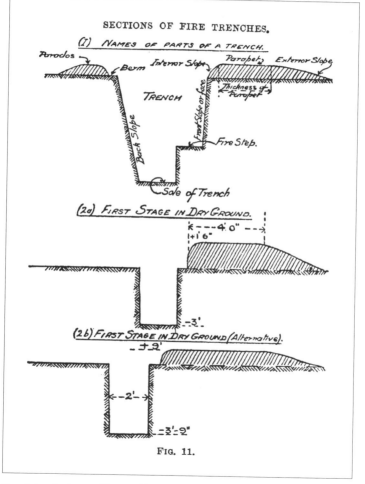

Trench terminology as illustrated by a War Office Manual, 1915.

PARAPET AND PARADOS

The spoil removed in digging a trench was used to form a 'parapet' – a mound of earth in front of the trench on the enemy side – and a 'parados' – a slightly higher mound at the rear. 'Parapet' dates back to the sixteenth century, derived from Italian *parapetto* (literally meaning 'defend the breast'); 'parados' is nineteenth century, from the French art of fortification, meaning 'defend the back'. There were numerous other words employed in trench engineering: for instance, the 'berm' (or 'burm'), a ledge or shelf in front of the trench and before the parapet; and the 'fire-step', a step to allow soldiers to fire over the parapet. Today, the phrase 'put your head above the parapet' endures – implying bravery, or foolhardiness. Each fire trench was equipped with a fire-step ideally 2ft high and 18in wide, sufficient to raise an average man's head above the protection of the parapet when necessary.

> The silhouette of parapet and parados must follow a natural contour. An irregular parapet is essential to hide men's heads, for it is obvious that a man's head is easily seen if exposed over the top of a trench made like a straight wall, but seen with difficulty if his head emerges with numerous undulations.
> (Concealment Applied to Trench Warfare, *1915*)

> I sat down on a fire-step in a reserve trench and looked up, and there they were on the parapet above my head, leaning over in the breeze, glowing in the bright green grass that rimmed the parapet; poppies, blood-red, swarthy, virile, the same poppies that you have in your fields at home.
> (Pte J. Hodson, Told in the Trenches, *1916*)

When I first began to walk up Manchester Avenue, my thought was, 'there's nothing much to grumble about'. For several hundred yards it cuts through a ridge of chalk. Its parapet and parados tower white, clean and unbroken a foot or so over your head. Its sides are like the sides of a house or a tunnel; good, dry, solid chalk...
(Captain A.J. Dawson, A Temporary Gentleman in France, *1916)*

'Burm' – A narrow ledge cut along the walls of a trench to prevent the earth from caving in. 'Burm' to Tommy is a cuss word, because he has to go over the top at night to construct it.
'Firing step' – A ledge in the front trench which enables Tommy to fire 'over the top'. In rainy weather you have to be an acrobat to even stand on it on account of the slippery mud.
(Arthur Guy Empey, *Over the Top*, 1917)

"There goes our blinkin' parapet again."

'There goes our blinkin' parapet again': Bruce Bairnsfather cartoon illustrates the soldier's lot, 1915.

SAP

The term 'sap', describing both the means and type of excavation, has a venerable history dating back to at least the seventeenth century and derives from the Italian word *zappa*. Saps were important in the protracted sieges of the 1600s, when they were shallow tunnels dug beneath the walls of the besieged fortresses; the term *Sapper* was applied to military engineers from the seventeenth century, a predecessor to the Royal Corps of Engineers being the 'Royal Sappers and Miners'. During the First World War, saps were usually open extensions from the frontline into no-man's-land, serving as advanced observation or listening posts, or in preparation for an attack. The covered version in this case was a 'Russian Sap', with a blind end that could be breached to allow men to break out into an advanced position without being observed.

'Sap' – A small ditch, or trench, dug from the front line and leading out into 'No Man's Land' in the direction of the German trenches. (Arthur Guy Empey, *Over the Top*, 1917)

JUMPING-OFF TRENCH

A 'jumping off trench', often hurriedly constructed in no-man's-land at night, was shallow and was intended to advance the frontline a few yards forward, thereby gaining some ground before an attack.

When the fire on any sector increases tenfold, while the roads behind the lines are thronged with five times the normal traffic of troops and lorries, the attack or 'jumping-off' trenches are being dug in front of the line, a commander cannot fail to know that an attack is preparing.
(John Masefield, The Old Front-line, 1917)

TRENCH SIGNBOARDS

It was necessary to direct soldiers through the maze of trenches, for although they were theoretically constructed in parallel lines – at least in the early stages of trench warfare on the Western Front – the re-entrants, salients and wired strongpoints known as 'redoubts' were interconnected by communication trenches (CTs) and minor trenches intended for latrines, entrances to dug-outs, trench mortar batteries, and so on. Most soldiers would travel to the frontline from the rear areas along crowded CTs at night; bustling, narrow thoroughfares 6ft deep with barely enough room for men to pass. Although relieving battalions were guided to the front by experienced soldiers from the battalion about to be relieved, to direct them, signboards would still be necessary, picked out by candlelight. Many of the long CTs were named after main thoroughfares, such as Sauchiehall Street or Oxford Street, while fire and reserve trenches often had picturesque names: Lovers Lane, Lavender Walk, Idiots Corner, International Trench, Nonsense Trench, Chaos Trench, Gangrene Alley. These names were painted on rough and crude boards to aid in direction finding. Such boards existed in the frontline; and others, with a more urgent message, might warn of the dangers from snipers, artillery fire or the physical hazards of loose or low wires, or treacherous duckboards.

The naming of trenches themselves has been left largely to local enterprise. An observant person can tell, by a study of the numerous name boards, which of his countrymen have been occupying the line during the past six months.
(Ian Hay, Carrying on After the First Hundred Thousand, *1918*)

We swung into the country road in the gathering twilight, and turned sharply to our left at the crossroad where the signboard read, 'To the Firing-Line. For the Use of the Military Only'.
(James Norman Hall, Kitchener's Mob, *1916*)

SURVIVING TRENCH SIGNBOARDS

'DEATH VALLEY' (IWM) – The Somme, France

'DO NOT STAND ABOUT HERE. EVEN IF YOU ARE NOT HIT SOMEONE ELSE WILL BE' (CWM)

'GAP D UNDER M.G. FIRE' (AWM) – Hangard Wood, France

'HEAVY ARTILLERY <u>GAS DEPÔT</u> IS YOUR RESPIRATOR <u>SOUND</u>? IF YOU ARE NOT <u>SURE</u> WALK RIGHT IN AND <u>HAVE IT TESTED</u>' (CWM)

'HELLFIRE CORNER' (NAM) – Ypres Salient, Belgium

'KEEP TO THE TRENCH IN DAYLIGHT' (IWM)

'MONTREAL CROSSING' (CWM) – France

'PICCADILLY CIRCUS' (IWM) – Trench System, Gaza

'SUICIDE CORNER' (IWM) – There were 'Suicide Corners' on the Somme and in the Ypres Salient

'TO STINKING FARM & CURIE AVE' (AWM) – The Ypres Salient, Belgium

'TO FRONT LINE' (AWM) – Bullecourt, France

'TO THE FRONT LINE' (IWM)

'THAT TIN HAT YOU PASSED JUST NOW IS WORTH MONEY – PICK IT UP AND TAKE IT TO THE SALVAGE DUMP' (IWM)

'ROODEKANGA' (AWM) – St Quentin, France

'WALKING WOUNDED' (AWM) – Villers-Bretonneux, France

'WIND DANGEROUS' (AWM) – dangerous in gas attacks, from Nieppe

Signboards preserved in the Australian War Memorial (AWM), Canadian War Museum (CWM), Imperial War Museum (IWM), National Army Museum (NAM)

'THE BAGS'

According to Fraser and Gibbon, 'the bags' was the term commonly applied to the parapet, mostly built up from sandbags. This was particularly the case in wet ground, where sandbags had to be stacked to create a 'High Command' trench, with more bags than excavation – often simply called a 'parapet' or 'barricade'. Not surprisingly, soldiers more often than not described the act of leaving the trench as 'mounting the bags' or 'going over the bags'.

'Sandbag' – a filled sandbag (usually made of sacking) measures 20 ins. By 10 ins. By 5 ins. In building a parapet, sandbags are 'dove-tailed' alternatively lengthwise and breadthwise in the way usual in brick walls. A sandbag laid with its side towards the enemy is called a 'stretcher', while one with its end towards the enemy is called a 'header'.
(G. Belton Cobb, *Stand to Arms*, 1916)

STOP-GAP

Little stacks of sandbags,
Little lumps of clay;
Make our blooming trenches,
In which we work and play.

Merry little whizz-bang,
Jolly little crump;
Made our trench a picture,
Wiggle, woggle, wump

(The Wipers Times, *No. 2, Vol. 1, 26 February 1916*)

LOOP HOLE

In common with many terms used in trench warfare, 'loop hole' is ancient, dating back to at least the sixteenth-century development of siege warfare – the term 'loop' probably derived from the Dutch word *luipen*, meaning 'to watch'. A small opening or gap cut into a wall or defensive position, 'loop-holing' was a common military necessity. In the trenches, loop holes were most commonly produced in steel 'loop hole plates' to be built into the parapet, with the hole itself covered by a small rotating door opened to allow observation of the enemy. Snipers commonly had them in their sights.

Sketches of Tommy's life Up the line — N° 3

We marched into the Trenches, late in the evening, going across fields on « duck boards ». There is nothing to be seen but shell-holes, and wintry looking trees.

Sketches from Tommy's Life: Private Fergus Mackain's depiction of the duckboard track to 'the trenches'.

DUCKBOARD

The term 'duckboard' arguably first arose in the First World War, as the need to adequately floor damp trenches was met with slatted flooring in sections, designed to fit together when laid. Presumably derived from similar boards used to allow access for ducks to steep-sided ponds, duckboards came into their own in the wet conditions of Flanders. An alternative was 'bathmat', or simply 'mat'. Duckboard tracks were also often laid across damp, boggy or shelled ground – and were exceedingly difficult to walk upon when wet.

DUCK-BOARDS, by the way, or duck-walks, are a kindly invention (of the R.E., I suspect) to save soldiers from the bottomless pit, and to enable officers on duty to cover rather more than a hundred yards an hour getting along their line of trench.
(Captain A.J. Dawson, *A Temporary Gentleman in France,* 1916)

> *The fellows now are on fatique, and that is what they feel;*
> *The weather clerk has given them a very shabby deal.*
> *The heavy 'bath mats' make them groan; the 'bee-hives' make them swear;*
> *To have to do the R.E.'s job they think is most unfair.*
> *(P.A. Savi and E.M. Savi,* Bosh and Boches, Reminiscences, *1919)*

SUMP

A 'sump' or 'soakaway' was often dug under the duckboards to allow water to drain away from the trench or an area where duckboards lay over an area frequently covered by rainwater. 'Who took a bath in a sump?' asked the *5th Gloucesters Gazette*, December 1915.

BARBED WIRE

Barbed wire was part of trench warfare from its inception on the Western Front. The earliest successful use of barbed wire dates back to the late nineteenth century (patented in 1874, in Burlington, Iowa), where it was used in the American West as a means of cattle control; deterring humans instead of cattle was an obvious development, and the military use of wire was advocated from the 1880s onwards. By the early twentieth century, wire had become accepted by the military and was used extensively in the South African War. It became one of the most potent symbols of trench warfare – as in the 'battalion hanging on the Old Barbed Wire.'

> Barbed wire. *What could be more simple, for instance, than barbed wire?*
> *It is a wicked thing – those thickets of thorns that have borrowed*
> *the bitingness of the bramble, and translated the sinister graces of a*
> Rubus *[e.g. blackberry] into terms of iron ... war flora represented by*
> *the snarls of* Barbedwiria volubilis *in the depths of a crater.*
> *(The botanist Reginald Farrer,* The Void of War, *1918)*

ENCYCLOPAEDIA OF MILITARY TERMS

BARBED WIRE – Some one has written that this was invented by
Mephisto. After what we have heard about him it is surprising that he
should invent anything of such an affectionate and 'clinging' nature. At
the front it is used for giving an artistic finish to a trench. No trench
is complete without it. It is planted at night in order that the artillery
may plough it up in the morning. A good crop of barbed wire has been
known to prevent opposing armies from arguing the 'point'. When
a soldier gets tangled up in it he says things which are not taught at
school. This may be the reason why the Padre never goes on a wiring
party or leads an attack.
(Made in the Trenches, 1916)

'Gott Strafe this barbed wire'
(Captain Bruce Bairnsfather, Fragments from France, *1917)*

If you want to find the old battalion,
I know where they are, I know where they are, I know where they are
If you want to find the old battalion, I know where they are,
They're hanging on the old barbed wire,
I've seen 'em, I've seen 'em, hanging on the old barbed wire.
I've seen 'em, I've seen 'em, hanging on the old barbed wire.

(Soldiers' Song, *J. Brophy and E. Partridge,* Songs and Slang of the
British Soldier, *1931*)

The building was surrounded by a strong wire entanglement, built,
where stakes could not be driven into the paved courtyard, on
wooden frameworks known as chevaux-de-frise *('wire horses').*
(G. Belton Cobb, Stand To Arms, *1916)*

'Knife-rest' – The name at the Front for a portable X-shaped wire-entanglement framework, resembling a knife-rest, used for stopping gaps in wire-entanglements in No Man's Land.
(E. Fraser and J. Gibbons, *Soldier and Sailor Words and Phrases*, 1925)

WIRING

The act of constructing barbed-wire entanglements, usually in no-man's-land, and usually on working parties at night.

A pleasant job is wiring when you're near to Fritzie's line,
The landscape looks so peaceful when the brilliant star-shells shine:
The gentle shell explosions sound like music to your ears;
They do not always land on you, so you need have no fears!
(P.A. Savi and E.M. Savi, Bosh and Boches, Reminiscences, *1919)*

VEREY LIGHTS

No-man's-land at night was regularly lit up brilliantly by flares, star shells fired by artillery, coloured warning rockets launched from the frontline, and smaller 'Verey lights' usually fired by officers from hand-held pistols throwing up 'light balls'. Star shells and Verey lights would cause working parties to be starkly silhouetted against the skyline; warning rockets were fired to alert the artillery in case of attack. The term originated from its American inventor, Edward W. Very, and though 'Verey' was commonly used for the lights and pistols, 'Very' was actually the correct form.

I think, says one gravely, both sides ought to club together and shove arc-lamps up between the front lines. Consider the awful waste of all those 'Verey' lights that are sent up. They're pretty, of course, but if they're for beauty why not more red and green ones, and what's wrong with purples? What about a competition every night for the best display?
(Pte J. Hodson, Told in the Trenches, *1916)*

> *I was put on sentry with two others to look for anything strange happening, strange lights, and so on. By now, of course, I knew all the usual lights – red, green and so on – that the Germans threw up.*
> *(Pte Albert Andrews, 19th Battalion, Manchester Regiment, 29 June 1916)*

DUG-OUT

The term 'dug-out' had two definitions during the war, very different from each other. The first, and most commonly understood, was a shelter or underground dwelling associated with trench warfare. This usage would have been familiar to some at least, as it had been reported in the British press during the Russo–Japanese war of 1904, which saw the widespread use of trenches – and was based on a civilian term implying an underground shelter or excavation made to escape difficult weather conditions. This usage was supplemented by another meaning, again used early on in the war – that of retired officers called back to the colours in the wartime emergency, and typically placed in command of the new battalions of Kitchener's Army. Frequently, popular works of the day made a play on the two uses.

Tales of a Dug-out, by an officer of the "Die-Hards": book written by a 'dug-out' retired officer of the Middlesex Regiment ('The Die Hards'), the book title reflects its twin meaning.

DUG-OUT – A hole in the ground with a lid on. There are three kinds of dug-outs at the front. The 'Bungalow' for Officers, the 'Love in a Cottage' for Sergeants, and the 'Noah's Ark' for privates. They are built for men, mice, rats and cats to sleep in. A dug-out is decorated with jam, cheese, photographs and fleas.
(*Made in the Trenches*, 1916)

DUG-OUT – Of two kinds. The name originates in a habit of the early natives who excavated holes for themselves to avoid the slings and arrows of the enemy. Another kind is the erection in which Area Commandants dwell.
(*The BEF Times* No. 1, vol. 2, 15 August 1917)

My dearest John,
I am living in a little cave just behind the trenches, they call it a dug-out, & it is like a rabbit's burrow & every now & then I go through a little passage into the trench to have a look through a spy-hole at Mister German, but he is very careful & does not show himself much, as he is frightened Daddy might shoot him!
(A soldier's letter to his son, 11 February 1915)

SOME DUG-OUT NAMES:

'My Little Gray Home in the West'
'The Ritz Carlton'
'The Rats' Retreat'
'The Suicide Club'
'Vermin Villa'

(James Norman Hall, Kitchener's Mob, 1916)

AT THE RITZ
GEORDIE: 'Well I'm blowed! They'm named yon place after 'owd doog-out on t'Somme!'
(Punch, *5 March, 1919*)

ALTERNATIVE DUG-OUT TERMS

Dug-outs deepened as the war progressed and as the effectiveness of artillery bombardments increased; howitzer shells in particular being capable of penetrating the ground before exploding. The Germans had constructed 'deep-dug-outs' in the chalk areas of France, protecting their troops from the British preliminary bombardments at Loos in 1915, and on the Somme in 1916. Less effective were shelters cut into the trench sides, which served to keep soldiers out of the worst of the elements, but which could only hope to give protection from spent rounds – those bullets that had lost their velocity. These shallow excavations were variously described as 'cubby-holes', or, more tellingly, 'funk-holes'.

One day they shelled our trench, and we lost 120 men in an hour. Some who had lain in a cubby hole and had dosed off for a few minutes were buried alive.
(Diary entry, Pte John T. Lawton, 5th King's Liverpool Regiment)

'Funk hole' – Tommy's term for a dug-out. A favourite spot for those of nervous disposition.
(Arthur Guy Empey, *Over The Top*, 1917)

MESPOT

Soldiers of the Mesopotamian 'sideshow' campaign most commonly referred to the theatre as 'Mespot', modern-day Iraq. Alternatives were 'Mesop' and 'Mess-up'. 'Mesopolonica' was, according to Fraser and Gibbon, 'a composite expression for an unknown or doubtful destination', and was clearly a mixing of two 'forgotten fronts', Mesopotamia and Salonica.

MR. PESSIMIST (cheering up for once): *'British Mesopotamian success.'*
MRS. PESSIMIST: 'That's the worst of it. They mess up all of their successes.'
(Punch, *8 December 1915*)

'ELEPHANT'

On 2 January 1917 Lance Sergeant C.P. Harris noted in his diary that he had seen a 'large semi-circular iron structure'. Consisting of sturdy curved and corrugated sections – much more robust than a Nissen-hut section – this was an 'elephant'. Elephants were dug into the ground to serve as protective coverings, creating sturdy shallow dug-outs, often stacked high with materials. There were two sizes, the smaller being called a 'baby elephant'.

There was no concrete in any part of the line, very few iron girders and not many iron 'humpies' or 'elephant backs' to make the roofs of dugouts.
(John Masefield, The Old Front-line, *1917*)

We found a corrugated iron arch called a 'baby elephant' and used for the support of shallow funk-holes and dugouts. We crawled under this, and with no protection against the cold ... we slept like hogs until a red sun winked in our eyes and finally woke us.
(Pte Alfred M. Burrage, Artists' Rifles, War is War, *1930*)

PILL-BOX

'Pill-box' was the term introduced for a concrete fortification used to strengthen defensive lines, particularly deployed by the Germans. In the wet ground of the Ypres Salient, though the German positions had the topographical advantage of height, they were challenged by ground conditions. Here the digging of deep dug-outs such as those seen on the Somme was difficult, as instead of well-drained chalk there were particularly difficult water-bearing layers. Here, from 1915 onwards, the Germans built a system of block-built or cast steel-reinforced concrete structures known as MEBUs (*Mannschafts Eisenbeton Unterstände*) that were intended to both withstand shellfire and provide covering machine-gun fire against the attackers. The term 'pill-box' presumably derives from British descriptions of the fortifications, which were copied by the Allies as the war progressed, though 'pills' had been a slang term for ammunition since the Boer War.

> The pill-box was the only piece of good cover in the whole battalion area. Imagine a small room ten feet square and six feet high with walls of thick rough concrete. There is only one opening, the door, over which a waterproof sheet is draped.
> (*Charles Edmonds*, A Subaltern's War, *1929*)

NO-MAN'S-LAND

The concept of a piece of land that fell between two territories, or of waste, unowned ground, has long fascinated writers and it is not surprising that such an expressive term as 'no-man's-land' should appear repeatedly throughout history. The *Oxford English Dictionary* lists at least four categories of meaning, the earliest dating back to the fourteenth century when *nomannesland* was a place of execution just north of the London City wall. First used in a military sense in the late nineteenth century – describing a no-go area between warring peoples – its specific association with the land between trench lines is claimed by Major General Sir E.D. Swinton in his book *Eyewitness*: 'To the best of my knowledge this term, which became part of the English language during the war, was first used by myself in 1907 in a story called *The Point of View*, to describe this neutral zone between two opposing trench-lines.'

> *Had a glimpse of 'No Man's Land' for the first time through a trench periscope. An amazing sight. Earth pounded to atoms – all heaps and holes. Trees shorn of all branches and splintered cruelly. Long grass growing out of the muck heaps, and here and there bodies of men.*
> *(Pte J.C., KRRC, Told in the Huts, 1916)*

SHELL HOLES

The *Manchester Guardian* for 25 July 1916 records the words of a company commander: 'The Boche was crumping us all the time … On the stroke of twenty-five, I got a good jump from my rum-box, and fell headfirst into a little pool; whizz-bang hole I suppose; something small.' Many soldiers had close personal experiences of the effects of a whizz-bang, with *The Scotsman*, 6 October 1916, reporting the 'words of 'an infantryman': 'A whizz-bang came over, passing so close to my face that I actually felt the breath of it. It passed through a tin of bully-beef, a tin of jam, a good-sized cheese, and a water-filled petrol-tin, and immediately buried itself in the earth.' While the resulting hole of the high-velocity whizz-bang was small, that of the heavier-hitting 'Jack Johnson' was much larger, as recorded in the letters of Lieutenant Colonel (Lt Col) E.W. Hermon on 30 May 1915: 'I saw a Jack Johnson hole as well & you never saw such a hole. I haven't seen one actually burst yet & I don't want to if it is at all close.'

> *'IF YER KNOWS OF A BETTER OLE, GO TO IT'*
> *(Captain Bruce Bairnsfather, Fragments from France, 1916)*

CAMOUFLAGE

'Camouflage', according to Partridge, was 'originally from the slang of the lively, vivid, ingenious Parisians, with its *camoufler*, "to disguise"'. Perhaps more likely, it could have evolved from the term *camouflet*, meaning a bomb in a hidden space – and such bombs were widely used in mine warfare. Ernest Weekley noted that it was 'naturalised with amazing rapidity early in 1917', and quoted George Bernard Shaw as saying 'I was in khaki by way of camouflage'. Though the word was in use among troops in 1915 (particularly in the sense of 'bravado'), it did not feature in newspapers before May 1917.

> *On some of the trees or tree stumps by the sides of the roads [on the Somme] one may still see the 'camouflage' by which these exposed places were screened by enemy observers.*
> (John Masefield, The Old Front-line, *1917*)

THE SALIENT

A salient is a curve in a fortification, a line that protrudes out into the lines of the enemy. Though thrusting forwards, trench lines within salients could easily be 'enfiladed', that is the enemy could fire along their length, with each salient facing the enemy on three sides. There were numerous salients in the frontline, and often limited trench raids or offensives were carried out in order to 'cut them off', to straighten the position. Perhaps the most important was the Ypres Salient, formed in late 1914 when the trench positions became stabilised after the series of battles known as the 'Race for the Sea'. The Ypres Salient was bisected by the Menin Road, which passes through the Vauban city walls at the Menin Gate, a feature that would become the focus for commemoration in the post-war period. The Ypres Salient was held by the British throughout the war. Though its shape and form would change over time, its basic purpose – the protection and holding of the city of Ypres at all costs – would remain the same.

The Ypres Salient was the ground on which the quality of British manhood was put to the test, most often, in the most frightful conditions, against heaviest odds, during the years of war.
(Philip Gibbs, The Immortal Salient, *1925*)

Our trench line, with its infinity of salients and re-entrants, is itself only part of the great salient of 'Wipers'. You may imagine with what methodical solemnity the Boche 'crumps' the area of that constricted area.
(Ian Hay, Carrying on After the First Hundred Thousand, *1918*)

'WIPERS'

Based in Belgian Flanders, the modern Flemish town of Ieper was known as Ypres by the British, though it was Yperen to both the Germans and the local Flemish population. A railway signboard in the Imperial War Museum reads 'Ypres' on one side, 'Yper' on the other. As one would expect, it is pierced by shrapnel. The British soldier's attempt at pronouncing the town's name was to produce some variation, and very quickly Ypres would become 'Wipers' or 'Wypers' (E.J. Kennedy, *With the Immortal Seventh Division*, 1916), made famous by the trench newspaper the *Wipers Times* (subtitled, in a typical play on words, the *Salient News*), the first of which appeared in February 1916. Other variants were Y-pree, Yips or Eeps. The town was shell-blasted throughout the whole time of the British occupation.

It is even hot in the wintertime at Wipers.
(Arthur Guy Empey, Over The Top, *1917*)

One of the many correct pronunciations of Y-P-R-E-S rhymes with *deeper*; we are getting tired of 'snipers', 'the breeze', 'sleeps', 'I guess', and 'chips'.
(The Brazier, *trench magazine of the Canadian Scottish (16th Battalion, CEF), 18 July 1916)*

I made a serious blunder when I asked one of them a question about Ypres, for I pronounced the name French fashion, which put me under suspicion as a 'swanker'. Henceforth it was 'Wipers' for me, although I learned that 'Eeps' and 'Yipps' are sanctioned by some trench authorities.
(James Norman Hall, Royal Fusiliers, Kitchener's Mob, *1916)*

'POP'

'Pop' was the familiar name for Poperinghe, 8 miles east of Ypres and the first town between the front and the Channel ports of any size out of range of all but the largest German guns. It was from 'Pop' that many men made their way 'up the line' to the Salient, and it would be to 'Pop' that men returned when out of the line, perhaps visiting Talbot House – or 'Toc H' in signalese, an everyman's club that had a sign above the door 'Abandon rank all ye who enter here'.

SOME PLACE NAMES:

Armenteers: *Armentières*
Bally-all: *Balleul [sic]*
Hazy-Brook: *Hazebrouk*
Plug-street: *Ploegsteert*

(James Norman Hall, Royal Fusiliers, Kitchener's Mob, *1916)*

Étaples was another stumbling block, but 'Eatables' soon revealed Tommy's way out...
(Chaplain Major E.J. Kennedy, With the Immortal Seventh Division, *1916*)

It is evident that the Battle of the Somme is going to add some fresh household words to our War vocabulary. 'Wipers' is a veteran by this time: 'Plugstreet', 'Booloo', and 'Arminters' are old friends. We must now make room for: 'Monty Ban', 'La Bustle', 'Mucky Farm', 'Lousy Wood' and 'Martinpush'.
(Ian Hay, Carrying on After the First Hundred Thousand, *1918*)

THE SOMME

Prior to the British arrival on the Somme in late 1915 it had been a quiet sector, occupied by the French and run on a 'live and let live' principle. When the British took over, the 'offensive spirit' was asserted, leading to the major Anglo-French offensive of July–November 1916 – The Battle of the Somme. Thomas Livingstone of Glasgow noted in his diary that the 'Big Push' had opened in July 1916, and in the weeks that followed, newspapers were full of news of the British attacks and the mounting casualties. It was for this, and for the decimation of Kitchener's 'Pals' battalions that the Somme became infamous. And in August 1916, the public got to experience some of the flavour of the attack, with the release of the film *The Battle of the Somme*, which featured a mixture of real and reconstructed battle sequences. It would have a lasting effect on the public consciousness. 'On the Somme' or just 'the Somme' soon became familiar phrases.

PALS

The term 'Pals' – as applied to a group of men who joined the army together, effectively to maintain class-consciousness – was coined by Lord Derby in a speech made in St Anne Street, Liverpool on 28 August 1914; following a letter to the Liverpool press the day before, he expressed his intention to raise battalions of 'commercial classes' that could be offered wholesale to Lord Kitchener to help fulfil his manpower appeals. With the requirement of the first thousand-strong battalion met, his speech made reference to the raising of another battalion:

> *I am not going to make you a speech of heroics. You have given me your answer, and I can telegraph Lord Kitchener tonight to say that our second battalion is formed ... This should be a Battalion of Pals, a battalion in which friends from the same office will fight shoulder to shoulder for the honour of Britain and the credit of Liverpool.*
> *(Lord Derby, 28 August 1914)*

The 'Pals' concept spread like wildfire in 1914–15 throughout the North and Midlands. Becoming a matter of civic pride, each battalion was raised by local dignitaries, who fed, clothed and equipped these men until the unit was taken over by the War Office – the costs of raising them only then being met by the government. The idea caught on through the desire of some men to join together, either out of camaraderie, or from a desire to avoid mixing with working men outside their class. With the introduction of conscription in 1916, however, the concept became redundant.

Cap badge of a Pals Battalion: Public Works Pioneers Battalion, Middlesex Regiment.

'PALS BATTALIONS'

The Pals phenomenon soon spread; the name 'Pals' would never be accepted officially, but was prominent in unofficial titles. There were other terms used that signified a collective in Kitchener's 'New Army'.

Pals:

Accrington Pals (11th East Yorkshire Regiment)
Birmingham Pals (14–16th Royal Warwickshire Regiment)
Bradford Pals (16th, 18th & 20th West Yorkshire Regiment)
Leeds Pals (15th West Yorkshire Regiment)
Liverpool Pals (17th–20th King's (Liverpool) Regiment)
Manchester Pals (16th–22nd Manchester Regiment)

Chums:

Grimsby Chums (10th Lincolnshire Regiment)

Commercials:

Glasgow Commercials (17th Highland Light Infantry)
Hull Commercials (10th East Yorkshire Regiment)

City & Civic:

Bristol's Own (12th Gloucestershire Regiment)
Sheffield City Battalion (12th York & Lancaster Regiment
Edinburgh City Pals (15th & 16th Royal Scots)
Stockbroker's Battalion (10th Royal Fusiliers)

Trades & engineering:

Hull Tradesmen (11th East Yorkshire Regiment)
Public Works Pioneers (18th, 19th & 26th Middlesex Regiment)

Sportsmen:

Football Battalions (17th & 23rd Middlesex Regiment)
Sportsman's Battalions (23rd & 24th Royal Fusiliers)
Hull Sportsmen (12th East Yorkshire Regiment)

Transport & infrastructure:

Glasgow Tramways Battalion (15th Highland Light Infantry)
Newcastle Railway Pals (17th Northumberland Fusiliers)

Other interest groups:

Glasgow Boy's Brigade Battalion (16th Highland Light Infantry)
T'Others (13th East Yorkshire (Hull) Regiment)
Public Schools Battalion (16th Middlesex Regiment)
Tyneside Irish (24th–27th Northumberland Fusiliers)
Tyneside Scottish (20th–23rd Northumberland Fusiliers)

'SIDESHOW'

With the war often characterised as a battle between those generals
and politicians who pushed for new offensives on the Western Front
in Europe ('the Westerners'), or for one of several options in the near
East ('the Easterners'), the term 'sideshow' came into use. Borrowed
from nineteenth-century circus usage, it was applied to any campaign
that was seen to divert activity away from the main event in France
and Flanders. Gallipoli, Mesopotamia and particularly Salonica were
tarred with the 'sideshow' brush: so much so that H. Collinson Owen's
1919 book *Salonica and After* was subtitled *The Sideshow that Ended
the War*. Yet it was in this 'sideshow' that Bulgaria was defeated in
October 1918; the first of the Central Powers to surrender.

'BIRDCAGE'

The term 'birdcage' was applied to any area of trenches protected by
barbed wire, and particularly where a strongpoint (known as a 'keep'
or 'redoubt') was surrounded by the wire. The most famous use was in
Salonica, where the British Salonica Force (BSF) was kept holed up in
a well-defended encampment surrounding the Greek city of Salonica
(now Thessalonica).

> General Sarrail at once set about the organisation of the 'Birdcage', and
> the British and French dug and wired feverishly. It was quite expected that
> the Bulgars would attack, and in the meantime the correspondents
> on the post were allowed to announce to the world that the Allies
> now found themselves in one of the strongest 'entrenched camps'
> ever made.
>
> (H. Collinson Owen, Salonica and After, *1919)*

A War of 'Things'

The Great War was a war of things, of materiel. Primarily an artillery war fought to break the siege conditions imposed by modern industrialised conflict, it required a vast logistical framework and extended supply train. For the British Army in France, this train involved bases in Le Havre – where Army Service Corps (ASC), Army Ordnance Corps (AOC) and other logistical specialists operated to support the fighting troops in the line. Both the AOC and the ASC were responsible for the supply of munitions and the materiel of war, from the simplest button to the largest calibre shell – a multitude of 'things' that required a huge infrastructure to provide adequate stocks, supply chains and issuing officers.

From the average soldier's perspective these things would include his uniform and boots, as well as what the army would term his 'necessaries' – knife, fork, spoon and so on. Responsible for their upkeep and safekeeping, soldiers could be docked wages for their loss – which in turn sponsored thieving and various acts of 'borrowing' (with slang terms to express these). From the British Army's perspective, 'things' would include myriad weapons of war, from the rifle (Short Magazine Lee Enfield, or SMLE), to the tank, howitzer or aircraft.

'Thingumyjig'

There was a wide range of words to describe something whose name you had forgotten, particularly in a war characterised by the development of military technology. A Lewis gun for example had packing glands, tumbler pins, cork plugs, gibs, split collar roller pins, and axis side lever bushes. Any of these might be called a 'thingumajig', a 'thingummy', an 'oojah', an 'oojiboo', an 'oojah-ka-piv', or an 'oojah-cum-pivvy'. Canadians had a 'hooza-ma-kloo'.

'SWAGGER STICK'

No off-duty soldier would be seen without his swagger stick in Blighty, a pure piece of military nonsense. Swagger sticks came in a variety of shapes and forms; the best have silver ends with the regimental badge, guaranteed to provide extra 'swagger' to the otherwise drab uniform. Purchased from local outfitters and suppliers eager to cash in on a new-found trade, these items appear in the soldier portraits produced by the photographic studios – more often than not provided as props by the establishment. Those men rash enough to splash out on a suit-able stick would leave it at home, consigned, like the officer's sword, to the storeroom, a vestige of nineteenth-century warfare.

'KITCHENER BLUE'

The first recruits to join Kitchener's Army were forced to make com-promises; they had little in the way of equipment, no uniforms and no barracks. Lapel badges stood in for uniforms in the first instance, and men 'went to war' training in flat caps and tweed suits with broom handles. As a stopgap, simple uniforms were supplied in what became known as 'Kitchener Blue' – blue serge in place of khaki. Unsatisfactory, it was replaced before the 'Pals battalions' proceeded overseas.

PUTTEE

Puttees were derived, like the khaki Service Dress, from the British experience in India; 'puttee' coming from the Hindi word for 'band-age'. They were intended to provide a covering for the lower leg that would give greater support and protection. In fact, tying the puttee too tight was to exacerbate the problem of 'trench foot', a condition akin to frostbite resulting from restricted blood circulation and prolonged water immersion. Puttees were used by most nations during the First World War, a military fashion that was to stagger on in one or two armies in a second world conflict. Consisting of long, wool serge strips provided with cotton tapes, puttees were wound around the leg from the ankle to the knee for the average infantryman. Mounted soldiers were distinguished by their practice of winding the puttee from the knee to the ankle, the tapes wound close to the ankle. Finding ways of exerting their own personality, some soldiers would also create, using judiciously applied folds, fancy patterns with their puttees.

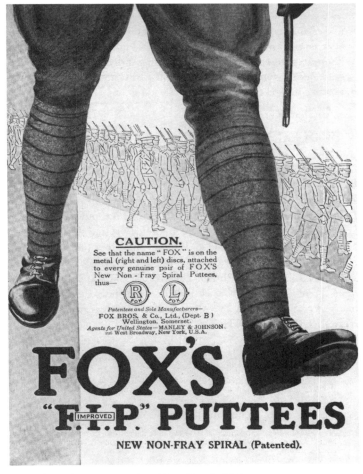

Advert for Fox's Puttees, aimed at officer clientele, 1916.

'MATERNITY JACKET'

The British soldier wore a simple khaki serge uniform known as Service Dress, comprising jacket, trousers, puttees and cap; officers wore a version with open jacket and collar and tie. But one uniform would establish above all others the style of the flying man, the double-breasted clean lines of the RFC tunic, known as the 'Maternity Jacket'. With no buttons showing, and worn with a stylish 'Field Service Cap' – worn rakishly on the side of the head – RFC men in uniform cut a distinctive profile.

'GORBLIMEY'

In 1914, with winter setting in, men in the trenches were resorting to most un-military looking woollen balaclava helmets in an effort to keep warm. The official response was the issue of a 'Winter Service Dress Cap', headgear that was well-padded and equipped with flaps to keep the ears warm. Ungainly, the mythology is that this cap, which became known as a 'gorblimey', was so nicknamed by the first sergeant major who cast his eyes upon one – the term deriving from cockney slang for 'God bless me', though the pre-war maritime song *My Old Man's a Fireman on the Elder Dempster Line* includes the lines 'My old man's a fireman, An 'wot d'yer think o' that? He wears gorblimey trousers an' a little gorblimey 'at.'

> Most of the infantry now wear the soft 'Gorbli'me' hat which looks horrid, but does not give mark as the flat-topped 'Brodrick'.
> (A.D. Gillespie, Letters from Flanders, *1916*)
> (The Brodrick was a shortlived pre-war peakless cap)

> ### 'TEDDY BEAR' COATS.
>
> Second Lieutenant Leonard A. Elgood, on active
> service with the 5th Battalion (Angus and Dundee)
> Black Watch, in a letter to his father, writes: 'You
> have no idea of our clothes! We have been served
> out with coats lined with fur, and they are jolly
> warm. I must add the 'fur' is goat skin – at least,
> that's nearer it. Then with scarves, helmets, hose
> tops, &c., you can imagine we look rather funny.
> These 'fur' coats was be worn either with the fur
> outside or inside, just as you prefer it. They are,
> of course, called 'Teddy bears'.

The *Daily Telegraph*, November 1914. (2nd Lt Elgood would survive the war as a decorated soldier)

'BRITISH WARM'

The 'British Warm' was a short woollen coat, then, as now, designed to be worn over the standard officer's uniform – though it was an optional, non-standard piece of kit. According to Fraser and Gibbon, the term derives from Indian Army usage, where it was listed as 'Coats, Warm, British', in contrast to 'Coats, Warm, Native'.

'HUG-ME-TIGHT'

Rifleman Bernard Britland, taken prisoner in August 1915, was in the November of the following year knitting a 'hug-me-tight', a sleeveless jacket which crossed over in front. These originated in America as women's garments; but Rifleman Britland had a go at making more than one. With touching cheerfulness he wrote home to his 'best girl': 'I will try and make you a hug-me-tight worth wearing, but I think I should be a better hug-me-tight than anything made from wool, don't you eh?'

'GREYBACK'

The standard pullover-style grey flannel shirt of the Great War period was known as the 'greyback'. Worn by all other ranks, the seams of these shirts were regularly tested by the application of candle flames – as soldiers searched for the body lice that would favour the woollen shirt, and which themselves would sometimes be referred to as 'greybacks', a term in use from the mid-nineteenth century in the USA.

'BURBERRY'

The 'Burberry' was a quintessential item of officer's clothing; essentially a 'trench coat' (a number of companies lay claim to the invention, including Burberry and Aquascutum), it was made from waterproofed gabardine material. 'Burberrys' had been worn by pre-war Antarctic explorers and were much in demand 'in the trenches'.

I hung my soaking Burberry to the brazier
(The Morning Rire, *Issue 5, 1915*)

TRENCH COATS IN DEMAND.

Military supply dealers here report a growing demand for the British trench coat on the part of the recently-commissioned army officers from Pittsburg. The coat in question has been designed specially for use in trench warfare. It has a high collar with a wide turn-over, and is close-fitting to the waist. Below the waist it flares out ... as for length, it comes down about to the soldier's ankles. The wide skirt effect gives plenty of leg room for running or climbing in and out of trenches.

The New York Times, *August 29, 1917*

'Burberry Trench Warm' advert, 1917.

'Four-by-two'

As a 'soldier's best friend', it was mandatory that the rifle should be
kept clean. This was not just part of the military obsession with cleaning; it was essential if the principal weapon was to be effective, and
not jam when needed most. As such, in and out of the trenches, rifles
were subject to inspection, with the breech and barrel examined carefully for any sign of the dirt that would jam a round irretrievably in
the barrel and render the weapon unserviceable. In order to clean his
rifle, each soldier was provided with 4in wide flannel strips marked
out in 2in portions – 'four-be-two' in the language of the day, which
passed through the barrel with the aid of a brass-tipped, and therefore
weighted, cord known as a 'pull-through'.

The 'hussif'

The housewife – or 'hussif', presumably derived like many army terms
as the form of the words as they left the sergeant major's mouth – was
an essential piece of kit that held sewing materials, thread, needles, a
thimble, wool, buttons and so on. The ravages of army life meant that
some repair would be necessary – the housewife provided a means
of keeping the uniform in at least some semblance of order; and by
1917–18, with the proliferation of badges and patches, it also allowed
the soldier to add insignia to his tunic. The 'hussif' was simple in construction: a pocket of cotton material with a piece of serge for patching
(and holding needles), closed by a flap. 'You might send me a hussif
as I lost mine when captured', wrote Rifleman Bernard Britland from
a prisoner-of-war camp in Germany in November 1915, though two
months later he asks for 'a housewife and opener'. The *Manchester
Guardian* on 9 March 1918 included a list of items most requested
from the Front, which included hussifs and 'bachelors' buttons', buttons which attached through a simple riveting process rather than
having to be sewn on.

FINNIGANS SOLDIERS' COMFORT BOXES NO. 6

```
2 towels
1 Unbreakable Mirror, nickel-plated, in pigskin case
1 Tommy's cooker
1 Tin of boric acid powder
1 Tube of Tooth Paste (Euthymol)
2 Tablets of Soap (specially prepared)
1 Safety Razor, including 12 blades
1 Shaving brush
1 Stick of shaving soap
1 Rubber Shaving Mug
1 Hussif
1 Tin of Boric Ointment
1 Tin of Anti-Fly cream
1 Tooth Brush

Cost 25/-
```

The Manchester Guardian, *1915*

Every man was in full marching order. His pack contained the following articles: a greatcoat, a woolen shirt, two or three pairs of socks, a change of underclothing, a 'housewife,' – the soldier's sewing kit, – a towel, a cake of soap and a 'hold-all,' in which were a knife, fork, spoon, razor, shaving brush, and comb. All of these were useful and sometimes essential articles, particularly the toothbrush, which Tommy regarded as the best little instrument for cleaning the mechanism of a rifle ever invented. (James Norman Hall, Kitchener's Mob, 1916)

'Button stick' – A contrivance made of brass ten inches long which slides over the buttons and protects the tunic in cleaning. (Arthur Guy Empey, *Over the Top*, 1917)

I'VE LOST MY RIFLE AND BAYONET

I've lost my rifle and bayonet,
I've lost my pull-through too,
I've lost my disc and my puttees,
I've lost my four-by-two.
I've lost my housewife and hold-all,
I've lost my button-stick too.
I've lost my rations and greatcoat–
Sergeant, what shall I do?

(John Brophy and Eric Partridge, Soldier Songs and Slang, *1930)*

IDENTITY DISCS

Identity discs have not always been part of the soldier's traditional accoutrements. Now known as 'dog tags' – because of their obvious similarity to the small pieces of metal used by pet-owners to identify their charges – this term has a US origin, dating back to the nineteenth century, and appears not to have been commonly used in British circles. Pre-war, identity in the British Army was provided by the Pay Book. Inadequate, this form of identification was supplemented by the addition of a single stamped aluminium disc with the soldier's details, replaced in 1914 by a single red fibre disc, and in August 1916 by a two-disc system; the green to stay with the body, the red to be removed. By the end of the war they were known by the grimly ironic name 'cold meat ticket'.

Little circles of soft vulcanite, known as 'Identity Discs,' and inscribed with each man's regimental number, name, regiment and religion, were handed out, to be worn on a piece of string round the neck –forbidding things, for obviously they would only be needed when the wearer was hors de combat *and unable to speak.*
(G. Belton Cobb, Stand to Arms, *1916)*

Medals

Campaign Medal Groups: (1914–15 Star, War Medal and Victory Medal): Pip, Squeak and Wilfred after cartoon characters, or Gieves, Matthew and Seagrove, from the naval outfitters.
DSO (Distinguished Service Order): Dick Shot Off
MC (Military Cross, first awarded 1915): Maconochie Cross
MM (Military Medal, first awarded 1915): Maconochie Medal, Many Muddles, Mother's Meeting
OBE (Order of the British Empire, first awarded in 1917): Other Bugger's Efforts

Tommy Cooker

Tommy cookers were solid fuel heaters that were manufactured 'for the man in the trenches'. Usually consisting of a simple frame to support both a cake of solid fuel and the soldier's mess-tin, there were a number of commercial types available, including 'Kamprite' and 'Anglo', which were 'perfect for use in trenches, camp and in the field'. 'Tommy cookers' are still made today.

> *We had to brew our tea on fiendish contrivances called Tommy Cookers, which took on an average two hours to boil half a pint of water.*
> *(Pte Alfred M. Burrage, Artists' Rifles,* War is War, *1930)*

Flea-bag

The 'flea-bag' was an officer's valise-come-sleeping bag, part of the extensive kit recommended to newly commissioned officers; the derivation of the term was obvious.

TRENCH WADERS

Local circumstances dictated that some trenches – particularly those deeply dug into clay soils – were water-logged, thereby promoting the debilitating condition known as 'trench foot', caused by excessive water immersion. To prevent this, rubber waders, or 'gum boots', were issued as 'trench stores' to the men in the frontline, kept there to be worn by successive occupants of the trenches.

> 'Gum boots' – Rubber receptacles for holding water. Also used in the game of slipping the slippery slip in wet and muddy trenches.
> (The War Budget, *30 March, 1916*)

STEEL HELMET

Given the importance of the steel helmet, introduced in the autumn of 1915, it is perhaps odd that there were so few variations on its name. Though collectors today call it the 'Brodie' (after its inventor, John Brodie), there is no evidence to suggest this was used at the time. 'Tin hat', 'battle bowler' and 'steel jug' seem to have been sufficient; 'tin hat' was such a succinct phrase, so clear and quick to say and understand, that further variation was probably unnecessary. Variants were 'tin lid', 'lid', 'toby' and 'pudding basin'. It is notable that 'tin hat' was also the term most favoured during the Second World War. More than a decade after the war, 'tin hat' was still in use in the expression 'to tin-hat the lot', as in 'to top it all' (H.Z. Smith, *Women of the Aftermath*, 1931). The term 'shrapnel-helmet', used occasionally, shows the main purpose of the helmet in protecting the wearer's head and neck from shells bursting above.

> I was struck on the 'Tin helmet' as we call them, by a large piece of shrapnel two inches long.
> (Diary entry, Pte John T. Lawton, 5th King's Liverpool Regiment)

'**Steel helmet**' – A round hat made out of steel which is supposed to be shrapnel proof. It is until a piece of shell goes through it, then Tommy loses interest as to whether it is shrapnel proof or not. He calls it a 'tin hat'.
'**Tin-hat**' – Tommy's name for his steel helmet which is made out of a metal that is as hard as mush. The only advantage is that it is heavy and generally adds to the weight of Tommy's equipment. Its most popular use is for carrying eggs.

(Arthur Guy Empey, *Over the Top*, 1917)

'This puts the tin hat on it!': Donald MacGill postcard, *c.* 1916. The reverse of this card carries the message: 'This is what I look like in some of the stunts we have to do'.

'This puts the tin hat on it !!'

C'est ça qui vous complète un homme !

PICKELHAUBE

The German spiked helmet that had been worn since the mid part of the nineteenth century, and which had spawned a Victorian military fashion for spiked helmets in both Britain and the USA, was to define the image of the German soldier in numerous cartoon images, usually impossibly worn perched upon a large head. The *pickelhaube* was a favoured souvenir of Allied troops.

> *The walls [of the dug-out] were all panelled and lined with a double row of bunk, on which lay blankets, ruffled from recent use. A greatcoat or two hung on the walls, and (joy!) there were five 'pickelhaubes' lying about.*
> *(Charles Edmonds*, A Subaltern's War, *1929)*

BLACK VEILING RESPIRATOR

The use of poison gas by the Germans on 22 April 1915 during the Second Battle of Ypres caught the Allies unprepared. Primitive respirators were extemporised on 23–24 April, with General Headquarters (GHQ) of the BEF issuing a directive that field dressings should be soaked in bicarbonate of soda, an alkaline, to combat the suspected chlorine – although urine was equally effective. Scientific advice mustered by the British was to devise a respirator in May 1915 based around a pad of cotton waste soaked with sodium hyposulphite, sodium carbonate and glycerine; this was held in black mourning gauze, used to tie the mask to the face.

HYPO HELMET

The gas or tube helmet, a flannel hood designed by Captain Cluny MacPherson of the Newfoundland Regiment, was introduced in May 1915 in response to the first German gas attack. The hood covered the whole head, its tail being tucked into the tunic to provide a seal, and a simple mica window was provided for vision. The 'Hypo Helmet' (officially, 'Smoke Helmet') was soaked in sodium hyposulphite solution or 'hypo', which would counteract the effects of the gas drawn in through the material by breathing. By the autumn of 1915, this was replaced by a more sophisticated version, the 'Phenate (P) Helmet', using the same basic gas hood design, and developed in response to the introduction of phosgene, ten times more toxic than chlorine. This mask was made from cotton flannelette soaked in sodium phenate, with two circular glass eye-pieces and a tube valve and rubber outlet to expel carbon dioxide held in the teeth. This contraption gave rise to another term, the 'tube helmet'. This nightmarish creation was famously recorded as the 'goggle-eyed [or googly-eyed] bugger with the tit' by Captains Robert Graves and J.C. Dunn of the Royal Welsh Fusiliers. From January 1916 all P Helmets were dipped in hexamine – highly absorbent of phosgene gas – to become the 'Phenate-Hexamine' or 'PH Helmet'. All were clammy, cloying and unpleasant to wear.

If a whiff of gas you smell,
Bang your gong like bloody hell,
On with your googly, up with your gun –
Ready to meet the bloody Hun
(Captain J.C. Dunn, The War the Infantry Knew, *1988)*

The Trench Times, *May 1916*

SMALL BOX RESPIRATOR

The Small Box Respirator (SBR) was developed in order to provide universal protection from a range of gases, without being an encumbrance to free movement. The face mask was linked by a hose to a 'box' filled with lime-permanganate granules between two layers of charcoal, and was carried in a haversack that could be worn either slung over the shoulder, or, through the use of a lug and leather strap, hitched up onto the chest into the 'alert' position. When wearing it, the soldier gripped an inner rubber mouthpiece between his teeth, using the integrated nose clip to ensure his breathing was through the 'box'. When first issued universally with these in August–October 1916, each soldier was acclimatised to gas exposure (when wearing the mask) in a tear gas chamber for five minutes. This mask was highly effective.

PERISCOPES

In the trenches, looking over the parapet during daylight hours was most unwise; snipers would have weapons fixed in position, targeted at dips in the parapet, at latrines and crossing points, and at loop hole plates. There was continual loss of life on the Western Front through the actions of snipers in this way. From early on, the need to be able to look over the parapet to observe activity in no-man's-land led to the production of specially designed 'trench periscopes'. In an issue of the *Transactions of the Optical Society* for 1915, the basic parameters were laid down for trench periscopes, the object of which, it was stated, was 'to give the soldier a view of his front whilst his head and person are sheltered'. Soldier names for periscopes included a 'look see', or a 'look stick', presumably for the slender types often carried by officers.

BAYONET

Despite the proposal that between the Boer War and 1914 that 'there was to be no shock-combat in future' (Gen. I.H. Langlois, *Lessons from Two Recent Wars (Russo-Turkish & South African),* 1909), the bayonet was retained on the grounds of its success as a morale-booster and intimidatory weapon. The ambivalence in using the bayonet is revealed in the words of 'a junior officer' quoted in *The Scotsman* as having 'stuck [his] man' in July 1916, while C.E. Montague in *Disenchantment* (1922) claimed that 'the bayonet does not win battles – it claims battles already won ... the bayonet thrust is more of a gesture.' Called 'Josephine' or 'Rosalie' by the French (there was some dispute concerning the promotion of 'Rosalie' by the French press, which was resisted by the troops), British soldiers used the terms 'cat-stabber', 'meat-skewer', 'tin-opener' and 'tooth-pick' (corresponding to the German slang term *Zahnstocher*).

Dear Kitty,
You should have seen us today on bayonnet fighting we were half mad the man who can pull the uglyiest face and do the most shouting is the best...
(Pte P. Edwards, 1st Battalion Royal Welsh Fusiliers, July 1918)

TRENCH KNIVES

In most cases, the average bayonet was too long to be of any effective use as an offensive weapon in trench raids. While the Americans, the Germans and the French were to be issued with short knives for battle use, the British would resort to privately purchased examples from stores like *The Army and Navy* in London, or to manufacturing their own close to the frontline. Typical of this industry was the use of cut-down bayonets, but any other suitable piece of metal that would carry a blade was also to be pressed into service. Nevertheless the trench club would be the weapon of choice in British trench raids.

THE GREAT GAME

SUBALTERN (wounded four times at Gallipoli, and about to rejoin after four months' sick leave: *"Can I get a trench dagger here?"*
SHOPWALKER: 'Trench dagger?' Certainly, Sir. You'll get that in the Sports Department."
(Punch, *24 May 1916*)

TRENCH CLUBS

Of all the items associated with trench warfare, the rediscovery of clubs and knives as weapons is identified with the descent of warfare from the ideal of open battle to the extended and stalemated nightmare of the trenches. In the strict confines of the trench, rifles with fixed bayonets could not be wielded effectively, and where a modicum of surprise was needed, the club, knife, revolver and grenade found favour in night-time trench raids. In most cases, clubs were fashioned from whatever was to hand – and there was no official issue of such weapons in the British Army. With the British experience in South Africa, the term 'knobkerrie' (from Cape Dutch) made a resurgence, while 'Kosh' or 'cosh' had been around since the mid-nineteenth century, although its origin remains unknown.

HIPE

Names for the rifle include 'bondook', from nineteenth-century Indian Army slang, but also 'Hipe'. This was a term used as a substitute for 'arms' by NCOs when giving orders on the parade ground, such as 'Slope Arms'; becoming, in this instance, 'Slope hipe'. Associated with the Regular Army, 'hipe' was picked up by the civilian armies of the Great War, finding its way into the poems of Patrick MacGill, who served with the London Irish Rifles at Loos in 1915.

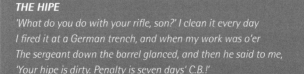

THE HIPE

'What do you do with your rifle, son?' I clean it every day
I fired it at a German trench, and when my work was o'er
The sergeant down the barrel glanced, and then he said to me,
'Your hipe is dirty. Penalty is seven days' C.B.!'
(Extract from Patrick MacGill, Soldier Songs, 1916)

MACHINE GUN

Of all the weapons associated with trench warfare, the machine gun is perhaps the most infamous. *The Times* during the early months of the war used the word '*mitrailleuse*', only introducing 'machine-gun' on 2 September 1914, and thereafter using both terms until November 1916, after which *mitrailleuse* was used only for air and naval combat. *The Soldiers' War Slang Dictionary* (1938) reports the use of 'makki' and 'mangle' as terms for the machine gun, mangle coming from the rotating handle of early *mitrailleuse*. 'MG' was a common term in use among British soldiers, who also used the proprietary names such as 'Vickers' or 'Lewis.' The Germans had a vivid collection of metaphors for the weapon, which translated as 'death-organ', 'stuttering aunt', 'stone-knocker', 'stutterbox', 'tak-tak', 'mowing machine', 'butcher-machine' and 'diarrhea-machine'. While a range of literary uses of language assign the qualities of the human voice, or writing, to different kinds of gun, one metaphor is found repeatedly – 'rattle' for the sound of the machine gun. Empey in *Over the Top* combines both ideas in comparing a machine gun to a 'typewriter', while in French trench-slang it was a 'coffee-grinder'.

BOMB

In the early stages of the war the British were out-bombed by the Germans, who deployed their efficient stick grenade (*stielhandgranate*) – known as the 'potato-masher' by both sides. The British version from 1914, a 16in stick grenade ('policeman's truncheon'), had a fatal flaw – as it was detonated by a percussion striker, the bomber had to be extremely careful not to hit the side of the trench when preparing to throw it. By 1915 soldiers were making their own 'bombs', ignited by a slow-burning fuse. Typical of these was the 'jam-tin' bomb – literally a tin filled with explosive gun cotton and shrapnel balls. Another bomb involved a slab of gun cotton on a handle, nick-named the 'hairbrush'. In France, the 'Battye Bomb' – named after its inventor Major Basil Battye RE – was manufactured at Béthune, and consisted of a cast-iron cylinder containing 40g of explosive ignited by a Nobel fuse.

The Type 15, or 'Cricket-ball', was the first grenade to be mass produced, again in 1915. Also ignited by friction, the grenade was badly affected in wet weather, the special friction brassards issued to bombers rendered useless. Despite their limitations, half a million grenades of this type were eventually produced. Unreliable, they were replaced by the Mills Grenade in May 1915, named after its inventor, William Mills. Officially designated the 'Number 5' grenade, but sometimes called a 'Mills spud' by the soldiery, the secret of the Mills' success lay with its ignition system: the striker was activated when a pin was removed and a lever was released to trigger a four-second fuse, during which time the bomber had to throw the grenade. Other grenades included the German *diskushandgranate*, a flat discus-like bomb with detonators around its edge that was christened the 'tortoiseshell' by the British, as well as the *eierhandgranate*, the egg grenade, the German answer to the Mills Grenade but small and of limited effect.

> *A dozen varieties of bombs were in use … The 'hairbrush,' the 'lemon bomb,' the 'cricket ball,' and the 'policeman's truncheon' were the most important of these, all of them so-named because of their resemblance to the articles for which they were named.*
> (*James Norman Hall*, Kitchener's Mob, *1916*)

German 'potatomasher' or *kartoffelstamper*.

TANK

The 'tank' was one of the most important weapons to be developed during the war, first used in the Battle of the Somme at Flers in September 1916. Originally called 'landships' or 'land cruisers' (reflecting the interest of the Royal Navy in their early development), the codename 'tank' was first used by Colonel Ernest Swinton to disguise their actual purpose, the idea being that they were 'water tanks' for the British campaign in Mesopotamia. The first prototype was named 'Little Willie', and the next, 'Big Willie' (the first with a rhombohedral shape), would also be called 'Mother'. It was 'Mother' that set the pattern for British tanks in the Great War. German slang names for a tank reflected their use: *Grabenrampe* ('trenchramp') or *Chauseewalze* ('road-roller').

> I was instructed ... to try to find some non-committal word to take the place of 'landship' or 'land cruiser' ... The structure of the machine in its early stages being boxlike, some term conveying the idea of a box or container seemed appropriate. That night ... the word 'tank' was employed in its new sense for the first time. And thus, on Christmas Eve, 1915, was given a new significance to a simple little English word ...
>
> (*Major General E.D. Swinton,* Eyewitness, *1937*)

Alternative names for the tank

Early names
Armoured machine gun cruisers
Armoured machine gun destroyers
Caterpillar
Caterpillar machine gun destroyer
Landcruisers
'Land ironclads' (H.G. Wells, 1903)
Landships

Names for the prototypes
'Little Willie'
HMS *Centipede*
'Mother'
'Big Willie'

Alternative codenames
Cistern

Container
Receptacle
Reservoir

Press nicknames
'Boojum'
'Jabberwock with eyes of flame'
'Giant Toad'
'Hush-hush'
'Land dreadnought'
'Old Ichthyosaurus'
'Motor-monster'
'Slug'
'Touring fort'
'Travelling turret'
'Whale'

Major-General E.D. Swinton, *Eyewitness,* 1937

Tommy and Poilu, on taking leave of each other:
Tommy: Au reservoir.
Poilu: Tanks, tanks
(The Brazier, *the magazine of the Canadian Scottish (16th Battalion,
CEF), 20 December 1916)*

ANZAC

The term ANZAC was first used in Egypt, where the Australian and New Zealand Army Corps were in training prior to their deployment to a battlefront. An obvious acronym for the army corps, its use is nevertheless credited to Sergeants Little and Millington, who had cut a rubber stamp with the initials 'A & NZAC' for the purpose of registering papers at the corps headquarters, situated in Shepheard's Hotel, Cairo. When a codename was requested for the corps, a British officer, Lieutenant White, naturally suggested ANZAC.

While ANZAC was the official designation, the term would soon become applied to the area of the Gallipoli Peninsula where soldiers themselves first saw action: Anzac Cove, which has become a formal geographical term in Turkey since the 1980s. It would also encompass the men from both Australia and New Zealand who served at Gallipoli, and who later saw action in France, Flanders, Palestine and elsewhere. As the Anzac forces in Gallipoli also included the Ceylon Planters Rifles, one correspondent to *The Times*, 6 September 1915, suggested a modification: 'The dispatches from the Dardanelles vividly suggest that Anzac should in future include an "I" for India. May I suggest Ainzac?'

With losses mounting at Gallipoli, there were moves in December 1915 to name the fledgling new capital of Australia 'Anzac', rather than Canberra. In order to raise interest and investment in the English south coast housing estate he was promoting, Charles Neville in 1915 set up a competition to name the new town; the prize was awarded in January 1916 to the name 'New Anzac-on-Sea', by which time the Allied forces at the Dardanelles had been evacuated. As the news filtered through, Anzac-on-Sea was soon renamed Peacehaven. Later in the year, Parliament moved to protect the word itself, with a bill presented and introduced in October 1916 with the following words: 'The origin of the word "Anzac" is well known to us. It is a word which has become almost sacred from its being associated with deeds of heroism and sacrifice. It is not right or fitting that a word associated with hallowed memories of brave and gallant men should be used for trade purposes and as a trade mark, and that we should have "Anzac soap" and an "Anzac Motor Company" … Worst of all, everybody will recollect that the word "Anzac" was used in the "Anzac-on-Sea" case when it was certainly put to a very base and improper use'.

Accordingly, on 18 December, Parliament passed the *'Anzac' (Restriction on Trade Use of Word) Act,* which stated that 'it shall not be lawful to use in connection with any trade, business, calling, or profession the word "Anzac", or any word closely resembling that word, without the authority of a Secretary of State, given on the request of the Government of the Commonwealth of Australia or of the Dominion of New Zealand, and this prohibition shall apply notwithstanding that such word forms part of any trade mark, or of the name of any company or society or other body, which has been registered before the passing of this Act.' Companies which had been using the name were required to abandon it, this specifically referring to The Anzac Motor Company, which, after a debate in the Commons, was given three months to change its name.

Australian 'ANZAC Day' badges from 1919.

FROM 'STAND TO' TO 'STAND DOWN'

Life in the trenches was dominated by its routine; the beat of daily existence which commenced with 'stand to' (from 'stand to arms') at one hour before dawn, when all troops in the frontline would stand upon the fire-step armed and ready to confront an attacker in the early light. Stand to would last at least an hour-and-a-half, but would finish when the enemy parapet could be seen through the periscopes set up along the line of the trenches. Following stand to, most men were stood down, but leaving sentries on duty, one per platoon, to man the fixed box periscopes. With stand down, a tot of rum was issued to each man, a welcome respite from the often freezing conditions.

Breakfast would follow, with the meal comprising rations that had been brought up at night and meant to last a forty-eight-hour period. This included tea, bacon and bread – these were the staples – but often it could be simply bully-beef and biscuits. Night fatigue parties would bring up hot food in specially designed carriers where possible; all other goods were brought up in sand bags, often a hopeless jumble of loose and tinned rations. Corned beef – 'bully' to the troops – was a variously received staple. Other tinned food staples included 'pork and beans' – beans with a small cube of pork fat – and a ration of Maconochie, which was a vegetable and meat concoction. Jam was a versatile ration, but the frequency of 'Tickler's Plum and Apple' variety was unpopular, with strawberry jam largely suspected to have been removed by transport men earlier in the chain. Fresh rations – meat, bacon, vegetables – would also be supplied where possible, though C.W. Langley noted on 1 May 1915: 'We caught a cabbage today, a sturdy, tough old thing of last year's hatching (1st green food since September).' Water was from petrol tins, and would never quite lose its petrol taste – something even the strongest tea could not defeat.

After breakfast, it was time for platoon commanders to make their inspection of rifles – which the men had cleaned during their meal

– attention being given to the breech and chamber, parts of the gun liable to fouling from mud and dirt. Those men not on 'sentry go' were detailed for 'fatigues', working parties for trench repairs; similar activities in no-man's-land would have to wait for the cover of darkness.

INFORMATION AND MISINFORMATION

The incessant flow of information between the frontline and headquarters (HQ) put junior officers under a lot of extra pressure, every incident having to be reported to the 'Cuthberts' (desk-workers). Information coming from HQ was, as far as the ORs were concerned, 'bumf' (bum fodder), 'eye-wash', or, after 1917, 'camouflage'. At the front, rumours were known as 'gup', 'clack' (an old term for tongue), 'guff', and among Australian troops 'furphy', adopted from 'Furphy carts', water and sanitary carts manufactured in Victoria for the ANZAC forces. Information would be processed by 'column-dodgers', who, as far as the troops were concerned, were 'swinging the lead', or 'swinging it'.

> *E is for Eye-wash, a wonderful lotion, employed by the man who is keen on promotion.*
> (An Anzac Alphabet, *J.W.S. Henderson, RGA,* The Anzac Book, *1916*)

> **FURPHS**
>
> *There's rumours and rumours of rumours*
> *A-travelling along the line;*
> *There's rumours of rumours rumoured*
>   *As an art cut very fine*
>
> *In soldier's palaver 'furphs' they are called,*
>   *And busy as busy they be*
> *In variety most inexhaustible*
>   *Of happenings on land and sea.*
>
> (*J.M. Harjkins*, Blighty, Summer Number, *1917*)

'KAMERAD'

Meaning literally 'comrade', the term was used reputedly by German soldiers on the point of surrender, an act that would, it was hoped, ensure their safety – and survival. It was instinctive for surrendering soldiers to call upon fellow combatants – comrades in arms – for quarter. The term was adopted early on by the British press and in cartoons, often accompanied by the usual image of oversized men in small uniforms, or of thin specimens in spectacles. The term was also to see extensive use in the plethora of 'war books' that appeared in the late 1920s and early 1930s. 'To Kamerad' logically meant 'to offer surrender'.

Kamerad: typical negative stereotyping of German troops, *c.* 1916.

'FUNK' AND 'WINDY'

In a period when the mentioning of fears was not considered a thera-
peutic way of dealing with them, there were a number of ways of
avoiding saying 'afraid' or 'frightening'. A correspondent in the June
1918 issue of *Kia Ora Coo-ee*, the magazine of the ANZAC forces in
Egypt, Palestine, Salonica and Mesopotamia, wrote: 'it is a very windy
proposition to sit in a "bus" that is performing all the insane tricks
a pilot can think of', 'windy' being a development from 'having the
wind up'; 'wind vertical' was a popular version among airmen. Even
an avoidance term like 'getting the jitters' was altered to the expression
'to get 'em', while 'batchy' was a pre-war army term for 'temporarily
unhinged by fright'. Later in the war, 'wind-up jackets' were ordinary
soldiers' tunics worn by officers – thereby removing the possibility of
being targetted by snipers.

'Funk' was originally 'smoke'; Ned Ward in the late seventeenth-
century *London Spy* talks about the 'funking society', those who
spent time in tobacco shops. By the nineteenth century, army slang
was using 'funk' to mean 'fear', as in the diary of Assistant Surgeon
Henry Kelsall during the Indian Rebellion in 1857, when he
describes a soldier 'bolting home in a great funk'. 'Funky' was occasionally used to mean 'afraid', while a 'funk-hole' was any hole you
dived into in no-man's-land to shelter from gunfire. Other words
and phrases include the obscure 'bar poo' and 'to go to bar poo' (to
lose your nerves).

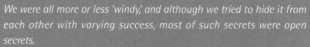

*Wind-up, immediately, everyone thinking we were about to embark
[for France]. Nothing further happened, however.*
(*Pte Sydney Thomas Fuller, 1/1st Cambridgeshire Regiment,
23 December 1917*)

*We were all more or less 'windy,' and although we tried to hide it from
each other with varying success, most of such secrets were open
secrets.*
(*Pte Alfred M. Burrage, Artists' Rifles,* War is War, *1930*)

Sometimes at night an unaccountable outburst of firing is heard far away in the north: it runs like a wind down the trenches, getting louder and louder: we stand to, and pour rapid fire into No-Man's Land. They call it a 'wind-up', and 'getting the wind-up' is becoming quite a regular term for the panic.
(*26 January 1915*, A Soldier's Diary of the Great War, *1929*)

'I thought you said Scotch soldiers never got the wind up!': play on words on a postcard, *c.* 1915.

'CARL THE CARETAKER'

As trench warfare required trench-dwellers to keep under cover and not to look over the parapet in daylight, a mythology arose that suggested that the trenches in front were not garrisoned, but rather looked after by a solitary individual – 'Carl the Caretaker'.

> *I had actually seen a German, although Tommy insisted that it was only the old caretaker. 'Carl the caretaker' was supposed to be a methodical old man whom the Emperor had left in charge of his trenches on the western front ... Sometimes he was 'Hans the Grenadier,' owing to his fondness for nightly bombing parties. Sometimes he was 'Minnie's husband.'*
> (*James Norman Hall*, Kitchener's Mob, *1916*)

'STAND TO'

'Stand to' was an abbreviation of the term 'Stand to Arms', meaning to stand on the defensive, armed ready and waiting for an attack. As those attacks most commonly came at dawn or dusk, in the trenches, Stand to also came to be associated with these specific times, when the garrison of the frontlines would stand on the fire-step ready to meet a potential attacker. In some cases, Stand to was a time to fire off a prospective warning fusillade of small arms – also known as the 'morning hate', or 'mad minute'. Stand to was followed by 'Stand down.'

> *Just after the first streak of dawn had appeared behind the German trenches, an order was passed down the line, 'STAND TO,' and Allan was awakened from a doze and told to stand on the firestep. 'Stand to,' he was told, was an abbreviation of 'Stand to arms.'*
> (*G. Belton Cobb*, Stand to Arms, *1916*)

> May 26th, 1915. *A typical day in these trenches begins at dawn, with 'Stand to.' The N.C.O.'s jerk the men out of their heavy sleep – the private soldier seems to have the power of dropping off into deep slumber in the most uncomfortable positions – and plant them on the fire-step, where they yawn and rub their eyes, and begin to clean their rifles, before the inspecting officer comes round.*
> (A Soldier's Diary of the Great War, *1929*)

'MAD MINUTE'

The British Regular Army that formed the bulk of the original BEF sent to France in August 1914 was highly trained; famously, at Mons it was this army that was capable of maintaining a rate of fire of fifteen rounds a minute fired from the bolt action Short Magazine Lee Enfield (SMLE) rifle. Trained in what was termed the 'mad minute' – the act of firing this many rounds in the alloted time – the soldiers that followed would rarely be able to exhibit the same level of professionalism in their musketry. In the trenches, the mad minute would also be exercised at Stand to.

> *We had our training amongst the hills and dales. There had the first taste of the 'Mad Minute', load and fire 15 rounds of ammunition in 1 minute, scores being recorded in the butts.*
> (*Pte Ralph I. Smith, D Coy, 12th Battalion, Gloucestershire Regiment* (*Bristol's Own*))

'SUICIDE CLUB'

A term given to a machine-gun ('Emma-Gee') company, trench-mortar ('Toc-emma') battery or bombing company – all hazardous occupations. None were popular with their neighbours, the infantry; singled out for particular attention by the opposing artillery after deploying their weapons, their positions would be mercilessly bombarded.

> 'The joke's on you ... you have joined the suicide club'. We asked the chaps
> to explain ... when in the line or trenches, the bombers got most of the
> risky jobs and were exposed to more danger.than the ordinary man of
> the regiment.
> (*Harry Stinton, 1/7th London Regiment* (*Diary entry, published as*
> Harry's War, *2002*))

'SENTRY GO'

'Stag' was sentry duty, otherwise known as 'sentry go' or 'picket (piquet)
duty'; 'doing stag' involved two hours on duty followed by four hours
off; soldiers were 'told off' for sentry duty. Twenty-four-hour guard
duty was known as 'doing one for the King'. 'Gillo' was a common term
for 'look alert'. The sentry challenge took the form: 'Halt, who comes
there?' 'Friend.' 'Advance one and give the countersign'.

FAGS

With cigarettes being in such plentiful supply, chain-smoking was
inevitable, helped along by organisations like the Tobacco Fund of

the *Weekly Despatch* newspaper, which
provided 'comforts' to the troops. So
important were cigarettes to the men
that some would risk serious injury
to get a 'fag' (derived from a term
for 'something that drooped'), or
would keep their 'emergency fags'
and matches in their field dressing pocket. Rifleman Groom of the
London Rifle Brigade recalls that
cigarettes cost one franc for a tin of
fifty – his usual ration for six days
in the line was six tins – and that

Handy Black Cat Dictionary, 1915; given
away in 'fag packets'.

chain smoking was the norm in the line, a remedy for frayed nerves. The most popular cigarettes were Woodbines, Gold Flakes, Navy Cut and Capstan (these were those suggested for purchase in the *British Prisoner of War Gazette*), while also frequently mentioned were Turf, Flag, Three Castles and Black Cats, while De Rezskes and Kensitas were specifically advertised to officers. The commonest slang term for cigarette, after 'fags', were 'coffin nails' and 'yellow perils', while the term 'gasper' was common enough to be used as the name for the trench paper of the 18th–21st Battalions, Royal Fusiliers.

W the Woodbines they smoke by the score like Oliver Twist we are asking for more.
(*Joyce Denys, Hampden Gordon & M.C. Tindall,* Our Hospital ABC, *1917*)

On Active Service
28-12-16

Dear Sir, Please accept my heartiest thanks for the cigarettes which have just reached me in the desert. I need not say how very acceptable they are. It is 14 months now since I left Penarth but I can see they have not forgotten the Penarth boys.

Hon. Sec.

Penarth Xmas Present Fund

Penarth

S. Wales

Postcard to the Cardiff Evening Press *Tobacco Fund from Pte Ben Walker, E.E.F.*

TRENCH LIGHTERS: 'THREE ON A MATCH'

To the average cigarette-obsessed soldier, the means of obtaining a light was of prime importance. The phrase 'three on a match' supposedly relates to a wartime superstition that lingering too long on a shared match was a dangerous pastime, the third man being the potential recipient of a sniper's bullet – though this could just as easily be a post-war invention. Matches being prone to dampness, a range of lighters were commercially available (including the simple, 'tinder lighter' issued with the Princess Mary Gift Tin in Christmas 1914). 'Trench art' lighters were common too, made from scrap brass or bullets, and produced in ordnance and engineer workshops of the AOC, RE and ASC.

Pack up your troubles in your old kit-bag,
And smile, smile, smile,
While you've a Lucifer to light your fag,
Smile boys, that's the style.
(Pack up Your Troubles, *by George Henry Powell, 1915*)

A 'DUCK'S BREAKFAST' AND OTHER MEALS

The mere existence of the phrase 'duck's breakfast' (a face-wash and a drink of water) in the environment of the trenches serves to indicate how irregular and often meagre food supplies were for frontline troops. The ubiquitous 'biscuit' gave its name to square mattresses of horse hair occasionally available to billeted soldiers. Chocolate, when available, came in 'sticks', and 'coco' was an infusion of liquorice available in estaminets (small café). By August 1915, C.W. Langley was feeling that 'No one can stand bully beef now' ('corned willie' – corned beef – was unpopular enough to be linked to the Kaiser's name), especially when the estaminets held the promise of 'Bombardier Fritz' (pomme frites). 'Oofs' and 'lay' could be bought from French peasants. The most desired food was sent from home, and might be cake, chocolate or even roast chicken. The canteen of the 7th Canadian Infantry Battalion offered Peak Frean cakes (2 francs for 1lb), milk,

Nestles (1 franc per tin), and lobsters (2 francs per tin). Pte Bernard Britland in a PoW camp in October 1915 sent a card home asking for tinned tongue, salmon and rabbit; in June 1916 he wrote: ' I received your parcel of cakes last week, in very good condition'.

HOGMANAY EVE DINNER, 1916

Soup – Puree of Mud, Cream of Tomato
Fish – Salmon Croquettes a la Hand Grenade
Entrees – Macaroni au Pull-Through, 'Colt' Mutton
Roasts – Turkey and P.P. Sauce, Old English Roast Beef and Yorkshire Pudding. The function of the turkey is to transmit motion and energy to the mechanism of the M.G. Section.
Salad – A la German Kultur (Boche!)
Game – Sniper, Potted au Telescopic Sight
Vegetables – 'Bombardier Fritz' (fried potatoes), Creamed Carrots, 'Shrapnel' (shelled peas)
Sweets – 'Belt-fillers' with Ammunition Sauce (plum pudding), 'Jack Johnsons' (a trifle?), 'Bomb proofs' (mince pies), Cheese, Nuts and Raisins. Coffee.

The Brazier, trench journal of the Canadian Scottish, 16th Battalion CEF, 1916

November 19th, 1914. 'Pommes de terre frites' is anglicised into 'Bombardier Fritz' by the Tommies.
(A Soldier's Diary of the Great War, *1929*)

'Bully beef' – A kind of corned beef with tin around it. The unopened tins make excellent walls for dugouts.
(Arthur Guy Empey, *Over The Top*, 1917)

BULLY BEEF

Corned beef – 'bully' to the troops – was imported then, as it is now, from South America. The origin of the term 'bully beef' is obscure, though the strongest contender is from the French *bouilli* (boiled beef), or it may equally have been derived from the use of bull images on the tin. Other tinned food staples included 'pork and beans' – tinned beans with a small cube of pork fat at the bottom of the tin. Bully beef was so prevalent that it was surprising that some soldiers could record a preference for one brand over another – for Pte Hodges serving in 1918, 'Fray Bentos' was the preferred brand.

IRON RATIONS

In the war, 'iron rations' comprised a tin of 'bully beef', biscuits, and a tin containing tea and sugar. It was a 'crime' to dip into these rations unless the order was given to do so from an officer, the intention being that these would be used only in an emergency. According to Fraser and Gibbon, the term derives from German seventeenth-century usage, and was certainly prevalent in the British Army two centuries later, perhaps relating to the tin – or the accompanying army biscuits. These were so hard that men had to have reasonable teeth – a requirement of the medical inspection on enlistment – to bite into them (they were sometimes called 'the dentist's friend'), or they had to be ground into a powder and mixed with water to make rudimentary desserts or to bulk up food in the frontline. The term was also used for German shelling on the Western Front – 'iron rations' for light shelling and 'iron foundries' for heavy shelling.

> They're hiking over muddy roads in sunny Picardy,
> They've heard about the roses ... but no roses can they see!
> If walking makes one healthy they should be a sturdy bunch,
> They've just done eighteen kilos on an iron ration lunch.
> (*P.A. Savi and E.M. Savi*, Bosh and Boche, Reminiscences, *1919*)

'DIXIE'

A Dixie or Dixy was a large cooking pot with a lid that was also carried into the trenches by soldiers 'out on rest', but otherwise on a fatigue. Each dixie held twenty pints of food to be divided between twenty men.

> *Each company had its own field kitchen, a sort of two-wheeled cart,*
> *containing a fire and five large metal pots known as 'dixies'. Each of*
> *these dixies held enough tea or stew for fifty men.*
> (*G. Belton Cobb,* Stand to Arms, *1916*)

'JIPPO'

'Jippo' referred to any kind of meat fat or dripping, especially bacon fat, but was sometimes used to mean 'stew'. There were many variant spellings to this word, indicating its primarily spoken usage: jippo, gippo, gypo, gypoo, jippy, and more. Though officially first documented in 1914, it was clearly a development from 'jipper' or 'gipper', variously given as Isle of Wight dialect, navy slang, and an army slang word for 'Irish stew'. It probably derived from the word 'gippo', used in the seventeenth and eighteenth centuries to denote a scullion or kitchen servant.

MACONOCHIE RATION

Maconochie was a tinned vegetable and meat concoction that at least served to break the monotony of bully beef. This issue was to be memorable enough to warrant an epic poem, *The Rubaiyát of a Maconochie Ration* by 'T.I.N. Opener' (based loosely on the four-line verse format of the ancient Persian *Rubaiyat of Omar Khayam*), which was published just after the war in 1919:

Thou! Oh Thousand Mysteries in a Can
Ingeniously contrived as food for man –
On Moab's Mountains [i.e in Palestine] or in Flanders Mud –
You're welcome unto us as Tickler's Jam!

A tin full of anything, which when heated was a something that made
you feel like nothing.
(*Definition of maconochie in* 5th Gloucesters Gazette, *April 1917*)

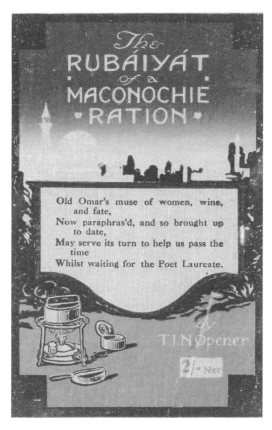

The Rubaiyát of a
Maconochie Ration,
1919.

PROPRIETARY COMFORTS

'Comforts' was the term used for parcels of goods sent to the front by well-wishers. The same names appear again and again, some of them already generic by 1914: Vaseline, Keatings (an insecticide), Lysol, Rowntree's Clear Gums, Zam Buk, Lifebuoy, but also malted milk tablets, whale oil (a protection against trench foot), and chocolate. A parcel sent to the front was a 'blow'; food would receive a 'caning' (enthusiastic despatch). In nineteenth-century slang, your 'whack' was your share or lot when prize-money (or something illegally obtained) was being divided up. During the war, parcels from home would be 'whacked out' or 'whacked round' to denote being shared among friends. This would also be the case when the parcels belonging to soldiers killed in action were shared around. Partridge thought the term derived from the sound of porridge being portioned out onto plates, but Francis Grose's *The Vulgar Tongue* (1785) defines the word as 'a share of booty obtained by fraud'.

> **COMFORTS FOR THE TROOPS FUND, NORTHAMPTON**
> *Sir, I received your parcel quite safe and I heartily thank you for your kind appreciation. A Merry Xmas to you all. No. 8611, Alexander Thorpe, 1st N. Fus.*
> (Postcard from Pte Thorpe, 15 December 1915)

BRAZIER

Braziers – buckets with holes punched in them – were a means of keeping warm, as well as cooking, but their glow could be seen for some distance. Pte Groom of the London Rifle Brigade was impressed by an 'old sweat's' approach – using a candle stub, cigarette tin and 'four by two' flannel, water could be boiled, slowly, enough for a mug of hot 'char'. Most coveted was the paraffin-fuelled Primus pressure stove – a rare luxury in the trenches.

'POZZY'

Jam – 'pozzy' in soldier's slang – was another welcome ration; but the frequency of Tickler's Plum and Apple variety raised Bruce Bairnsfather's 'eternal question' – 'When the 'ell is it going to be Strawberry?' For most soldiers there was a belief that the most popular flavours – strawberry in particular – was appropriated by ASC men in the rear areas.

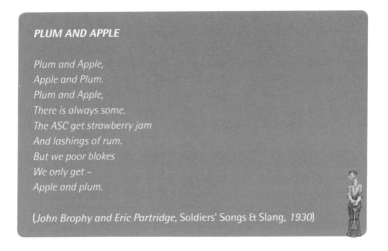

PLUM AND APPLE

Plum and Apple,
Apple and Plum.
Plum and Apple,
There is always some.
The ASC get strawberry jam
And lashings of rum.
But we poor blokes
We only get –
Apple and plum.

(*John Brophy and Eric Partridge*, Soldiers' Songs & Slang, *1930*)

SRD

The issue of a rum ration in the armed forces was a British institution. Service rum was thick and fiery; its positive effects after a night on the fire-step are remembered in most soldiers' memoirs. Rum was issued from ceramic jugs labelled 'SRD', which spawned a host of explanations, from 'Soon Runs Dry' and 'Seldom Reaches Destination' to 'Service Rum Dilute' (this last one was included, as the official definition, in Brophy and Partridge's book on trench slang); but dilute it was not. An enduring mythology, the initials nevertheless stand for something rather more prosaic, for 'Supply, Reserve, Depot', a large establishment based in Woolwich, the repository of many such stores.

SRD rum jars.

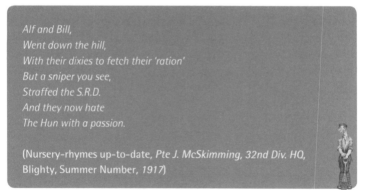

Alf and Bill,
Went down the hill,
With their dixies to fetch their 'ration'
But a sniper you see,
Straffed the S.R.D.
And they now hate
The Hun with a passion.

(Nursery-rhymes up-to-date, *Pte J. McSkimming, 32nd Div. HQ,*
Blighty, Summer Number, *1917*)

Rum Jar

Rum was issued at dawn and dusk, usually following Stand to; its fiery warmth was intended to dispel some of the ague brought on by the cold, wet and miserable trench conditions. Famously, it was also to be issued to those men about to go 'over the bags', either at dawn with a large-scale attack, or at night prior to a raid. The rum ration was issued by a senior NCO from a ceramic jug (marked SRD), known as a 'rum jar'. Given that drunkenness was a serious offence, the ration could not be accumulated and saved for later; poured into mug or mess-tin, it was to be drunk in the presence of the officer. It was a long-held belief that, like the issue of strawberry jam, any rum residue left in a jug was taken by the sergeant – a perk of his position. Because of their shape, German trench mortar projectiles were quite often called 'rum jars' too.

THEY DIDN'T BELIEVE ME

Don't know how it happened quite
Sure the jar came up alright?
Just as full as it should be
Wouldn't touch it, no, not me!
Sergeants very seldom touch
Rum, at least, not very much,
Must have been the A.S.C.
Anyway, it wasn't me!

Yet when I told them that I hadn't touched the jar,
They didn't believe me, they didn't believe me;
They seem to know a sergeant's thirst,
I fear they all believe the worst,
It's the rottenest luck that there could be;
And when I tell them, and I'm certainly going to tell them,
There'll be fatigues for them where'er I be,
They'll never believe me, they'll never believe that
The man who tapped the jar could not be me!

(The BEF Times, No. 5, Vol. 1, 10 April, 1917)

CHATS

'Chats' and 'chatting' refer to body lice and the communal activity of their removal – often by running a candle flame along the seams of uniforms (and thereby weakening them). The potential for merging two meanings of the word is seen in the heading for a column in the *5th Gloucesters Gazette*, September 1918: 'Chats from an editor's flea-bag' (the 'fleabag' was the officer's sleeping-bag). 'Chat' dates back to the eighteenth century and was possibly a joke based on the idea of 'chattels', movable goods. Alternatives were 'coot' and 'cootie', possibly from a Malay word for a parasitic insect, though *kootee* was Anglo-Indian for 'a house', with a rhyming slang relation to 'louse'. Partridge also lists the following terms: greybacks, crabs, live-stock, bosom chums, dimback, seam-squirrel, toto. If you were infested you were 'lousy, crummy, or ticky'.

'Cooties' – Unwelcome inhabitants of Tommy's shirt.
(Arthur Guy Empey, *Over the Top*, 1917)

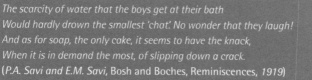

Our chief fatigue which was 'self inflicted' was 'chatting'. It consisted of stripping to our waist, then burning our shirts, etc, with a candle to kill the lice.
(*Pte Ralph I. Smith, D Coy, 12th Battalion, Gloucestershire Regiment (Bristol's Own)*)

The scarcity of water that the boys get at their bath
Would hardly drown the smallest 'chat'. No wonder that they laugh!
And as for soap, the only cake, it seems to have the knack,
When it is in demand the most, of slipping down a crack.
(*P.A. Savi and E.M. Savi, Bosh and Boches, Reminiscences, 1919*)

'RATS AS BIG AS CATS'

This phrase has become a metaphor for life in the trenches, perhaps derided and devalued today as a wartime cliché. But rat hunting was often a pastime of the trenches, as recorded in the anonymous *A Soldier's Diary of the Great War* (1929), for 17 June 1915: 'We had some rat hunts, too, with terriers; sticks, and some half bricks. Talking of rat hunts, there were some rats as big as cats in our trench (or seemed so by moonlight), and we started potting at them with revolvers.'

We had amusing incidents such as 'rat bashing'. At the rear of some of the sheds in the reserve positions there were piles of rubbish and tins, etc. We would creep out in the dark and surround it ... one would go to the centre and switch on a torch while we killed them with pieces of wood and sticks.
(*Pte Ralph I. Smith, D Coy, 12th Battalion, Gloucestershire Regiment (Bristol's Own)*)

FLIES

Flies were a constant companion to the troops in the trenches, especially in summer (and in the heat of Gallipoli), and particularly where there were dead and unburied bodies crowding no-man's-land. 'The flies were buzzing obscenely,' wrote Charles Edmonds in *A Subaltern's War*, but for the editor of the paper for 5th Corps of the Signal Company, 14 July 1917, ('published' via carbon paper) 'Flies, extermination of' was the responsiblity of the 'officer i/c fly papers'.

Blow-flies deposit their eggs on fresh or decaying flesh, and this is one of the great sources of trouble to the officers of the Army Service Corps. But they are not content with killed flesh. They will lay their eggs on any living flesh which is exposed, or in sores or tumours, and here their larvae will thrive.
(*Dr A.E. Shipley F.R.S.,* The Minor Horrors of War, *1915*)

THE WINGED HUN

When I write of the enemy with wings, it has nothing to do with the Taube, the Aviatik, and the Fokker. Only with the fly. We can and will beat the Germans; but if the length of our stay in France depended on a success all along the line against the fly we should arrive home in the year 1950 with beards.
('X', Told in the Trenches, *1916*)

SCROUNGING

Scrounging was a way of life in the army, particularly overseas, and involved the appropriation of anything useful from anywhere. Allegedly derived from north country dialect, the term came into its own in the mass citizen army of the First World War. As described by J.C. Dunn in *The War the Infantry Knew*: 'a form loomed up in the darkness and held out to me something which I found to be a canteen with stewed rabbit in it. It was a present from a group of men who were the best foragers in the Regiment. This accomplishment was afterwards known as "scrounging"'.

EXPRESSIONS FOR GETTING SOMETHING FOR NOTHING (NOT STEALING, BUT OFTEN VERY CLOSE TO IT):

Boning: Used by Dickens and many others to mean 'steal'.
Bunce: Originally money, but later something you found and claimed (by saying 'bunce'); leading to the expression 'stick up for your bunce' (your share).
Click for: Though this could be used in a negative sense, you could also 'click for' something good, in the sense of making a good connection.
Hot-stuffing: From 1914.
Humming: cadging (Australian).
Making: From the late 1600s, hovering on the border of legality.
Mumping: Originally 'cheating' or 'deceiving', from the seventeenth century.
Wangling: A pre-war term.
Winning: 'not quite lawfully or officially'.

I have 'wangled' another man's candle ...
('Wagger' (C.W. Langley) Battery Flashes, 1916)

The job I 'clicked for' nearly every other day was to get water for the
R.E.'s, pumping it from a well close by Madame T.'s estaminet.
(Pte Alfred M. Burrage, Artists' Rifles, War is War, 1930)

LIFTING

The line between 'using' and 'stealing' was very fine in the stressful
conditions of the trench when a stray bullet could make such nice-
ties meaningless. 'Pinching', known from 1670, and its 1914 rhyming
slang version 'half-inching' were, according to Partridge (*Dictionary
of Slang and Unconventional English*), 'very general among soldiers
1914–18'. Variations were 'winning', 'nicking' (from about 1826, and
originally meaning 'cheating'), 'making' and 'boning' (known from
the late 1600s), 'nailing' (from about 1810), 'knocking off' and 'sou-
veniring' (known from 1915). Cpl F.R. Ingrey wrote in his diary that
his paybook and jacket was stolen (he found both, but minus his
money); personal theft occurred as well as widespread theft of supplies – 'skilcuring' was a term used for stealing army supplies to sell
to civilians. George Copeland enlisted in the Highland Light Infantry
on 20 January 1915 aged 15 years and 10 months; he was discharged
medically unfit on 13 November 1915 having previously been court-
martialled and sentenced to fifty-six days' detention for 'when on
active service stealing goods, the property of a comrade ...'. Given the
shortages of food and comforts, the prevalence of petty theft was inevitable, but dealt with severely.

SWEARING

Swearing is essentially a phenomenon of spoken language, and obscenity laws heavily circumscribed the printing of obscenity in the early twentieth century. Sensibilities ensured that writing offensive language could cause problems, so it is not surprising that there should be little documented use of swearing. But it is equally surprising that there is so little reference to it, though official records – such as the service papers for Private Alfred Smith of the West Yorkshire Regiment, a hardened 'old sweat' and inveterate drinker – indicate that swearing was very much part of soldiers' lives. Smith was fined seven shillings and sixpence and given three days C.B. (Confined to Barracks) for drunkeness and 'using highly obscene language.'

Donald McNair's letters home referred to a 'most respectable looking young man' whose 'torrent of pure and unadulterated swearing, punctuated with incessant blasphemies, was unique'; later he had to share living space with four men who were 'utterly low-class and foul-mouthed louts – I certainly have nothing in common with them, and find it difficult to put up with their wantonly pointless, witless and filthy conversation.' But McNair was a member of the Exclusive Brethren, a rigorously self-controlled religious sect.

The occasional use of dashes in transcribed speech shows the natural use of swearwords in situations of stress: Private Albert Andrews' account of an encounter on 28 January 1916 – 'Look at this ––er ... he thinks he's going to Blighty' – shows a natural use of what may be any one of a number of words. Private Paxton Dent of the Seaforth Highlanders 'somewhere in France', noted in his diary for 15 March 1915: 'It was far from pleasant, sliding into that slimy water, and a little

Good-bye, Pat ;–and when you meet the Bulgars, knock ⌊L out of 'em!

'Knock the L out of the Bulgars', postcard, c. 1916

while after we emerged, we felt very uncomfortable, and then we were told we had gone too far and should have to turn back. You should have heard the swearing.'

There were several ways to get round social or official prohibitions on swearing; the 'accidental on purpose' dropping of the L in 'Bulgar' allowed reference to a word which it was illegal to print at the time, and the arrival of Fokker aeroplanes gave provision for double-entendres. But the key point was made by John Brophy, that when you were ordered to 'get your fucking rifles' this was considerably less urgent than the order to 'get your rifles'. 'Fucking' was thus an endearing filler, working in much the same way as 'old' in 'the old barbed wire'. Swearing was part of the normal speech, albeit not the normal writing, of a very large proportion of the men at the front.

As to what the defining words were, the best indication of word and accent comes in an Australian war glossary, *Digger Dialects* (W.H. Downing, 1919), in a couple of definitions: Carksucker – American soldier; Fooker – English private.

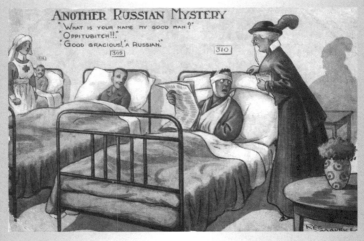

'Oppitubitch'; 1915 postcard showing how the power of swearing changes through time.

GROUSE

Partridge points out that 'the best of soldiers considered that they had a right to *grouse*, a word used by Kipling in 1892' – actually he had used it at least five years earlier. Grousing was not complaining so much as grumbling without expectation of remedy; regional origins for the word existed in terms for 'worrying and scratching', in use in Oxfordshire, Middlesex and Sussex according to the *Manchester Guardian* in 1918, while Partridge linked it to the words 'grudge' and the American 'grouch'. A more tenuous link traces it back to 'grutch', meaning 'to complain', which is documented in English from the thirteenth century but fading in use by the seventeenth century. Grousing was traditionally 'the soldier's privilege' but, while it was an acceptable pastime, soldiers were less inclined to put up with a 'moaner'.

There is nothing Tommy likes better than a mild grouse at everything in general and everything else in particular – with the exception of charging Fritz with the bayonet, which little pastime, according to a writer in the Daily Mail, *is Tommy's favourite. (Funny how these writers for the daily press get to find things out, isn't it?) We scarcely know ourselves when we read, in the daily papers, accounts of our habits and hobbies...*
(The Grouser, *in* The Brazier, *20 December 1916*)

Grousing, grousing, grousing
Always bloody well grousing.
Grousing at the rations,
And grousing at the pay
(*Soldiers' song,* c. *1915*)

'Whizz-Bangs' and 'Flaming Onions'

Commonest among all slang from the Great War are the terms applied to shells and guns, and these were to appear with great regularity in both trench newspapers like *The Wipers Times* and the wartime press at home. At the outbreak of war there was little in the way of formal reporting arrangements, and the army itself appointed Lt Col Ernest Swinton to be its official reporter, who chose the pseudonym 'Eyewitness'. According to Fraser and Gibbon (1925), it was Swinton who introduced the term 'Jack Johnson' to the public in September 1914. 'Jack Johnson' and 'whizz-bang' remained popular throughout the war, at home and at the front – though 'coal box', 'crump' and 'pip-squeak' were equally descriptive. Given that up to 70 per cent of casualties – dead and wounded – on the Western Front were caused by shellfire, it is not surprising that artillery should figure highly in both wartime and post-war soldiers' accounts. And with one of the most destructive weapons of trench warfare being the German trench mortar or *minenwerfer*, it is natural that 'minnies' were among the most feared – the fear of their power being hidden by a friendly term.

Aerial warfare was a new phenomenon and new slang terms developed to describe it. Aeroplanes were described as 'machines' or 'buses'; observation balloons as the inevitable 'sausage' due to their shape; anti-aircraft fire as 'archie' (after a West End theatre revue song), and successful aviators as 'aces'. With the glamour of the RFC, most of these terms were adopted by the press – and were thus devalued in the process.

BEING 'BUMPED'

For soldiers in the trenches, being shelled was a strong auditory experience, many never recovering their hearing – Robert Graves said that part of the inability to communicate with people at home was that you could not convey the incessant noise. Several expressions capture the sound of shells as well as the physical sensation of concussion (being 'bumped' or 'bonked'). Arthur Guy Empey (*Over the Top*, 1917) talks of the 'plunk' of a bomb landing at a distance, but the most common word used was 'crump'. As the bomb itself was mostly not seen, the sound became the thing itself – 'One solitary crump landed beside them' and 'The enemy put 96 crumps (5.9s) into a field' (F.C. Hitchcock, *Stand To*, 1937). It was also used to describe the action itself: 'The Boche was crumping us all the time', wrote a soldier correspondent in the *Manchester Guardian* of 25 July 1916.

Knowing the difference between the sounds of shells, particularly whether one was a 'goer' or an 'incomer', could save your life. Roland Leighton wrote to Vera Brittain on 29 April 1915 about 3.5in howitzer shells: 'Luckily you can always hear this sort coming and we had time to crouch down in the bottom of the trench.' Similarly, Christopher Haworth of the 14th Argyll and Sutherland Highlanders wrote: 'I am learning to judge by the whistle where the shells will drop'.

Attempts to describe the sound of a shell landing or flying past are seldom as memorable as 'whizz-bang'; individual observations such as Roland Leighton's 'the pounding of heavy guns, now fainter, now louder, but coalescing always into one dull, thundering roar ...' (11 September 1915) and Geoffrey Thurlow's 'tonight is strangely quiet save for a distant bumping of guns' (25 February 1917) give an eerily intimate idea of the sound experience of the war. Specific sounds carried their own importance, the sound of sniper fire reminding the soldier of constant danger: R. Andom's 'the snap of sniper-fire' or *The Observer*'s 'the intermittent pop – for that word expresses the sound best – of snipers on either side' (6 December 1914). But Charles Edmonds' rendering of a gas shell landing as 'Whirra Whirra Whirra Phut Phut Phut' is clearly based on a survivor's sharp observation.

BOMBARDMENT

Though artillery bombardment was the norm in trench warfare, it was usual to increase the intensity before offensives in the form of a 'barrage' (originally a French word meaning 'barring the way'). This was a means of subduing the enemy to allow the infantry to reach their objectives, particularly in the run-up to an 'over the top' attack. Increasing sophistication in ordnance techniques brought new barrage tactics. A 'moving barrage' or 'lifting barrage' was a way of directing artillery so that it laid down a curtain of explosives in front of advancing troops and the enemy could not advance to meet them. 'Losing the barrage' meant a breakdown in communication between artillery and infantry, often with disastrous results.

'Barrage' – Concentrated shell-fire on a sector of the German line. In the early days of the war, when ammunition was defective, it often landed on Tommy himself.
(Arthur Guy Empey, *Over The Top*, 1917)

BARRAGE TYPES

Preliminary barrage: bombardment of the enemy lines prior to the assault.
Straight barrage: barrage lines 'lift' progressively, the gun barrels being lifted up to attain greater distance, moving the bombardment forward at arbitrary intervals.
Lifting barrage: barrage lines lift to bombard successive trench lines, concentrating on strong points.
Piled-up barrage: barrage lifts progressively until the line to be attacked is reached, and fire is concentrated there.
Creeping Barrage (Rolling Barrage): the barrage line moving forward at set time intervals.
Box Barrage: A method of isolating an area from reinforcement by curtain walls of gun fire.

> *Near Thiepval the brigade went over the top behind a 'creeping barrage'*
> *of shrapnel, a device newly invented, which threw into our*
> *hands a strong German trench redoubt with two hundred and*
> *fifty prisoners.*
> (*Charles Edmonds*, A Subaltern's War, *1929*)

'DRUMFIRE'

A term that was most often used in the context of Allied bombardment of German lines; it described a continuous bombardment that resembled the rolling of drums.

```
On a comparatively small area the French on one day
threw a hundred thousand shells! We found a French
document in which the Commanding Officer calculated
that 18 bombs must be the allowance per metre of
German trench, there 18 bombs to be used, not in a day,
but in one or two hours! The rapidity of the artillery
fire was, therefore, as great as that of an ordinary
machine gun, but the shells hurled against us were
not infantry shells, but grenades of every calibre.
'Drumfire' is the name for this sort of artillery fire,
and its effects were simply dreadful — unspeakable.
```

German report on a bombardment, The Times, *6 December 1915*

> *It was zero hour and our barrage had fallen, blotting out the German bombardment with a drumfire forty times as great.* (*Charles Edmonds,* A Subaltern's War, *1929, describing the preparation for the Third Battle of Ypres*)

'**Healthiness**' – army slang for liability to shell-fire: 'healthy' means comparatively safe; 'unhealthy' dangerous.
(G. Belton Cobb, *Stand to Arms*, 1916)

Trench slang, a glossary of picturesque phrases used at the front

Crump – any high explosive shell

Black Marias – 11.2 [inch] shells, which, when exploded, give off a very black smoke

Jack Johnsons – from three different sources come three different types of shells called by this expressive name. One authority describes them as 8.27 [inch] shells, another as a 17in howitzer shell, but a Tommy writing from the front describes a 'J.J.' as a 15in shell

Portmanteau – a synonym for Jack Johnson

Coal Box – According to some a big shell, but generally understood to be a sort of high-explosive shrapnel which seems to burst in the air with a cloud of thick black smoke which whirrs around like a catherine wheel

Woolly bear – a 4.23 [inch] howitzer shell

Whiz-bang – mixed shrapnel and high-explosive shell – defines the noise made by the shell when hurtling through the air, and also the explosion

Dud – a term of satire, descriptive of any shell that fails to explode

The War Budget, 23 March 1916

SCORN FOR 'BLACK MARIA'

From WILLIAM MAXWELL. FRANCE Oct. 5. There is no doubt that when our men first made the acquaintence of 'Black Maria' these monstrous engines of destruction which have been the mainstay of the German army had a certain moral effect. But familiarity is breeding contempt. At first these terrible missiles did much damage, but since our soldiers have dug themselves in they have begun to despise them. The smaller shells, known as 'Whistling Rufus,' never had any terrors.

William Maxwell, The Daily Telegraph, 5 October 1914

'PIP-SQUEAK'

The term 'pip-squeak' was used for a high-explosive, high-velocity shell fired from a field gun. Fraser and Gibbons (*Soldier and Sailor Words and Phases*, 1925) state that the name comes from 'the sound of its discharge and flight. The word was often used by young officers in semi-official and official documents until an order was issued condemning its employment.'

'Crump' – A name given by Tommy to a high explosive German shell which when it bursts makes a 'Cru-mp' sort of noise.
(Arthur Guy Empey, *Over The Top*, 1917)

'JACK JOHNSON'

Jack Johnson was an American world heavyweight boxing champion at the outbreak of war, the first black man to hold the title, his name being a synonym for physical power: in 1914 Frances Grenfell wrote, 'I now felt like Jack Johnson instead of an old cripple'. Johnson held the title from 1908 until 1915, and held it despite various racially induced attempts to pit white heavyweight boxers against him, so-called 'white hopes', one of which had been the British heavyweight champion, Bombardier Billy Wells, who had been expected to fight the world champion in October 1911. Wells himself went on to serve with the British Army. The adoption of 'Jack Johnson' for German heavy artillery shells was apposite: packing a heavyweight punch, the shells arrived in a cloud of black smoke. There were inevitably variations: in his diary entry for 18 November 1914, Cpl J. Bremner of the Royal Garrison Artilllery stated that 'a Johnson burst right amongst them', while Amar Singh, aide-de-camp (ADC) to General Brunker, called it a 'Jack Jamison', and C.W. Langley wrote in 1915 of 'going to bathe in a Jack Johnson hole'.

The Revd Andrew Clark of Essex noted in his diary on Friday 3 March 1916: 'Dr Smallwood called. He says he has just talked with a Berkshire officer. This man told him about the names of shells–(i) the *pip-squeak* and the *whizz-bang* are two names for the same thing, and describe the explosion of the smallest shell – the 77 millimetre shell; (ii) Little Willie is the next largest; (iii) White Hope is a size larger still; (iv) Jack Johnson is bigger still.'

Jack Johnson, heavyweight world boxing champion, photographed by the Bain News Corporation sometime between 1910 and 1915.

'WHIZ-BANG' OR 'WHIZZ-BANG'?

The term 'whiz-bang' was in use from the 1830s to describe the sound of a firearm, and was thus in place to be applied to the small shell fired from a high-velocity gun from the inception of the war – specifically applied to German shells – and the term quickly became semi-official. The *Manchester Guardian*, 19 January 1916, reported from a 'young private in the 20th Service battalion [Manchester Regiment], in a letter received by his parents in Withington: "… yesterday Captain __ was buried by the debris thrown up by a whiz-bang. He was terribly shaken at the time. These whiz-bangs are murderous things. I don't know their weight exactly, but their great advantage is that they have a very flat trajectory, and therefore give little if any warning. All you hear is a whiz just over your head, and before you have time to duck, there is a terrific bang.'" The term was also used for the speedily written and despatched Field Service Postcard.

> *Johnny [Turk] started shelling us. We were there all day, and they shelled right up till nearly dark with nearly all 'whizzybangs'.*
> (Pte Henry Smith, *Letter from Palestine 13 December 1917*, Soho Monthly Paper, St Anne's & Soho Westminster, *March 1918*)

'TO WHIZZ-BANG'

Whizz-bang could also be used as a verb. The *Manchester Guardian*, 1 March 1917, reported a soldier's words: '"Fritz" began to "whizz-bang" the trenchboards over which they [a stretcher party] were travelling.' And the name reflected how important sound was in the trenches: the *Daily Express*, 5 July 1917, reported an interview with Arthur Pearson, 'the well-known campaigner on behalf of the blind – "I know now the difference between a whizz-bang and a bang-whizz," said Sir Arthur, smiling. "When the bang comes first and the whizz afterwards you know it's your own shell. When the whizz comes first then it's the other fellow's. I had practical experience of both."'

> *Hush! Here comes a Whizz-bang*
> *Hush! Here comes a whizz-bang,*
> *Hush! Here comes a whizz-bang,*
> *Now, you soldiers, get down those stairs,*
> *Down in your dugouts and say your prayers.*
> *Hush! Here comes a whizz-bang,*
> *And it's making straight for you:*
> *And you'll see all the wonders of No-Man's Land*
> *If a whizz-bang (bump!) hits you.*
>
> (*John Brophy and Eric Partridge,* Soldier Songs & Slang, *1931*)

> *The south-east corner of [the] wood, where a reserve company are dug in,*
> *is visited by 'Silent Susans' for about five minutes each noontide ... (Silent*
> *Susan, by the way, is not a desirable member of the opposite sex. Owing*
> *to her intensely high velocity she arrives overhead without a*
> *sound, and then bursts with a perfectly stunning detonation*
> *and a shower of shrapnel bullets.)*
> (*Ian Hay,* Carrying on After the First Hundred Thousand, *1918*)

'WIPERS EXPRESS'

The Second Battle of Ypres in April–May 1915 saw the deployment of a large calibre gun whose 42cm shell made a noise like a passing express train as it thundered overhead. According to Fraser and Gibbon, this was nicknamed the 'Wipers Express' by men present at the battle.

> *Tuesday 2 May 1915. Battle still in progress, though not so intense. I had*
> *11 420 mm shell more than 100 yds over my guns this morning. A truly*
> *terrifying noise they make going through ... and when they strike the hole*
> *they make is big enough to build a house in. Glad they did not*
> *hit me. When will it end?*
> (*Diary entry by Lt William Edgington, who was killed by*
> *'Wipers Express' shellfire four days later*)

SHRAPNEL

The term 'Shrapnel' dates back to the Peninsular War (1808–14), when shells filled with round musket balls and containing a bursting charge were termed 'Shrapnel's shells', after their inventor, General H. Shrapnel, RE. In the Great War, it has been estimated that almost 70 per cent of all casualties were wounded or killed by artillery fire on the Western Front. The high-explosive charge in heavy artillery shells would kill by tearing apart fortifications and human flesh alike, and wounds from the molten, jagged shell fragments were particularly feared. Quick-firing guns could also deliver high explosive, but were often packed with, in the case of the British version, 240 lead shrapnel balls that were propelled with force out of the body of the shell in flight. These were most often referred to as 'shrap'. The wide brim of British 'shrapnel helmets' was designed to protect the wearer from such airbursts.

Shrapnel burst over our head – pieces of shells whizzed across our backs, and I thought I was for it.
(Pte Rueben Stockman, Queen Victoria's Rifles, June 1916)

'DUDS' AND 'BLINDS'

Shells that were fired and failed to explode were 'dud', a term previously used to describe a useless or counterfeit object. With the War Office struggling to control the supply of artillery shells early in the war, the supply of munitions from overseas brought problems of faulty fuses and weak drive bands. 'A Dud is a generic term for everything that ought to go off but doesn't', reported Bombardier Drew of a trench mortar battery (*Made in the Trenches*, 1916). This shortcoming resulted in the 'Shell Scandal' of May 1915, following the Battle of Neuve Chappelle, and would ultimately see the fall of the Liberal Government and the formation of the Ministry of Munitions. Duds were also called 'blinds', as reported in the *Manchester Guardian* in July 1918, and in the diary kept by Cpl J. Bremner of the Royal Garrison Artillery: 'A great quantity of their shells are blind, we banged off a few today in quick time' (21 November 1914).

The Dud Shell, or the Fuse-cap collector, Bruce Bairnsfather cartoon, *c.*1915.

Bystander copyright.
THE DUD SHELL—OR THE FUSE-TOP COLLECTOR
"Give it a good 'ard 'un, Bert; you can generally 'ear 'em fizzing a bit first if they are a-goin' to explode."

A FEW MORE MILITARY TERMS DEFINED
DUDS – These are of two kinds. A shell on impact failing to explode is called a dud. They are unhappily not as plentiful as the other kind, which often draws a big salary and explodes for no reason. These are plentiful away from the fighting area.
(The *BEF Times,* No. 2, Vol. 2, 8 September 1917)

'**Dud**' – A German shell or bomb which has not exploded on account of a defective fuse. Tommy is a great souvenir collector so he gathers these 'duds'. Sometimes when he tries to unscrew the nosecap it sticks. Then in his hurry to confiscate it before an officer appears he doesn't hammer it just right–and the printer of the casualty list has to use a little more type.
(Arthur Guy Empey, *Over The Top,* 1917)

CLOTH HALL
YPRES.

THIS WEEK

THE
THREE DUDS
WORLD'S BEST KNOCKABOUTS

BOUNCING BERTHA
THE LITTLE MARVEL,
Only 17 ins. High.

THE
JOHNSONS
A Shout. A Scream. A Roar.
This Season the Johnsons have
Carried all before them.
ETC., ETC

• Entire change of Programme Weekly •

Best Ventilated Hall in the Town

Dud Corner – the British memorial to the Battle of Loos, September 1915. 'Duds' were particularly prevalent in this battle, as they had been at Neuve Chappelle, in May of the same year.

COMMON NICKNAMES FOR GUNS

Asiatic Annie (Gallipoli) – firing from the Asiatic Shore
Beachy Bill (Gallipoli) – another name for Asiatic Annie
Big Bertha (*Dicke Berthe* in German) – the legendary heavy howitzer
Billy Wells – any British heavy howitzer, after British heavyweight
champion and artillery NCO Bombardier Billy Wells
Grandma – a British howitzer at Ypres
Heavies – a general term covering all large guns
Long Tom – any large gun
Percy – a 4.7in naval gun in the field
Quick Dick – a German high-velocity gun
Shooting iron – an 18 pounder field gun

There's a certain darned nuisance called 'Beachy'
Whose shells are exceedingly screechy;
But we're keeping the score,
And we're after your gore –
So look out, 'Beachy Bill', when we meet ye.

(The Anzac Book, *1916*)

SEVENTY-FIVE

The 75mm was a French quick-firing field gun with a unique hydraulic
recoil system that allowed for a rapid rate of fire. The gun was rightly
celebrated in all Allied armies, and though not used by the British
Army, the BEF had plenty of exposure to its activity. Usually referred
to as 'the 75', for the French it was the 'soixante-quinze', or the more
enigmatic 'Josephine'.

Trench mortars

Men of the trench mortars – TMs or 'toc emmas', in signallers' phonetic alphabet of the day – were described as the 'suicide club'; a group of soldiers who were likely to be targeted for retaliatory action by their opposite numbers across no-man's-land. For this reason, TM men were unpopular in the frontline. Trench mortars – simple trench-scale artillery capable of firing high-trajectory shells or bombs – were used as a means of destroying or reducing enemy trenches, and were capable of killing large numbers of men.

'Toffee apple'

The 'toffee apple' was a British mortar shell resembling toffee-covered-apples-on-sticks common at fun fairs – the visual comparison was an obvious one. The mortar comprised a 2in diameter tube, and this projected a spherical explosive charge mounted on a long shaft towards the enemy lines with a wobbling flight. An alternative (from the film *The Battle of the Somme*, 1916) was 'plum-pudding'.

Minenwerfer

The *minenwerfer* was a German trench mortar that was effective at both destroying sections of the frontline trench and reducing the morale of its occupants. As the shell could be observed in flight, sentries with whistles were placed in the frontline, their duty to observe the flight of the mortar shell and alert their comrades.

An unpleasant machine called the minenwerfer *... despatches a large sausage-shaped projectile in a series of ridiculous somersaults, high over no-man's land into the enemy's frontline trench, where it explodes and annihilates everything in that particular bay.*
(*Ian Hay*, Carrying on After the First Hundred Thousand, *1918*)

'**Minenwerfer**' – A high power trench mortar shell of the Germans, which makes no noise coming through the air. It was invented by Professor Kultur. Tommy does not know it is near until it bites him; after that nothing worries him. Tommy nicknames them 'Minnies'. (Arthur Guy Empey, *Over The Top*, 1917)

There is no explosion which, for sheer gut-stabbing ferocity, is quite like that of a minenwerfer. The bursting of one close at hand was like one's conception of the end of the world. (*Pte Alfred M. Burrage, Artists' Rifles, War is War, 1930*)

FLYING PIG

Large and unwieldy, the mortar bombs lobbed by the *minenwerfer* were likened to 'flying pigs' by the troops. During daytime, sentries with whistles and periscopes were spaced out along the trenches to help give warning of the menace. Pte H.S. Clapham of the Honourable Artillery Company (HAC), writing near Ypres in 1915 (*Mud and Khaki*, 1930), described the mortar shells as 'sausages'.

Agony Column

```
Minnie. - Meet me at the flying pig 8.30.- Toc Emma
```

The BEF Times, *No. 4, Vol. 1, 5 March 1917*

It is natural, when you are up the line, dodging 'minnies' and 'whizz-bangs' in the trenches, to pour withering scorn on 'the blighters at the base,' the 'Ac Esses See' (otherwise the Army Service Corps). (*P. J. Fisher, C.F., Khaki Vignettes, 1917*)

CASHIMBO

'*Kaichimbo – hau ihn; gib ihm!* (roughly – belt him, give it to him) from Graff and Bormann, *Schwere Broden, 1000 Worte Front Deutsch* (German Trench Slang Dictionary, 1925); this phrase, probably acquired from soldiers taken captive, came into English as 'to catch cashimbo', meaning 'to be shelled'. Kaichimbo/cashimbo may have had something to do with the Brazilian Portuguese for 'a pipe', may have been connected to the sound of a shell exploding, or may have been a meaningless word (like shouting 'Geronimo!'); Cpl J. Bremner of the Royal Garrison Artillery wrote in his diary several times of giving the enemy 'What Oh'. Perhaps this avoided having to recognise the reality of trench warfare – the term 'to go it' was also used for firing heavy artillery.

AIR BATTLE

The term 'dogfight' for a fight between aeroplanes emerged just after the end of the war; the term used till then was 'air battle'. Air battles fascinated troops on the ground, sympathy often being expressed for the pilot of a plane shot down, whatever his flag. In July 1915, Rifleman Britland had 'an interesting experience' watching a German plane being hit and bursting into flames – 'it must have been terrible for the two men ... the men must have been terribly burnt before they died.' Two years later, Pte T.L. Lester of the Auckland Light Infantry wrote in his diary: 'witnessed a big air battle. British airmen fight against big odds. 3 Germans attack one of our planes and set it on fire, and came down in flames with airman burnt to death. 1 French scout brought down, observer killed, pilot wounded.'

AIRMEN'S SLANG

On 16 September 1916, the *Daily Mirror* reported the RFC's use of the term 'hickyboo' for a Zeppelin; Partridge noted this as 'hick(a)boo' as an air force warning that a raid was imminent, with the quote from Manchon that it was derived from the Hindi word meaning 'eagle'. Other flying slang included 'flat spin', and a 'flip' (a flying trip).

Some terms from the war in the air

Arsey-tarsy: a plane landing upside-down

Circus: squadrons in the air together, famously enacted by the German 'ace', Baron von Richtofen

Comic business: flying

Conk-out: engine failure

Baby elephant: a scout plane used by the No.1 Australian squadron in Egypt

Blimp: a balloon: 'Curiously deceptive in view of its smug corpulent appearance'. (*The Soldiers' War Slang Dictionary*, 1939)

Blind spot: area below and behind the aeroplane, where the pilot could not see an attacker

Flaming onions: pyrotechnic anti-aircraft fire from the German *Licht pucker* gun

Flechette: a steel anti-personnel dart thrown from an aircraft

Harry Tate: RE8 aeroplane; Harry Tate was a popular music hall impersonator

Hun: used in the RFC for an officer training as a pilot

Hun-hunting: active searching out of enemy aircraft

Hunland: location of the enemy

Joy-wagon: training aircraft at the flying school

Office: cockpit of a plane, 'with its many instruments, writing pad, speaking tube, the name was an apt one'. (*The Soldiers' War Slang Dictionary*, 1939)

Pile up your bus: crash your aeroplane

Quirk: British 'BE' aircraft

Rupert: kite balloon

Scout: fighter aircraft

Tripe, Tripehound: Sopwith Triplane, a British aeroplane

ARCHIBALD? CERTAINLY NOT!

The words of a George Robey music hall song were the inspiration for the RFC slang term for anti-aircraft fire, 'Archie' (as well as the guns and their gunners). According to legend, aviators would see the all-too-ineffective shells burst in a puff-ball of smoke, and be moved to exclaim: 'Archibald? Certainly not!' It was derived from Robey's hit of 1911:

> It's no use me denying facts, I'm henpecked, you can see!
> 'Twas on our wedding day my wife commenced to peck at me
> The wedding breakfast over, I said, 'We'll start off today upon our honeymoon.'
> Then she yelled "What! Waste time that way?"
> 'Archibald, certainly not!'
> 'Get back to work at once, sir, like a shot.'
> When single you could waste time spooning
> But lose work now for honeymooning!
> 'Archibald, certainly not!'
>
> (*George Glover and John L. St John, 1911*)

> All along the road there are 'Archies' mounted on motor lorries, and these, at intervals, wake into paroxysms of gun-fire and deafen the unlucky one who happens to be under their muzzles.
> (*Major F.N Baker, RGA, 4 November 1916*, Field Guns in France, *1922*)

'BUS'

'Bus' was the usual slang term for an aircraft used by flyers; it was also used occasionally as a slang term for a lorry. According to Fraser and Gibbon's *Soldier and Sailor Words and Phrases* (1925) the term quickly lost currency through overuse by novice airmen.

'SAUSAGE'

Applied to the German kite balloon, used to observe enemy trenches, it could just as easily have been used for the British example of a similar shape. Both were favoured targets by the opponents. Confusingly, 'sausage' was also a nickname for *minenwerfer* shells.

> Editor's Note:
> As an evidence of the lack of encouragement given to us by both the Huns and the elements, we might mention that, as we penned the above, the Sausages dropped five-twelfths of a dozen assorted coal boxes amd whiz-bangs in our Editorial back yard, and we betook ourselves and our staff to the deepest trench we could find ... the river being in flood, the floor is twelve inches deep in decidedly icy water.

RMR Growler *(Canadian Trench Newspaper), 1 January 1916*

TAUBE

Early war, the Rumpler *Taube* ('dove') was a German monoplane of pre-war design with distinctive, swept-back wings; slow and difficult to manoeuvre, the *Taube* was largely unsuccessful and withdrawn from frontline service. Despite this, the name stuck; it was in common use, in English, French and German, for any type of German aircraft.

'Taube' – *Flugzeug* (aeroplane)
(Graff and Bormann, *Schwere Broden, 1000 Worte Front Deutsch* (German Trench Slang Dictionary), 1925)

> *Someone saw a monoplane coming, a queer flat squarish thing. It didn't look British. It came straight for us. Was it a Taube? There was a little panic of pleasant excitement. It dived. It swooped straight at us, crowded in the field. At last we saw the Allied marks on it.*
> (*Charles Edmonds*, A Subaltern's War, *1929*)

'FOKKER SCOURGE'

With the air war very much a matter of technical superiority, the arrival of the *Fokker Eindecker* over the Western Front in April 1915 led to the destruction of a large number of Allied aircraft, termed 'Fokker Fodder'. The success of the monoplane lay with its use of an interrupter gear that allowed machine guns to be fired through the rotating propellor. With the Fokker in the ascendancy from July 1915 to early 1916, the period was known as the 'Fokker Scourge'; it would be overcome by the British use of 'pusher' aircraft, with a rear-mounted propellor that afforded a clear field of fire forwards.

'IRON-ARSED FRITZ'

In *Stand To* (1936) F.C. Hitchcock refers to the name given to a German aircraft ('Taube') reinforced with metal sheeting against ground fire – 'iron-arsed Fritz'.

'ACE'

Derived from cards, aces being the best four cards in the pack, this term was first given by the French to those pilots who were successful in shooting down at least five enemy aircraft; it then passed to the other Allied air services. According to Fraser and Gibbon, in the RFC (and later Royal Air Force), 'ace' gained an almost derogatory meaning for a flashy airman.

THE ALPHABET

(As learnt 'Somewhere in France')

A is the Arm Drill of which we are so sick: We loathe the Non-Coms when they bawl out, 'Look Slick!'

B is Battalion the one that's out here, The other, at home, gets the skittles and beer!

C's the Commission we'll some day receive, Perhaps, if we're lucky, by next Christmas-eve.

D stands for Dixie, with stew or with tea; To clean it you need half the sand of the sea.

E's for "Extend," to a score or so paces, On arrival we drop in the gorse on our faces.

F is "Fatigue"; when we say when it's hot Is best represented by dash and by dot.

G is for Grousing, a luxury great, And not really evil, like U-boats and Hate.

H is for – Well, to the place we'll consign The stingy Estaminet's watered-down wine.

I's for Inspection of Quarters or Rifles; A wonderful fuss is kicked-up about trifles.

J is the jump of delight we achieve When we hear there's a glimmering prospect of leave.

K is the Kit which the Army supplies; Some items, however, the soldier-man buys.

L is the 'Langour' which over us steals, When doing "grub orderly" just after meals.

M is Maconochie, food of renown; When it's served up, the bulk of us trot off to town.

N is the "Numbers" by which we salute, They're mighty particular here how you do't.

O if for Officer, given to straffing; Indecorous privates at times can't help laughting.

P is for "Physical," though it sounds queer, The expert can tangle his toe and his ear.

Q is the Quandary in which we are placed When answering friends who advise greater haste.

R is for Route March, in August a bane, The heat and the flies and our packs give us pain.

S is the Song which our march should beguile; At a hundred and one in the shade, 'tain't worth while.

T is the Training we hope to complete Before the daisies we turn up our feet.

'**U-P**' is the manner in which we are 'fed', At 5.30 a.m. when we're pulled out of bed.

V is the Victory we're hoping to share in, Perhaps as processional troops into Berlin.

W's Webbing, the stuff to make kits, for comfort it beats the old leather to fits.

X is 'Xpectancy, strained to the utmost, While waiting for parcels which may come by the next post.

Y is our Youth, which behind us is slipping, Like its ties and its socks which we used to think 'ripping'.

Z is the Zeal, with which, grousers' despite, We'll answer the call when the time comes to fight.

Artists' Rifles Journal, Vol. 1, No. 3, November 1916

OVER THE TOP

With the artillery war claiming more lives than any other area of conflict, soldiers in the trenches were more likely to be killed or maimed by shells or shrapnel than in direct action with the enemy. And the psychological damage of continued bombardment would induce a condition that would take time to be recognised officially as 'shell shock'.

Though most frontline troops faced the trial of going 'over the top' at least once in their experience, many injuries were attributed to the vagaries of trench warfare. Carelessness over the use of cover – or lingering at vulnerable points, such as latrines or gaps in the sandbag parapet – meant quick death from snipers, and novices tempted to peer over the parapet were soon claimed as casualties. Head injuries were understandably common; the number of deaths decreased after the introduction of the steel helmet in late 1915. Large-scale battles were relatively few – 'the Big Pushes' of popular imagination – but the British commitment to the 'Offensive spirit' meant that there were patrols and working parties nightly, and that trench raids were common. All took their toll.

The rate and scale of casualties in the Great War is breathtaking: infamously, the opening day of the Battle of the Somme on 1 July 1916 saw at least 60,000 men killed, wounded or reported missing. In fact, the term 'casualty' is misleading, as it refers to anyone effectively taken out of action, with deaths forming a smaller proportion of the whole. It was relatively rare for a soldier to survive the war completely unscathed, and wounding was a common experience. The British Empire fielded almost 9.5 million men; almost a million lost their lives, while a further 2.1 million were wounded.

GOING OVER THE TOP

The act of leaving the trench to assault the enemy was to be a pivotal experience in the life of a Great War soldier. Confined to a ditch, with just a strip-like view of the sky by day, or a periscope view of no-man's-land, it was a foolish soldier indeed who was to put his head 'above the parapet'. Though death was often random and continual while in the trenches, there could be nothing to compare with the act of rising bodily out of the protecting earth and advancing into the face of enemy guns. With trench warfare set by late 1914, most soldiers would have to experience going 'over the top', that is, over the top of the parapet constructed in front of the trench to protect its occupants, at least once. And with the parapet in most cases stacked high with sandbags, it was inevitable that the phrase 'over the top' (used as the title of at least two contemporary books) would be transformed to 'over the bags', or to 'hopover', as the act of the soldiers mounting the bags in an attack.

> As soon as we 'went over the top' our artillery opened a terrific barrage on the German defences, it was a wonderful yet terrible sight. It is not much use going into further details, it is almost impossible to describe the scene.
> (*Pte K.S. Wyatt, 8 Royal Fusiliers, letter home 14th April 1917, describing the Battle of Arras*)

> We 'went over the top' five times in five days and on the 5th day we succeeded in gaining our objective.
> (*Diary entry, Pte John T. Lawton, 5th King's Liverpool Regiment, on the Somme*)

SPORT

The wide potential of the word 'sport' leads to what can seem to the modern reader to be some rather startling usages. In *Troddles in the Trenches* by R. Andom, printed for *Newnes' Trench Library*, the protagonist is described as having 'not lost his genial gentleness in this new sport of shooting Germans.' Even the Revd Andrew Clarke makes no comment on reporting a story from a soldier that 'Easter Monday had been a great day's sport – something like following partridges from field to field at home and watching them run. The Germans had that day really run.' Cpl J. Bremner and his comrades on 29 October 1914 'had a bit of sport during the morning [as] two German aeroplanes flew over our heads. We were ordered to get our rifles down and let fly'. A few days later: 'we have had a bit of sport, a hare came through our lines – great sport seeing half the Batt'y chasing it'; and the following day, 'It is fine sport especially when there are a few sitting round the fire and one [shell] bursts in the air, we all make a dive for cover.'

The narrated story of junior officers leading the advance on the first day of the Battle of the Somme by kicking footballs into no-man's-land is one of the abiding images of the war; though this was a direct copy of an earlier experience, the 'Footballer of Loos' in September 1915. Perhaps its poignancy derives from the persistence of an ingenuousness that had somehow survived; as early as November 1914 the Revd Clark had reported that 'when a British cavalry force charges, the younger officers dash off, letting forth the usual hunting yells, and the men yell out any call that comes to their fancy, as they gallop; "This way to the stalls" – "Threepenny entrance this way" – "Three shies a penny"'. Irony has always been an essential part of the soldier's armoury.

I never finished a hun myself although I potted a few, but they ran so fast that you could not see them for dust.
(*Letter home from Pte W.G. Green, 1/20th London Regiment, 1 October 1915, describing the Battle of Loos*)

The Times *on 5 October 1915 reported 'A Rugby Football Player's Account' of a 'Real Live Battle' – practically the whole day we advanced by short rushes, the Germans taking advantage of it to play skittles with us ... When they gave themselves up it was like the end of an international Rugger match.*

FUSSBALLINDIANER

For some soldiers, sport was the obvious paradigm by which they could understand what was going on around them. The Christmas 1915 issue of *Depot Review*, trench newspaper of the British Stationery Depot, Rouen, included an allegorical football match between Britain and Germany, delayed at the outset as the German Crown Prince was 'looting the dressing room' (Britain eventually wins 21–1). *The Iodine Chronicle* in May 1916 gave a set of football results tracing the course of the war, including French 2 – Germhun 2, Russia 4 – Germany 3, Anzacs 1 – Turks 1. Two trench glossaries published in Germany, *Wie der Feldgraue Spricht* (1916) and *Schwere Brocken, 1000 Worte Front-Deutsch* (1925) state that after 'Tommy' a common German epithet for British soldiers was *Fussballindianer* – football indians.

'STUNTS' AND 'SHOWS'

Though 'stunt' was used by the RFC to imply acrobatics (often while 'stooging around'), the term was used, perhaps in a darkly ironic manner, for trench raids, and even larger attacks. Another term for an offensive was 'a show', generally considered a greater, more protracted affair than a 'stunt'.

'STUNTS' – The birthplace of the word is, I believe, America. It still means anything out of the ordinary, clever, etc., but the word has become the adopted child of the English fronts. 'Some stunt,' says a man to a comrade making a 'blighty' cup of tea. 'Some stunt,' says the same man a week later, in a hospital bed, as he describes how his battallion went over and took the Bosche trenches.
('Arnold Maxim', *With a Lewis Gun in France and Salonika*, 1917)

We had been expecting 'the stunt' for some days ... Then one afternoon our guns set up a heavy and concentrated bombardment, and we guessed what it meant, trying to picture the gallant band of carefully chosen and trained lads 'going over the top' and across 'no Man's Land' to bomb the German trenches.
(*Chaplain to the Forces, P.J. Fisher,* Khaki Vignettes, *1917*)

It was a hard-bitten fighting crowd, a 'stunt' division, with a bad name among the Germans and a good name at G.H.Q.
(*Pte Alfred M. Burrage, Artists' Rifles,* War is War, *1930*)

'Trench raid' – Several men detailed to go over the top at night and shake hands with the Germans, and, if possible, persuade some of them to be prisoners. At times the raiders would themselves get raided because Fritz refused to shake and adopted nasty methods.
(Arthur Guy Empey, *Over the Top*, 1917)

PATROLS

Patrols in no-man's-land were always in danger of meeting enemy patrols or being spotted. They might be 'nailed down' by a machine gun or 'hot fire', though from late 1914 this was unlikely to be from a 'fusillade'. With luck, they 'skinned through'. Larger troop movements could be disrupted by artillery fire – the Revd Grice-Hutchinson in

Artillery & Trench Mortar Memories (1932) describes how in March 1918 'we were all moving down to Arras, in a perfectly confident expectation of being snaffled by the Boche'.

> I had to go out on a patrol ... last night (a fighting patrol means you go out and positively ask the enemy to come out and have a scrap).
> (*Pte Donald McNair, Devonshire Regiment, 20 Oct 1917*)

> Open attacks in daylight involved advancing in waves or 'attacking by bounds', making good one position before advancing to the next.
> (*Major A.R. Richardson, University of London Officers Training Corps*, Trench Warfare, *1915*)

BOMBING

The term 'bomb' was used almost universally in preference to the now more familiar 'grenade', and the 'bomber' was specially trained in its deployment. Grenades would logically be thrown by 'grenadiers', but (according to Fraser and Gibbon) after a direct appeal to the king in May 1916, this term became reserved for soldiers of the elité Grenadier Guards. As a result, 'bombs' and 'bombers' replaced 'grenades' and 'grenadiers.'

BOMB-THROWER: a man specially trained to throw bombs (grenades); larger bombs are thrown by trench mortars.
(G. Belton Cobb, *Stand to Arms*, 1916)

> Smithers prided himself on being 'some' bomber from the first day he wore a bomber's badge, but when he was made lance-corporal he came to the conclusion that his equal at bomb-throwing wasn't living.
> (*Cpl C.C. Fowkes, Warwickshire Regiment*, Blighty, Summer Number, *1917*)

'SNAPSHOT'

A 'snapshot' was a quickly aimed and taken rifle shot at a target which was likely to disappear quickly. Snapshots killed many soldiers who inadvertently put their heads momentarily above the level of the parapet. In February 1915, Pte Britland trained at 'snap-shooting', firing five rounds at five separate targets which were raised and lowered in five seconds.

> KEEP your head down, chummy, keep your nut well down,
> When you're in the trenches keep your napper down;
> Bullets are a-flying, nasty bits of lead;
> It's all up to you, matey, if you stop one with your head.
> Drills you through the temple, comes out of your crown,
> If you want to see old 'Blighty'– keep your head well down.
>
> ('A Sergeant in the Royal Fusiliers', in Told in the Huts, 1916)

> Now and again we should see in the distance a 'Bosche' pop his square head above the trench and my pal would say, 'Are you going to have a shot, Tommy?'
> (Diary, Pte John T. Lawton, 5th King's Liverpool Regiment)

'SNIPED'

The term 'sniper' and 'sniping' derives from sports shooting or hunting of the small, long-beaked shore bird, the snipe. In some interpretations, a 'snipe hunt' is viewed as a near-impossible task. Sniping, which requires patience, concealment and skill, was first identified as such in a military context from the latter part of the eighteenth century – and was certainly in use from the mid-part of the nineteenth century. With the 'sniper' being the shooter and 'sniping' the act of shooting, to be 'sniped' was to be shot.

S is the Sniper; it's also his sickness on finding his cover is lacking in thickness.
(An Anzac Alphabet, *J.W.S. Henderson, RGA*, The Anzac Book, *1916*)

22. 2. 15
Left billet and moved to reserve trenches. We were there for 24 hours. The Germans were shouting across to us. Stood to in the early morning as this is the time when the Germans usually attack. Sniping usually starts now. Most of those who have been in the trenches do not trouble to return fire as it is only a waste of ammunition. However, being my first time in the trench I couldn't miss the opportunity.
(*Diary entry, Pte J. Underwood, CEF, 1915*)

It was his chum's sad duty to convey the news of their son's death to his parents: 'I am writing this in the trenches. I have just come back from seeing old Archie. He was killed by a sniper this morning at about 10.30 a.m. He was shot just above the right eye with an explosive bullet, and death was instantaneous. I am sorry there is no mistake about it.'
(*Pte Edgar Lee, writing of Pte Archibald Laird Gardiner, of the 8th Battalion, Royal West Surrey Regiment,* Eltham and District Times, *19 November 1915*)

'The Butt-notcher' – Snipers have a roving commission. It was a cold-blooded business, and hateful to some of the men. With others, the passion for it grew. They kept a tally of their victims by cutting notches on the butts of their rifles.
(James Norman Hall, *Kitchener's Mob*, 1916)

'MOPPING-UP'

With the development of static, positional warfare, the term 'mopping-up' became used to define those occasions where an advance had left small pockets of resistance behind, in dug-outs, machine-gun nests and the like. Moppers-up were those soldiers who were given the job of ensuring that the enemy left behind were dealt with efficiently.

18TH DIVISION
MOPPING UP COMPANIES

a)   Moppers-up are of two kinds: Area Moppers-up and Special Point Moppers-up.

b)   Area Moppers-up follow the leading lines, search the whole area passed over up to, but excluding, the final objective. They picket all dugouts, collect prisoners and ensure that no enemy are left active in the rear area of the assaulting troops.

c)   Special Point Moppers-up are formed up opposite the point for which they have been allocated and advance directly on that point.

(18th Divisional Orders, 18 October 1917)

THE DESTROYED BODY

The February 1917 issue of the *5th Gloucesters Gazette* carried the notice of a cross placed above a trench captured on the evening of 27 August 1916, bearing the words 'In loving memory of', followed by nine names, and then 'Missing', followed by six names. The absence of a term to describe the blunt reality that the body might be destroyed totally by a shell – 'blown to buggery' – or that soldiers died underground, or drowned in mud, meant that often identifiable remains were 'missing'.

MISSING

'Missing in action' was the official term used in communications after action; after a battle or raid, roll calls were held to determine the number and nature of casualties. For those men who could not be accounted for, some would be found by stretcher bearers, and others were identifed, dead, on the battlefield. For men captured by the enemy there would be the inevitable wait for information from the enemy itself. Official casualty figures would take into account: killed, wounded, missing and prisoners of war.

R.W. Surrey Record Office
May 24th 1917

SIR

I regret to inform you that a report has been received from the War Office to the effect that (No) 4868 (Rank) L/Corpl (Name) Rouse, P.S.V. (Regiment) R.W. Surrey was posted as 'missing' on the 23 Apr 1917. The report that he is missing does not necessarily mean that he has been killed, as he may be a prisoner of war or temporarily separated from his regiment.

Letter to Mrs Rouse; Lance Corporal Rouse was indeed a prisoner of war

POST OFFICE TELEGRAPHS To Perry, BHead. Capt. Samuel Perry Lpools Prisoner of War. Wounded. Camp not yet notified. Prisoners. South Kensington.
(Telegram to Captain Perry's wife, 25 September 1918)

Rifleman C.W. Ross, 4584 Queen's Westminster Rifles, missing since July 1st. Any Information gratefully received by his parents, 29c London Road, Forest Hill, S.E.
(The Times, 5 August 1916)

GASSED

On 29 May 1915, the *Morning Post* reported on the 'death of the gassed victims around Ypres', this being the first recorded use of the phrase 'gassed'. By 1925, Fraser and Gibbons were recording its ironic use to mean 'drunk', though Partridge recorded this usage from as early as 1917, an extraordinary instance of dark humour. The expression 'gassed at Mons' developed as a catch-all meaningless excuse to explain someone's absence: gas was not used at the Battle of Mons (August 1914). The use of gas in the First World War for a period affected the existing metaphorical sense of the word. From around 1910, in Ireland, and later in the United States, an enjoyable event could be described as a 'great gas'; from the 1930s such an event is recorded as a 'gas'. The term fell temporarily out of use, possibly from the association of the word in general consciousness with pain and awareness of the chronic effects of gas-poisoning during the Great War.

Private Frederick Walker's diary for October 1918 shows his battalion in support trenches, where he was gassed.

THE ANGELS OF MONS

The Battle of Mons of August 1914 was the first real engagement of the British Expeditionary Force as the small, professional BEF withdrew in the face of the advancing German Army. On 29 September the *Evening News* printed 'The Bowmen', a short story by Arthur Machen, in which 'a soldier' tells about how he and his comrades were on the point of being overwhelmed when he remembered the motto on the plates of a London restaurant – *Adsit Anglis Sanctus Georgius* (May St George be present with the English), together with an image of the saint. On repeating the words he is affected by a shock, hears voices shouting 'St George! St George!' and 'Harow! Harow! Monseigneur St George succour us!', and sees a shining throng of figures. Arrows fly towards the enemy, and instantly ten thousand of them fall with invisible wounds. Their counter-attack fails and the soldier 'knew … that St George had brought his Agincourt Bowmen to help the English'.

The *Evening News* was immediately inundated with requests for permission to use the story, sermons were preached on the theme, and psychic researchers asked Machen to reveal his sources, as the story quickly became *the* recognised experience of the battle. Attempting to convince the public that the story was fictional, Machen published *The Bowmen and Other Legends of the War* with three other unlikely visions providing a framework of myth. He explained that while a remembered ghostly story by Kipling was a possible source, the story really depended on his own imagination. By this time the bowmen had become angels in the public mind. Machen's disclaimer was refuted by Harold Begbie's *On the Side of the Angels: A Reply to Arthur Machen*, which attacked his 'callousness' towards the 'intense eagerness for consolation'. Machen must have been in telepathic contact with a dying soldier, now identified by Begbie as Lance Corporal —, who had given the story to a nurse, who passed it on to the Superintendent of the Red Cross. Other soldiers were quoted as having seen the same vision, and the nurse who had treated them produced a book in which atrocity stories contextualise the vision of Mons, with St George supported by St Michael, Joan of Arc and golden clouds. As late as 1966, A.J.P Taylor's *History of the First World War* gave this as the only documented intervention by supernatural powers in the conflict. The story of the Angels of Mons was maintained throughout the war and contributed to the postwar iconography of memorials.

SHELL SHOCK

While 'neurasthenia' was the term most often used early on to char-
acterise the feelings of anxiety developed during and after battle,
and particularly during protracted shellfire, the use of the term
'shell shock' was to become a lasting legacy of the war. Neurasthenia,
'impaired activity of the nerves', dating from the mid-nineteenth
century, gave way to 'shell shock' some time in 1915; it appeared in
the *British Medical Journal* for December 1915, and became com-
monplace in the newspapers around the same time. *The Times* for
20 November 1915 reported: 'Ernest Ball, of the Royal Engineers …
on his way home suffering from shell shock, the result of a chance shot
into a group of men engaged in sapping operations.' The army finally
recognised it under Army Order 265, Paragraph 2B1, 1917, as a condition that might allow for the medical discharge of a soldier.

```
        The vigorous self reliant soldier ... knows
      Phosferine was the only effective check to the
       nervous exhaustion and stunning of his senses
                    caused by shell shock.

        When you require the Best Tonic Medicine,
                       see you get
                    PHOSFERINE
```

The Daily Mirror, *20 October, 1915*

*A young man of not more than twenty years of age was brought from the
line to this collecting post. 'A bad case of shell shock,' the R.A.M.C man
described it. A man suffering from the modern warfare complaint is
usually as near the borderline of insanity, even if not death, as he can
be – he is a physical and mental wreck.*
('F.L.B.' Blighty, Summer Number, *1917*)

'FED UP'

Though there were few serious complaints, and soldiers were often dedicated to their junior officers (who had half the life expectancy at the front compared to ORs), for much of the time soldiers, when asked, said they were 'fed up'. This seemed to indicate a weariness, a desire for the war to end, not to go home individually, but for the whole rotten business to stop; it stopped short of serious complaint or protest. Even after nearly three years in the army, Pte Fred Walker wrote home that 'there it is, no use grousing, it all helps to win the war,' and the worst Pte Bernard Britland could say after two years in a prisoner-of-war camp was 'we are all fed up with prison life though we are treated quite well.' The state of being 'fed up' was accorded adhoc medical recognition in W.H. Rivers' paper presented to the Royal School of Medicine in December 1917, in which he proposed that discussion of war experiences by groups of soldiers away from the front would produce an emotional response: 'even among those whose memories are not especially distressing it tends to enhance the state for which the term "fed up" seems to be the universal designation.'

'BLIGHTY' WOUNDS

Leave was a luxury in the First World War, and it is not surprising that the common soldier hoped for a simple wound or debilitating illness that would take him home. Such injuries became 'Blighty' or 'cushy' wounds – or often just 'a Blighty one' – sufficiently serious to be sent home on a hospital ship, sufficiently slight not to be life threatening or debilitating. Australian soldiers naturally enough hoped for an 'Aussie'. If a soldier 'stopped one' then he hoped above all for a 'a jammy one', or to be 'pipped' by a 'tap', ideally 'a nice little tap on the shoulder'. He might also be 'nabbed' by being 'potted' (shot). The absence of slang terms for major and life-threatening wounds is eloquent in itself.

The whistle of an approaching shrapnel speaks of coming danger, and then a prone figure on the ground who has been 'pipped,' to use a colloquialism of the Front.
(*Chaplain Major, E.J. Kennedy,* Wth the Immortal Seventh Division, *1916*)

Dear Kitty,
Just a line hoping you are alright I am in hospital and as you will
see by the writing that I am not a very good position I am waiting to
come across to Blighty.
(*Pte P. Edwards, 1st Battalion Royal Welsh Fusiliers, 23 September*
1918. (*Pte Edwards died of his wounds on 28 September 1918*))

The R.A.M.C. men are good nurses, tender as women, always ready
with a cheery word. 'You'll be all right, sonny; you've got a lovely
'Blighty''.
(*P.J. Fisher*, Khaki Vignettes, *1917*)

LUCKY DEVIL!

Lucky Devil: 'Blighty wounds' were much hoped for by the average soldier.

'BLIGHTY TOUCH'

From a dramatic sketch in the *5th Gloucesters Gazette*, February 1917, designed to discourage soldiers from self-inflicted wounds (SIW), a very serious offence, punishable by death in some circumstances.

> Tommy: *I was goin' ter give meself a blighty touch.*
> Woman: *A self-inflicted wound! Yes I knew that.*
> Tommy: *Then what yer want to ask for?*
> Woman: *Because I wanted to hear you confess it.*
> Tommy: *Ow, did yer! Well if yer think yer goin' to get me shot at dawn every day for a week, yer bloomin' well mistaken.*
>
> *(The 'woman' turns out to be the 'Spirit of the Women of England', and inevitably 'Tommy' goes back to his comrades, having briefly 'lost his way in the dark'.)*

'BODY SNATCHER'

Graphically, a 'body-snatcher' was a stretcher bearer or 'SB'. Most SBs were infantrymen, who carried no arms but bore a brassard (arm band) with the simple initials 'SB'. Only RAMC men were allowed to wear the Red Cross of Geneva. For Arthur Guy Empey (*Over the Top*, 1917), however, a 'body snatcher' was a sniper, and the term had other applications too.

> *Our mess at the guns is dwindling fast ... even the 'Body Snatcher' or 'Cold Meat Specialist' (Corps Burial Officer) has left us to rejoin his battalion.*
> (*Major F.N Baker, RGA, 30 August 1917*, Field Guns in France, *1922*)

'Stretcher-bearer' – field-dressings are intended to be used by the wounded men themselves, or by the stretcher-bearers themselves, or by their comrades. The work of the stretcher-bearers is to carry the wounded to the dressing station, where they are bandaged by the medical officer. In each battalion 16 men are appointed as stretcher-bearers, while an additional 16 are warned as reserves. RAMC men do not, except in cases of emergency, work in the trenches.
(G. Belton Cobb, *Stand to Arms*, 1916)

> *These stretcher-bearers grunt and groan, their walk seems like a mile;*
> *Bill resting back in comfort now indulges in a smile;*
> *He cannot help but send his mental thanks back to some Hun*
> *Who by a very lucky shot gave him a 'Blighty One'.*
> (*P.A. Savi and E.M. Savi*, Bosh and Boches, Reminiscences, *1919*)

CASUALTY CHAIN

Ensuring that men survived their wounds was the responsibility of the army medical services, and particularly the Royal Army Medical Corps (RAMC), whose role it was to care for the wounded and to evacuate them efficiently from the frontline to, it was hoped, 'Blighty'. The chain was a long one: first to the Regimental Aid Post (RAP), run by a RAMC doctor and a small number of orderlies that was set up close to the frontline, usually in dug-outs or ruined buildings. Next in the chain was the Advanced Dressing Station (ADS), set up at the farthest forward limit of wheeled transport, and run by the RAMC Field Ambulance. The wounded would be transported from RAP to ADS through a variety of means, on foot, by cart, on a stretcher – the latter with a series of relay posts where there was a considerable distance between the two. Men could then expect to be transported down the line to Main Dressing Stations (MDS), beyond the range of medium artillery fire; Casualty Clearing Stations (CCS), set up beyond the artillery zone, and finally, still within the theatre of operations, General and Stationary hospitals. From here, Tommy would hope to receive his 'ticket' – a label that marked him for transportation on hospital ships bound for 'blighty'.

> *I then went to the 'Walking Wounded' place & got some bread &*
> *tea – Wilmot then saw the M.O. & got a lift home on the score of*
> *bad feet.*
> *(Geoffrey Thurlow, letter to Edward Brittain, 3 November 1916)*

ENCYCLOPAEDIA OF MILITARY TERMS
DRESSING STATION – The home of pills, poultices, plasters, cas-carettes, castor oil, and catgut, needles, knives, and 'nerves'.
(Made in the Trenches, 1916)

'CCS' – Casualty Clearing Station. A place where the doctors draw lots to see if Tommy is badly wounded enough to be sent to Blighty.
(Arthur Guy Empey, *Over The Top*, 1917)

THREE CASUALTY CLEARING STATIONS
IN THE YPRES SALIENT:

'Bandagehem': Haringe (Bandagehem) Military Cemetery
'Dozinghem': Dozinghem Military Cemetery
'Mendinghem': Mendinghem Military Cemetery
Soldiers' mock-Flemish names for CCSs retained by the Commonwealth War Graves Commission.

SICK AND WELL

Soldiers reporting sick, often called 'duds', were aware that doctors were duty-bound to get them back to active duty with due dispatch. Many were just exhausted by the sleep-deprivation of being shelled – they were 'whacked', 'done', 'puddled' (confused), 'ditty' (crazed), or they might find their 'nerves were beginning to feel the racket' (F.C. Hitchcock,

Stand To), or they were just feeling 'seedy'. A common complaint among staff officers and others was that the general poor health of so many city-dwellers meant that the stamina of new recruits was not up to soldiering. Pte Britland was surprised that during training he felt so well; in June 1915 he wrote home: 'I never seem to ail anything now. I am as hard as nails … it sounds funny to hear of so many of you ailing. We are living under conditions which 12 months since would have killed me and I never felt better in my life.' A soldier with reliable health was called a 'flier'.

'Number 9'

This was reputedly a pill doled out to men on sick parade, usually in the format 'Medicine and duties', the medicine being the pill itself – sometimes called 'the doctor'. According to Fraser and Gibbon, it derives its number from the ninth pill in the Field Hospital Case of drugs, and was usually prescribed where there was doubt over the claimed ailment. As such 'No. 9' was applied to anything dubious. According to some reports its ingredients had a laxative effect.

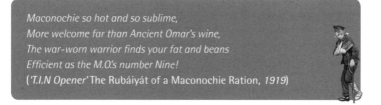

I went to the M.O., but all he could do was to give me a No. 9 pill – the universal specific of the army.
(*Pte H.S. Clapham, HAC, 4 February 1915,* Mud and Khaki, *1930*)

Maconochie so hot and so sublime,
More welcome far than Ancient Omar's wine,
The war-worn warrior finds your fat and beans
Efficient as the M.O.'s number Nine!
(*'T.I.N Opener'* The Rubáiyát of a Maconochie Ration, *1919*)

Trench fever and trench feet

The diseases most associated with the extreme conditions of trench warfare are 'trench fever' and 'trench feet'. 'Trench fever' (then a p.u.o;

Pyrexia of unknown origin) was a condition transmitted by body lice; 'trench feet' from prolonged immersion of the feet in water.

Trench fever – A malady contracted in the trenches; the symptoms are high temperature, bodily pains, and homesickness. A bad case lands Tommy in 'Blighty,' a slight case lands him back in the trenches, where he tries to get it worse than ever.
(Arthur Guy Empey, *Over The Top*, 1917)

What a strange complaint trench fever was. One got extraordinary temperatures, and it got one down most terribly but I never heard of a man dying of it.
(*Pte Alfred M. Burrage, Artists' Rifles*, War is War, *1930*)

'Trench feet' – A disease of the feet contracted in the trenches from exposure to extreme cold and wet. Tommy's greatest ambition is to contract this disease because it means 'Blighty' for him.
(Arthur Guy Empey, *Over The Top*, 1917)

The worst disease of that winter was 'trench feet' a sort of foot-rot caused by standing with one's feet continually wet and cold. At best it was extremely painful, and at worst it required the amputation of the patient's feet.
(*Charles Edmonds*, A Subaltern's War, *1929*)

'Trench foot' – a condition arrived at by dint of hard dodging of whale-oil parades and by having lots of water to stand in.
(*Listening Post*, the paper of the 7th Canadian Infantry Battalion, December 1917)

'Pushing up Daisies'

Not surprisingly, the soldier in the frontline, the stretcher-bearer, the
Voluntary Aid Detachments (VADs) and other nursing staff, were
imaginative in finding ways to describe dying and being dead. Terms
ranged from the sentimental 'go home' or 'go out', to the gently humorous 'push up daisies' or 'become a landowner', to the blunt 'snuff it'.
Phrases which originated in the First World War include 'becoming
a landowner in France', 'pushing up daisies', 'to stop' or 'cop a packet'
(though this was also used for being hit), 'to be buzzed', (from sending
a phone message on the 'buzzer'), 'to be huffed', 'to be booked', and the
adaptation of *il n'y en a plus* (there isn't any more) – 'napoo'.

All too often the soldier would use terms that avoided saying death:
'He could have done me quite easily', wrote Pte Albert Andrews of the
19th Manchesters (1 July 1916, but written up in 1917), and, of the
experience of finding an unexploded rifle-grenade just next to where
he was sheltering, 'I had been near before, but this was too near.'

Some terms for dying

Buzzed	Napoo
Copping it	Off it
Daisy pushing	Outed (from boxing)
Ditched it	Out of mess
Drawing your full issue	Number's up
Etre capout	Scuppered
Finee	Skittled
Get it	Snottered
Get done in	Snuff it
Go home, or out	Stonkered
Hop it	Taking the count
Huffed	Topped off
Knocked out	Wiped out
Loaf o'bread,	Written off
Mafeesh	

'Clicked it'; got killed; up against it; wounded.
(Arthur Guy Empey, *Over The Top*, 1917)

'GONE WEST'

The term 'gone west' is usually considered to be one of the most common terms for death, and, according to the *Oxford English Dictionary*, it certainly came to prominence during the war. Partridge considered that 'the finest, most beautiful of all these synonyms [for death]' had as its basis 'the idea of the setting sun' and that the phrase had 'occured in Classical Greek'. Another possible explanation is reference to the westward trip from Newgate Prison in London to the public gallows at Tyburn during the seventeenth century.

```
'Does anyone know the origin or meaning of the
soldiers' curious phrase for death, 'going west?'
  'Sir, I am loath to spoil any endeavours of your
correspondents to link this phrase with Wordsworth,
or Egyptian tradition, but I can assure them that
the origin is found in that splendid song which one
heard so much over yonder, at the impromptu bivouac
concert, entitled "Drake goes West".
  Anyone invalided from the front, as I am, will
corroborate me,
  I am, sir, yours faithfully, A Soldier
```

The Times, *31 December 1914 and 8 January 1915*

The King and Queen deeply regret the loss you and the army have sustained by the death of your son in the service of his country. Their majesties truly sympathise with you in your sorrow. Private Secretary, Buckingham Palace.

(*Telegram relating to death of Lt William Edgington, RFA, 8 May 1915*)

Copy   1st Sept. 17.

Dear Sir,

      I very much regret to inform you in reply to your letter of 23.8.17 that your Son was killed in action on 4th August - He had been out on a day-light patrol & was killed just out-side our Parapet on returning - Your Son was a most valuable Observer & a very gallant Soldier & this loss is greatly felt in the Battalion. - Please accept my deepest sympathy & that of the rest of the Battalion in your bereavement.

Your Son's Grave has a cross erected above it. - You can obtain its position from the Director of Graves Registration and Enquiries, War Office, London.

Your Son's courage - & the example he always set - is worthy of great praise. He was killed instantaneously.

           Yrs truly,
           G. B. Morris (Lt. Col)
           Commdr Battn.

Condolence letter from the Colonel, 1917.

BURIAL PARTY

Burial Parties were a consistent part of a soldiers life, both in the line and out of it.

13 July 1916: On the Monday I was put with the others burying the dead and this was when we realised the cost of our victory. Burying your own lads is not a job that I want again, some seeming by their looks to have died very easy, others very hard. Some we had to dig out – they had been half-buried. The job consisted of getting hold of them, taking their equipment off and emptying their pockets. You put the contents in the gas-helmet satchel and hand this to the Officer who is with you, giving the man's name, number and regiment if possible. Then they are put into a hole ready dug with boots and everything on. You put in about 10 or 15, whatever the grave will hold, throw about two feet of earth on them and stick a wooden cross on the top which is marked by the officers. For some it was the third day and you could hardly stand the stench as you got hold of them, often having to put them down, go out of the way and have a smoke. The game wanted sticking!
(*Diary entry, Pte Albert Andrews, 19th Battalion, Manchester Regiment*)

Rarely a night passed without its burial parties. 'Digging in the garden' Tommy calls the grave-making. The bodies, wrapped in blankets or waterproof ground-sheets, are lifted over the parados, and carried back a convenient twenty yards or more. Our chaplain was a devout man, but prudent to a fault. Therefore our burial parties proceeded without the rites of the Church. This arrangement was highly satisfactory to Tommy. He liked to 'get the planting done' with the least possible delay or fuss.
(*James Norman Hall, Royal Fusiliers,* Kitchener's Mob, *1916*)

CORPSE FACTORY

On 20 April 1917, *The Times* printed a story about the 'Corpse Utilisation Company' operating behind German lines, which according to 'Sergeant B–' of the Royal West Kents, who 'got the story from a captured German', was boiling corpses 'to make fat for ammunition making and to feed pigs and poultry, and God knows what besides ... Fritz calls his margarine "corpse fat", because they suspect that's what it comes from'. An article in a Berlin newspaper, the *Lokalanzeiger*, 5 April, had described a *Kadaververwertungsanstalt*, or 'carcass grading factory'. There followed in the British press a discussion of whether *Kadaver* could be used to describe a human corpse, the usual word being *Leiche* or *Leichnam* (the German slang for a sergeant major was *Leichenbitter*, or 'undertaker's man'). Some papers leapt at the chance to use the story for propaganda, *Punch* offering a cartoon of the Kaiser showing a soldier the *Kadaververwertungsanstalt* with the words: 'And don't forget that your Kaiser will find a use for you – alive or dead'. The government prevaricated, and though the British propaganda unit declined to promote the story, it gained some credence for a while, building outrage in an already traumatised nation who now feared the bodies of their dead sons were being eaten by the enemy.

What was missed was the strength of the morbidity of German trench slang, which viewed the front as a processor of *Kanonenfutter* (cannon-fodder); the commission for assessing conscripts' suitability for active service was known by soldiers as the *Kadaververwertungsgesellschaft*, or 'carcass grading company', easily translated to Allied soldiers as 'the corpse factory'. In a further twist of irony, the newspaper of the French 68th Regiment was called *le Bochefage*, 'the Boche-eater'.

Behind the Lines

If 'up the line' meant a spell in the frontline trenches, 'out on rest' could mean a great many other things, depending on the sector, the army or divisional commander, or the exigencies of battle. Away from the trenches, Tommy could resume some kind of normal life away from the constant danger of shellfire and bullets.

After a tour of duty in the frontline, on average seven days, a battalion was relieved. Its destination was the reserve trenches – less prone to sniping and trench mortars, but still subject to artillery fire. Men in reserve could be called upon to reinforce the front when under pressure, and were the main reinforcements when the front was under severe pressure. The welcomed withdrawal of a battalion out of the line completely was meant some rest, a chance for officers and NCOs to reassert military fastidiousness, and an opportunity for the average soldier to gain some mental freedom – washing, speaking to locals, and buying trinkets such as silks or other small souvenirs. Rest camps were set up in rear areas, though often still within range of the largest guns. Dependent on the theatre of war, they could be based in villages, set up in hutted or tented camps, or simply organised in the 'least dangerous' part of the battle area.

In many cases, soldiers out of the line could mix with civilians (those brave or foolish enough to be close to the battle area), talking at them in anglicised versions of the local language. They could also engage women in hopeful conversations. Out on rest, soldiers were paid in francs, dinars and other currencies, which they could spend on alcohol – often of lamentable quality – and other vices normally frowned upon at home: gambling, fraternisation with women of 'ill repute' and visits to brothels. Tommy would also have some freedom to make simple purchases, souvenirs, postcards and the ubiquitous '*oeuf-frites*' from estaminets. Hut-canteens provided and staffed by the YMCA, Church Army or similar organisations were 'dry' canteens, but such huts, funded through 'flag days' and the like, created a means for men to gather, drink tea, eat sandwiches and write letters home. Out on rest, however, military duties still prevailed: training, lectures, fatigues; but contemporary diarists all record the sense of relief at being set free of the random slaughter of the frontline, if only for a short time.

CATCHPHRASES

The meaningless phrases that triggered knowing laughter or just a smile of recognition came sometimes from comics, sometimes from songs, sometimes from sources now lost. 'Notarfonyer' appearing on a caricature drawing on the front cover of the *Open Exhaust*, January 1916, the trench magazine of 358 Company, ASC, was probably a phrase often used by the character portrayed. 'Listen to the phonograph' (used in *Troddles in the The Trenches*) meant something like 'we've heard it all before'. Australians used 'No farver, no muvver' to someone complaining, to which another would respond 'poor little feller', probably from the sentimental story *The Softening of Miss Cynthia* by Lucy Maud Montgomery. 'Do you want jam on it?' was another response to complaints, often shortened to just 'jam on it'. 'A land fit for heroes' was, according to C. Howarth, 14th Argyll and Sutherland Highlanders, 'a catch phrase to keep the troops from chucking up the war'.

'*C'est la guerre* (it's the war)' became a universal answer to finish any discussion on any topic, as did 'nuff said', while 'Remember Belgium' became a comment on the apparent meaninglessness of four years of trench-warfare, a response to 'what are we doing here?' The general fed-up-ness of the troops was expressed in the words 'Dear Auntie' or 'Dear Bill', from an apocryphal postcard that would challenge any encouraging or patriotic words from home. Australian catchphrases, whose irony in adversity sound as sharply honed now as they did under a bombardment, were 'we're winning' and 'nice day for it'. A pleasant surprise would be greeted with 'stuff to give 'em', while its development 'the give to stuff them' was applied to approval at the artillery's actions.

Things we must know – Who is the cook who asks, when you go to him for rations, 'if you want j-j-jam on it?'
(5th Gloucesters Gazette, *12 July 1915*)

'It's a Long Way to Tipperary'

No song during the period was the subject of as many pastiche versions as 'It's a Long Way to Tipperary', a song reputedly first sung by the Connaught Rangers in France in August 1914, a fact reported in the *Daily Mail* on 18 August. Its chorus was particularly celebrated:

It's a long way to Tipperary,
It's a long way to go.
It's a long way to Tipperary
To the sweetest girl I know!
Goodbye, Piccadilly,
Farewell, Leicester Square!
It's a long long way to Tipperary,
But my heart's right there.

The song was to remain popular throughout the war, yet a certain weariness as well as familiarity may be detected in Donald McNair's diary entry for 27 July 1917 when his troopship arrived at Cherbourg: '"Tipperary" was of course sung ...'. As a song with a rhythm which lent itself to marching speed, it must have had tedious connotations to most soldiers (Brophy notes that attempts to start it were often shouted or whistled down), as well as being taken up by civilians at home (after it was recorded by the Tenor John McCormack in November 1914) – soldiers on leave in England could not escape from it, even if they wanted to.

> *I wanter go where Tipperary*
> *Ain't whistled from morning to night*
> (*From* On Leave, *in* Depot Review No.5, *November 1915*)

Maybe for this reason it was used as a forum for expressing resentment towards those not undergoing the same kinds of deprivation and stress:

Another version of the lyrics was recorded by 2nd Lieutenant
F.T. Nettleingham in *Tommy's Tunes* (1917):

That's the wrong way to tickle Marie
That's the wrong way to kiss:
Don't you know that over here, lad,
They like it better like this.
Hoorary *pour la France!*
Farewell *Angleterre!*
We didn't know the way to tickle Marie,
But now we've learnt how.

According to him: 'If you ever hear the air of Tipperary, it's almost
certain that they will be singing the above.'

'It's a long way to
Tipperary', sheet music.

'ARE WE DOWNHEARTED?'

'Are we downhearted?' became a catchphrase in the early part of the war, having been appropriated, according to some sources, from a political slogan associated with the 1906 election. Called out from one group of soldiers to another (or ship to ship), the intended answer to the call was 'No!', but it very soon descended into 'Yes!', or even 'You bloody well soon will be!'

Are we downhearted? a popular catchphrase of the war years.

'In the pink'

'In the pink' has a long history dating back to at least the sixteenth century, when it meant the apex of achievement for almost anything (appearing as such in *Romeo and Juliet*, 1597). In the early twentieth century, this became more commonly associated with the 'Pink of Condition', in which form it was used during the war. The phrase was commonly used in letters home to perhaps cover the conditions at the front: 'I hope this reaches you as it leaves me, in the pink.'

> *Dearest Kitty,*
> *Just a brief note to let you know that I am in the pink hoping you are the*
> *same. I had a very pleasant journey across the water.*
> *Yours truly Percy*
> *(**Letter home from Pte Percy Edwards, South Wales Borderers,** 20 August 1918; he died of wounds sustained in action, September 1918)*

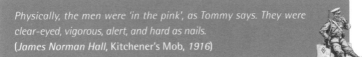

> *Physically, the men were 'in the pink', as Tommy says. They were clear-eyed, vigorous, alert, and hard as nails.*
> *(**James Norman Hall,** Kitchener's Mob, 1916)*

Nissen Hut

The Nissen Hut, developed in August 1916, was the design of Major P.N. Nissen of 29th Field Company RE, and was of prefabricated design made up of fifty-four separate semi-cylindrical sheets of corrugated steel. Each sheet measured 10ft 6in x 2ft 2in, and the hut could, by repute, be erected by six men in four hours, and be packed away on an army lorry. With accommodation at a premium for soldiers in the rear areas, Nissen Huts were preferred to damp and cold tents, and around 100,000 huts were produced during the war.

Rest Camp

From *Brackett's Army Dictionary* (1919): 'Rest camp: (theory) A nice quiet camp in a nice quiet spot, near a nice quiet village, where the troops can take a nice quiet rest after taking a long journey on boats, box cars, etc. (Practice) pick, shovel, rock pile, shovel and pick.'

> *My dear Charlie,*
> *When I got back off leave I found the Battn in rest billets but the following day we again went into the front line and only yesterday came into the supports. We had a pretty hellish time and rotten weather conditions and most of the time were wading up to our knees in water.*
> *(Letter from unidentified soldier, BEF, 21 August 1917)*

'Billet' – On active service a billet may be anything from a shed to a chateau. Usually the former. When troops are to be moved from one part of the front to another, a billeting party is sent in advance. These men receive explicit instructions to locate the most draughty and leaky barns in the country. At this they are experts. The generous-hearted farmers then inform their cattle and pigs that they must be very polite and wipe their feet before walking over a brave soldier's blankets. He also gives the hens and chickens warning not to lay eggs where a soldier may crush them. The farmer's wife then pours a jug of beer into a barrel of water, his daughters practice a 'No compres' smile and everything is ready for the reception of the 'Soldat Canadien'.
(Made in the Trenches, 1916)

> *Dear Gertie,*
> *Having lovely weather here just had a spell in the trenches but we are in billets at present.*
> *From your old friend Frank*
> *(Postcard from unidentified soldier in France, 21 May 1916)*

Estaminet

The estaminet (or 'staminet') was any small establishment set up to serve alcoholic drinks. Though some of these were on a formal bar footing, many others in the rear areas would be created to cater for the soldier fresh out of the line – and in need of refreshment. According to Brophy and Partridge (*Soldiers' Songs and Slang*, 1931), an estaminet must 'have a low roof, an open iron stove and a fug'. Its bill of fare was typically 'wine, cognac and thin beer, as well as coffee, soup, eggs and chips and omelettes'.

'Estaminet' – Translated into English means the 'Rendezvous de la Police Militaire'. It is where soldiers (including engineers) congregate to spend their unearned increment and to recount the many brave deeds they have done, also to listen to Mademoiselle's 'Arf an' Arf' language whilst drinking her 'Arf an' Arf' beer.
(Made in the Trenches, 1916)

TOMMY IN FRANCE
'Oh! Madamerselle, chery madamerselle,
You come for a nice promenay?
Yes, its always the same with your 'apres
la guerre',

And your 'me no compris' what I say,
Come along Bill to the old 'staminet,'
Though the beer may be rotten it still is
A 'wet',

A hunk off a loaf and a glass, me and you,
What's that old lady? Oh! Damn it,
'Napoo'.

(The BEF Times, No. 1, Vol. 1, 1 December 1916)

> *TOMMY* (to Jock, on leave): *'What about the lingo? Suppose you want an egg over there, what do you say?'*
> *JOCK. 'Ye juist say, "Oof".'*
> *TOMMY. 'But suppose you want two?'*
> *JOCK. 'Ye say "Twa oofs", and the silly auld fule wife gies ye three, and ye juist gie her back one. Man, it's an awfu' easy language.'*
> (Punch, *1916*)

'Y-EMMA'

The YMCA (and other organisations, such as the Salvation Army and the Church Army) were prevalent in the rear areas. With 'flag days' at home gathering funds for these charities for their special 'hut funds', these organisations provided comforts to the troops in even quite advanced areas on almost all fronts. The Y-emmas offered 'tea and a wad' as well as free stationery and a chance to buy small comforts that could be taken up to the frontline. With the badge of the YMCA being an inverted red triangle, the sign was refered to as 'Tommy's Triangle'.

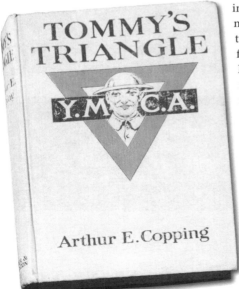

The triangle even made it into the frontline – fragments of mugs bearing the device have been found in recent digs in Belgium. The YMCA initials would also be interpreted as 'Young Mothers Call Always'.

The YMCA, 'the Y-emma' or 'Tommy's Triangle' supplied comforts for the troops while 'out on rest'.

SOUVENIR

'Souvenirs' were sought by most soldiers, though 'to souvenir' was also to scrounge, appropriate or steal. There was an active trade in battle items, especially in the rear areas, and in the early part of the war no Tommy would be seen without his *pickelhaube*; clearly supply did not keep up with demand, since the *Splint Record*, trench paper for the 2nd Field Ambulance, 1st Canadian Division, in December 1915 contained *A Soldier's Christmas Litany* which included: 'From all requests for German helmets ... Good Lord deliver us'. The paper's sequel, the *Iodine Chronicle,* in May 1916 advised that 'grub and socks are better at the end of a long march than shirts or souvenirs'.

'Souvenir' – A begging word used by the French kiddies. When it is addressed to Tommy it generally means, a penny, biscuits, bully beef, or a tin of jam.
(Arthur Guy Empey, *Over the Top*, 1917)

Dear Rowena,
Here's a souvenir for you a Hun Field Post Card, I got it from a Hun prisoner we captured. Things are rather noisy. Cheer-oh, Harris
(*From an unidentified officer in France, 9 September 1916*)

I is the Indian who cries 'Souvenir'
With a Teutonic head on the end of his spear.
(The Battalion ABC, 5th Gloucesters Gazette, *12 April 1915*
(*'It is extremely difficult to keep the Indians in the trenches; they always want to be charging'*, subaltern quoted in the Daily Express, *October 1914*))

SILKS

By far the most common souvenirs of frontline service are the silk postcards – known as 'silks' – a real phenomenon of the war. Though first produced in 1907, the new market provided by the influx of soldiers saw them gain popularity early on in 1915, as the locals realised the potential for the marketing of their skills; some estimates suggest that as many as 10 million cards were produced during the war. Each card was produced as part of a cottage industry which saw mostly women engaged hand embroidering intricate designs on to strips of mesh, the design being repeated as many as twenty-five times on a strip, before being sent to a factory for cutting and mounting as postcards and greetings cards. They were not cheap, each one costing as much as three times the daily pay of the average soldier. There is a huge range: sentimental messages (sometimes at odds with the military image on the front) 'friendship', 'birthday greetings', 'Home Sweet Home' and so on were popular, and the most common, as are cards celebrating festivals and holidays.

Hurray for Tommy! An unusual silk postcard; there were many variants.

Typical legends on Silk postcards

Patriotic
Hurrah for Tommy
Britons All
For the Liberty 1915
God Defend the Right
Vive La France 1915
Vive Les Alliés
Gloire au 75

Greetings
Happy Christmas
Christmas Greetings
I am the Christmas Kiss
A Happy Christmas to my Dear
   Wife
Happy Birthday

Souvenir
Souvenir from France
Souvenir de Belgique

Souvenir de France
Greetings from France
Good News from France

Sentimental & family
From Daddy
To my Dear Mother
Hope and Love
Kisses for my Darling
To My Sweetheart
Flowers from France
A Kiss from France
Love and Kisses
Yours Always
Remember
Remembrance from a Soldier
All Kind Thoughts
Good Luck
We Will be Happy Once again
Never Mind

Souvenir of the Campaign 1914–1915
Greetings from the Trenches

'Are we downhearted?'
Catchphrase used on silk
postcard.

'RED LAMP'

While the red lamp was originally the sign of a doctor's surgery in the early nineteenth century, by the twentieth it was universally accepted as the sign of a brothel. According to Sassoon, brothels frequented by officers were more often indicated by a blue lamp, while ORs queued at 'red lamps'.

'JIG-A-JIG'

The onomatopoeic term 'jig-a-jig' for sexual intercourse was already well established at the time of the war, appearing in Farmer and Henley's 1896 book *Slang and its Analogues*. It was one of many terms used by both soldiers and residents of the rear areas alike. While soldiers might hope to 'click' with a local girl, the more likely resolution of such desires would be beyond the red light of an OR-designated brothel, also known as a 'kip-shop'. The term 'tart' was the usual designation for a prostitute, and for roughly a week's pay a soldier could get ten minutes of not very private 'jig-a-jig'.

> We went to Amiens ... when we passed through there were a dozen or more little children all chanting the only English I think they knew 'Anglais soldat ... my sister 2 Francs, follow me.'
> (Pte Ralph I Smith, D Coy, 12th Battalion, Gloucestershire Regiment (*Bristol's Own*))

VD

Venereal disease was a constant worry for those supervising the health of troops. The rapid serving of customers and the low levels of personal hygiene in the ORs' brothels led to high incidences of sexually transmitted diseases. For Australians the 39 General Hospital and the No. 2 Stationary Hospital specialised in the treatment of VD, but ANZAC troops were at least prepared by being equipped with a preventative known as a 'blue light kit', presumably for officers only,

ORs getting a 'dreadnought'. British soldiers suffering from syphilis received an injection of '606', an organoarsenical compound also known as 'salvarsan', which was already being superseded by 1912. 'Short arm' inspections checked on groups of soldiers to ensure that sufferers were treated, a rather brusque application of public health.

TRENCH PAPERS AND NEWSPAPERS

Printed either in army offices or resuscitated printshops behind the lines or through regular processes in Britain, trench papers ranged from semi-official documents to the equivalents of college common-room rags. The closer to the front they were produced, the more they convey of the experience of the trench, while higher production values often accompany a sense of rank and deference (many of these are produced 'by permission of' the unit's commanding officer). The more interesting ones require the reader to read between the lines, as they are full of in-jokes and references to the foibles of individuals. Their titles range from formal descriptions of the unit producing them, to comic names – the *Morning Rire* ('laugh' in French) of the 2nd Irish Guards – or gallows humour, such as *Poison Gas*, the 'unofficial organ' of the 3rd Battalion, Queen Victoria's Rifles. Most famous of all was the *Wipers Times* (and its successors), which was published in facsimile after the war.

AVOIDING WORK

Work avoiders were 'skrim-shankers', an old army term, 'head-workers' or 'nut-workers' – thinking about how to avoid work. They would 'mike', or 'come the old soldier', or 'come the old man'. 'Lead-swingers' derives from navy usage; the man 'swinging the lead' was originally testing the depth of the sea with a lead weight – a job considered an easy one on board a sailing ship.

Lancs Fus. (Norwich). – The term 'lead-swinger' is army slang for a man who 'cracks the order' – that is, one who goes on sick parade without a reasonable excuse to get away from work.
(*Tit-bits*, 1 January 1916)

'The Leadswinger' – The Leadswinger has no particular habitat. It is of a shy, timid nature and has a furtive appearance. One of its chief enemies is the Emmo [M.O.].
(*Natural History in The B.S.F.*, The B.S.F. Library, Vol. 1, 1919)

'Blotto'

While rum was served out to men in the trenches twice a day (with a spoon, from a jar marked SRD), in rest camps the authorities were keen to try to keep men away from alcohol as much as possible. That this was unsuccessful can be seen in the spread of the word 'binge', previously only a Lancashire dialect word, meaning 'to soak'. This was also reinforced by the word 'bingo', a slang term for 'brandy'. Frequently used terms for 'drunk' were 'blotto', 'blindo' and 'blithero'.

'The Pictures'

With Charlie Chaplin a great favourite of the troops, a visit to a temporary cinema behind the lines was a highlight of leave from the front. 'The pictures' thus became applied to other areas of life in France and Flanders; the operating theatre of a field hospital was 'the pictures'; searchlight operators were also refered to as 'on the pictures' or 'on the movies'.

Sentry – 'Halt! Who goes there?'
Voice: 'Army Chaplain'
Sentry (a bit mixed): 'Pass Charlie Chaplin, All's Well!'
(*Humorous postcard*, c.1916)

Cox & Co.

By 1914 Cox & Co. had become the prime financial agents and bankers for most British regiments, and were even able to provide facilities for British officer PoWs to cash cheques in Germany. A cartoon in the April 1917 issue of the *5th Gloucesters Gazette* showed an officer stepping across the mud with the words:

> It is simply grand
> To cross No-mans-land
> On a nice little private war
> And a midnight raid
> Is part of our trade
> It's what Cox's pay us for.

Later in the issue an imagined demob course after the war includes '10 days at Messrs Cox & Co – Up-to-date methods of book-keeping.'

No   **D 951039**   Army Form W. 3241F.

ADVANCE OF PAY.

Agents :—Messrs. Cox & Co.

Rank and Name_____
(In BLOCK Letters)

Unit_____

RECEIVED from Cashier_____

the sum of_____francs.
(Figures)

Date_____   Signature.

Officers' pay advance slips, to be paid in Francs by Cox & Co. in the Field.

OFFICIALESE

By 1914 the word 'officialese' had been in use for thirty years, though few dictionaries recognised it. The use of a formal, distant and almost mechanical language achieved the removal of individualism or any sentiment that might affect efficiency, and tempered unpalatable reports with imprecise terminology. Often this meant that official bulletins communicated nothing by way of information, but assured the reader that events were proceeding, being observed, and to some extent managed.

'Official bulletins' managed by this means to annoy and frustrate – on 10 December 1916 the Revd Andrew Clarke wrote of the bulletin, 'it is insolent in its brevity: "Summary of Saturday's Official war news. There is nothing of importance to report on any front". Through the course of the war, the bulletin-writers developed a code by which news setbacks and failed attacks could be half-communicated through the balance of positive and negative terms. Alexander Aitken in *Gallipoli to the Somme* (1963) noted how fighting was described as 'sharp' or 'brisk' when 50 per cent casualties resulted. The official bulletin for 2 July 1916, after the beginning of the Somme offensive, stated: 'Attack launched 7.30 a.m. north of River Somme in conjunction with French. British troops have broken into German forward system of defences on front of 16 miles. Fighting is continuing. French attack on our immediate right proceeds equally satisfactorily.' Few would read this as implying anything other than a successful attack, while it states only that the front trenches were taken and the French attack was as successful as the British.

This careful selection of words developed into invention. Troops, having entrained and detrained to get from the Channel ports to training camps, continued their journeys to the front by 'embussing' and, on arrival, 'debussing'. Perhaps the most notable example of officialese was the selection, rather than 'truce' or 'ceasefire', of the word 'armistice', whose full implications allowed the German Army to claim not to have surrendered.

ATTRITION

On 2 September 1914, the military correspondent of *The Times* wrote: '… it was also clear that, owing to the numbers which Germany had massed in the Western theatre of war, annihilating victories for our side were difficult to obtain. We were faced with a war of attrition, a *combat d'usure* on a very gigantic scale, and we have to carry out this strategy to the bitter end …'

Such a state of affairs had been foreseen by many due to the nature of British and German military strategy: in 1909 in *Lessons From Two Recent Wars (Russo-Turkish & South African)* General H. Langlois had foreseen that a war between the two powers would centre on 'the form of a straight line without salient, and as envelopment is the only means of obtaining superiority of fire, the defence becomes unassailable. … A straight line cannot be invested and all the methods of procedure in siege operations fail against a front whose continual tendency is to become rectilinear and refuses to allow itself to be enveloped,' and the battle 'will go on eternally without result.'

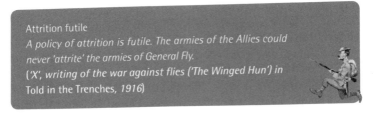

Attrition futile
A policy of attrition is futile. The armies of the Allies could never 'attrite' the armies of General Fly.
('X', writing of the war against flies ('The Winged Hun') in
Told in the Trenches, *1916*)

The *Depot Review* of the Army Service Corps' British Stationery Depot Rouen in Issue No. 5 in late 1915 included a playscript between two soldiers still bogged down in trench warfare in 1954.

A 'B.E.F.' ALPHABET

A is the ARMY, in which he's a veteran. Who's fought for a year from the Somme up to Meteren, finding in Winter each week is a wetter 'un, And passing his days in the trenches.

B is for old BLIGHTY, where so we hear, Prices are rising, and food is so dear, That a 'sub' can't afford to even go near: It is cheaper to stay in the trenches.

C is for the CAVALRY who, (so I've heard say) have not seen their gee-gees for many a day, But soon will mount them and gallop away, And we'll all say good-bye to the trenches.

D is for DUCKBOARDS – if placed end to end, They'd girdle the Earth, and to Heaven ascend, But I notice they've caused a peculiar blend, Of language to thrive in the trenches.

E is for the EDITOR, ruddy in hue, He'd blue-pencil this if I said all I knew, So I'll wish him good luck or – between me and you – He'll send me exploring Hun trenches.

F for the FLYING CORPS – here we express, Our admiration: could we do less? They often have helped us out of a mess, 'Cheer-oh!' from the men in the trenches.

G is for poisonous GAS that's emitted, By fighters behind the line only half-witted, But very pugnacious, and very much to be pitied, By those who live in the trenches.

H for the HUN who lives over the way: His future is black and his present is grey: Yet a Hun is a Hun, and as such he must pay, For making us live in the trenches.

I for the INFANTRY prefixed 'P.B.', One bob per diem and milk in their tea; They work day and night, after which they are free, To start on a job in the trenches.

J for JAR – if its contents are rum, A welcome awaits it whene'er it may come: Be it soon, be it late, there will always be some, To greet it with joy in the trenches.

K's for the KULTUR beneficient Huns, Endeavour to force down our throats with big guns: They send shells in packets, they send them in ones: But Kultur's NAR-POO in the trenches.

L is for LEAVE, our goal of desire, Ten days in Blighty away from the mire. Hope springs eternal, and ne'er will expire, In the breast of the men in the trenches.

M stands for MINNIE, whose shriek rends the night: They say that her bark is much worse than her bite, And if you can dodge her you'll sure be all right: But she isn't much loved in the trenches.

N for the NOMINAL ROLLS we send through, Daily and Weekly and monthly to 'Q': But we'd do it gladly and much worse things too, to finish the war in the trenches.

O the OBSERVER, who sees many sights, Such as stout German generals dancing in tights, And performing the most inexplicable rites, From his O-Pip in one of our trenches.

P's for PEDICULI, horrible pests, They make themselves happy in trousers and vests; Though dear little fellows, they're unwelcome guests, To the P.B.I. in the trenches.

Q? Well its obvious who fills this place – Princes of paper, the pride of our race –Every moment and minute be sure they can trace, And send back to the Man in the trenches.

R the RETURNS to be rendered by noon, Of the number of men who have seen a blue moon, Speak Japanese, or have been to Rangoon, Before they came out to the trenches.

S for the SAPPERS, who sin without shame, And in spite of all efforts will go down to fame, As the men who invented the five-bob 'A' frame, To keep up the sides of our trenches.

T for the TRENCHES themselves (this is where I must take heed what I write, or I'll swear!), Which have blackened our souls, and have whitened our hair: Oh! Life is a dream in the trenches.

U for the UNIVERSE, whose fat 'tis plain, Is now being settled in mud, slush and rain, By strafing which spreads from Nieuport to Lorraine, a line which is marked by our trenches.

V for the VICES soldiers posses, Discovered by those who have been more or less, Claimants to fame through a line in the Press, But have never shone in the trenches.

W is for WHISKEY and WHIZZ-BANGS as well: Of the former I've almost forgotten the smell, Whilst the latter contribute to make it like Hell, At various times in the trenches.

X for the unknown – and 'twixt you and me, Fritz is now thinking (and we all agree), That, hot as his present, his future will be, Much hotter that e'er in the trenches.

Y for the YARNS that one hears – some are true: Others – Well! Doubtless, though vivid in hue, Are spun by those 'back,' who have never been through, Or stood their whack of the trenches.

Z is for ZERO, the time we go over, Most of us wish we were way back in Dover, Making munitions and living in clover, And far, far away from the trenches.

The B.E.F. Times, No. 4, Vol. 1, 5 March 1917

'The Big Push'

Otherwise called the 'Great Push', the phrase came into prominence with the planning for the Battle of the Somme in 1916; yet it was to be used for any of the British offensives during the war, particularly that of the Battle of Loos in September 1915. A series of photographic postcards illustrated 'the Big Push in the West' at Loos, the battle itself described in Patrick MacGill's 1916 book, *The Great Push*. The phrase is now firmly lodged in the public consciousness, and is used in all situations where a greater effort is required.

> TOWARDS the end of June, 1916, it became apparent that the moment was at hand when the 'Big Push' on the Western Front, so long expected and so ardently desired, might at length be attempted with every prospect of success.
> (Sir Douglas Haig's Big Push, c. 1916)

Poor Fellow, were you wounded in The Big Push?: soldier in 'Blighty Blue', 1916.

"POOR FELLOW—— WERE YOU
WOUNDED IN THE GREAT PUSH?"
"NO MUM! IN THE LITTLE MARY."

Offensive Spirit

British official policy was not to rest in the trenches, but to continue offensive operations against the enemy, however insignificant.

> *Our generals never gave peace to the enemy, not allowed anything in the nature of a truce. They believed in the 'offensive spirit', and by raids, mining attacks, and the capture of forward trenches, which generally resulted in minor salients, they kept the great Salient active and abominable.*
> (*Philip Gibbs*, The Immortal Salient, *1925*)

> *The spirit of the bayonet must be inculcated into all ranks so that in an attack they will go forward with that aggressive determination and confidence which assures a bayonet assault.*
> (Musketry Regulations, Part 1, Bayonet Training, *1914*)

Quiet Sectors

Quiet sectors were those parts of the line where there was little offensive activity, and where the unofficial 'live-and-let-live' system was enacted. Usually, these sectors were at the extremities of the main offensive areas, and in some cases, 'quiet sectors' could transform, into 'offensive sectors', such as happened on the Somme in July 1916. Another term for a quiet sector was a 'health resort'.

> *It was summer and a so-called 'quiet' sector of the line, else no man could have stuck sixteen days of it off the reel. By the word 'quiet' it was meant to convey that there had been nothing more than a little friendly shelling on each side, and one or two almost formal calls in the way of raids.*
> (*Pte Alfred M. Burrage, Artists' Rifles,* War is War, *1930*)

Out on Rest

With each 'tour' of duty in the frontline trenches taking around one week or so, this was followed by one week in reserve, and a third 'out on rest'. For most frontline troops, the term 'on rest' was far from the truth; instead they were subjected to parades and the re-instigation of codes of cleanliness – as well as nightly returns to the trench lines, carrying the sundry stores and equipment that were required to prosecute effective trench warfare.

Force abbreviations

AEF: American Expeditionary Force. Sometimes referred to as 'After England Failed'.

AIF: Australian Imperial Forces. Applied to all Australian Forces wherever deployed. Confusingly, Australian military insignia was to bear another title, 'Australian Commonwealth Military Forces', referring to the Commonwealth of Australia.

BEF: British Expeditionary Force. The BEF was to take the left of the line in Flanders, as had been agreed in pre-war planning.

CEF: Constantinople Expeditionary Force. The first, naïve, abbreviation for the British troops bound for the Dardanelles. Painted on the sides of supply boxes, the term was a gift to Middle Eastern intelligence agencies. It was dropped in favour of the MEF early in 1915.

CEO: *Corps expéditionnaire d'Orient*, the French expeditionary force to the Dardanelles in 1915.

CEP: *Corpo Expedicionário Português*, the Portuguese Expeditionary Corps that served on the Western Front from 1917–18.

EEF: Egyptian Expeditionary Force. The British Army in Egypt, from 1916.

MEF: Mediterranean Expeditionary Force. The British Forces in Gallipoli in 1915, and then Salonica in 1916.

MEF: Mesopotamia Expeditionary Force. The British Army in Mesopotamia, from 1916.

COMIC CUTS

The term for the official 'Intelligence Summaries' that were issued on a regular basis by all echelons of command, and posted up on boards or even read to the troops. Often written in high-handed style, these communiques were often derided by the soldiery, who dismissed them as 'eye-wash'.

> *It was rumoured in* Comic Cuts. *(*Comic Cuts *is the stately Summary of War Intelligence issued daily from Olympus).*
> (*Ian Hay,* Carrying on After the First Hundred Thousand, *1918*)

'THE ACCESSORY'

The first use of gas in warfare by the British Army was the release of chlorine from cylinders at the opening of the Battle of Loos in September 1915, one of the first of the 'Great Pushes'. In order to maintain secrecy and ensure that the use of the gas would not be given away in a careless conversation, it was codenamed 'the accessory', with the soldiers of the Royal Engineers in charge of the new weapon being called the 'Special Companies'. Gas cylinders were known as 'dodgers'.

SHOT AT DAWN
ONE OF THE FIRST TO ENLIST
A WORTHY SON OF HIS FATHER

Epitaph on the grave of Private Albert Ingham, 18th Battalion, Manchester Regiment, Bailleumont CWGC Cemetery, France; executed for desertion, 1 December 1916

THE ARMY ACT. PART I. CRIMES AND PUNISHMENTS.

Offences in respect of Military Service
Every person subject to military law who commits any of the following offences; that is to say, Shamefully abandons or delivers up any garrison, place, post, or guard ... Shamefully casts way his arms, amunition or tools in the presence of the enemy...
Without orders ... leaves his guard, picquet, patrol or post; or
Being a soldier acting as a sentinel,

> (i) sleeps or is drunk on his post; or

> (ii) leaves his post before he is regularly relieved ...

Causes or conspires with any other persons to cause any mutiny or sedition...

Deserts or attempts to desert His Majesty's service; ...
Shall, on conviction by court-marshal ... be liable to suffer death, or such less punishment as is in this Act mentioned ...

Manual of Military Law, War Office, 1914

FIELD PUNISHMENT NO. 1

Field Punishment No. 1, usually abbreviated to F.P. No. 1, was also called 'crucifixion', as it entailed the shackling or tying of a man's arms and legs to a stationary object such as a gun wheel or a tree for several hours a day. The punishment was given for a variety of crimes and misdemeanours while 'on active service', and was common during the Great War, with an estimated 60,000 punishments served.

There were some twenty big trees dotted about, and to every tree a man was tied up, by a rope twisted many times round his body and arms, so that his toes, in some cases, only just touched the ground. It was the first time I had seen No 1 Field punishment in operation, and the sight was not a pretty one.
(*Pte H.S. Clapham, HAC, Ypres Salient, 15 June 1915*, Mud and Khaki, *1930*)

Greeting to the Sergeant
You've got a kind face, you old bastard,
You ought to be bloodywell shot;
You ought to be tied to a gun-wheel
And left there to bloodywell rot.
(*Soldiers' chant, J. Brophy and E. Partridge*, Songs and Slang of the British Soldier, *1931*)

RIOT

```
RIOT IN CANADIAN CAMP
12 KILLED AND MANY INJURED
V.C. TRAMPLED TO DEATH.
```

The Times, *7 March 1919*

By March 1919 there were still 19,000 Canadian soldiers stationed at Kinmel Military Camp, waiting for transport home. Following some weeks, during which they had been promised imminent demobilisation but had heard rumours of more recently conscripted soldiers who had seen no fighting being returned to Canada, they took over the camp, provoked apparently by the cry 'Come on Bolsheviks'. The rioting included looting stores, demolishing officers' quarters, and even dressing up in clothes taken from the women stationed in the camp. The disturbances were over within two days, the ringleaders removed, and assurances of quick demobilisation given. The word 'mutiny' was not mentioned in reports.

[The Buzzer] speaks a language of his own. His one task in life is to prevent the letter B from sounding like C, or D, or P, or T, or V, over the telephone; so he has perverted the English language to his own uses. He calls B 'Beer', and D 'Don', and so on.
(*Ian Hay,* Carrying on After the First Hundred Thousand, *1918*)

British Army 'Signalese' 1916

Ack	Nuts
Beer	Oranges
Charlie	Pip
Don	Queen
Edward	Robert
Freddie	Esses
Gee	Toc
Harry	Uncle
Ink	Vic
Johnnie	William
King	X-Ray
London	Yorker
Emma	Zebra

Some phonetic abbreviations

Ack Ack: Anti-aircraft guns
Ack Emma: AM (morning)
Ack Pip Emma: APM, Army Provost Marshall
Don Rs: Despatch Riders
Emma Gees: Machine guns

Emma Pip: MP, Military Police
Esses Emma: SM, Sergeant Major
O Pip: Observation Post
Pip Emma: PM (afternoon)
Toc Emmas: Trench Mortars

O pip, O pip on the tree top,
'Wind up,' 'wind up' when the shells drop,
Feeling you're due for the region of stars
Courage, O courage!
Observer from Mars
(Nursery-rhymes up-to-date, *Pte J. McSkimming, 32nd Div.*
HQ, Blighty, Summer Number, *1917*)

TERMINOLOGY, FOR STORES, OFFICIAL

Official terminology relating to stores and uniforms, all items given in the *Lists of Changes* which specified the current patterns to be adhered to at a given interval, had a peculiar means of listing the objects, starting with the object itself, then giving its decriptors separated by commas; army manuals had for decades been using convoluted descriptions of equipment such as 'Tools, artificers', small-arm cart, sets of' (*Manual for Regimental Transport*, 1877).

One thing you must never do in wartime is to call a thing by its real name.
To take a hackneyed example, you do not call a spade a spade;
you refer to it, officialy, as Shovels, General Service, One.
(*Ian Hay*, Carrying on After the First Hundred Thousand, *1918*)

PERSONAL CLOTHING, INFANTRY OF THE LINE
Boots, ankle
Cap, service dress
Drawers, woollen
Helmet, Wolseley pattern, with chin strap, cover, badge and bag
Jacket, service dress
Shoes, canvas
Trousers, service dress
Waistcoat, cardigan
(Regulations for the Clothing of the Army, *1914*)

Everyone is wearing 'boots, trench, gum, thigh'
(*Captain A.J. Dawson*, A Temporary Gentleman in France, *1916*)

FIELD SERVICE POSTCARD

The humble Field Service Postcard (also known as a 'whizz bang') was a means of getting a simple message home without having to go to the trouble of writing a long letter. Supplied by the military authorities (often in advance of offensives), all the sender had to do was cross out a few lines in order to get his message across, usually expressing the view that all was fine, and that 'letter follows at earliest opportunity'. Some provided more worry, however, with the sender in hospital, sick or wounded. Millions were sent (and parodied widely). In the Second World War they would become 'Reassurance Cards'.

Field Post Card – A card on which Tommy is allowed to tell his family and friends that he is alive; if he is dead the War Office sends a card, sometimes.
(Arthur Guy Empey, *Over The Top*, 1917)

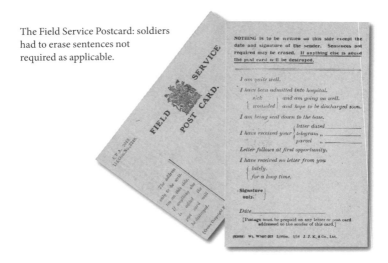

The Field Service Postcard: soldiers had to erase sentences not required as applicable.

GREEN ENVELOPE

Soldiers' mail home was subject to censorship; every letter of every postcard written home was read by an officer who would delete any words deemed likely to give the enemy knowledge of location or troop movements. Such passages were struck out with a 'blue pencil', with both the letter and its envelope signed by the officer. For soldiers seeking some level of intimacy, 'green envelopes' were issued, albeit rarely. These required the soldier to sign 'on his honour' that the letter inside would not contain anything of military importance. In ANZAC slang, a green envelope was either this official envelope, or anything cheap.

> Do you think I say too much, considering the signature on the green envelope? I am always afraid I do, but I say nothing of value to the enemy. I do rather 'translate the order generously' though; but what am I to do? I must tell you all I can, to let you know vaguely what is what. Of course I wouldn't 'give anything away' in a green one, which is really the spirit of the declaration.
> (Pte Donald McNair, Devonshire Regiment, letter home from Gaza, 27 October 1917)

ARMY POST OFFICE STAMPS (CACHETS)
(Used on envelopes that could not be delivered)

KILLED IN ACTION
RETURN TO SENDER
INVALIDED TO ENGLAND
NOT TO BE FOUND
PRESENT LOCATION UNCERTAIN
PRESENT LOCATION UNKNOWN
PRISONER OF WAR
RETURN TO SENDER
UNABLE TO TRACE

Alistair Kennedy and George Crabb, *Postal History of the British Army in World War 1*, 1977

OFFICIAL TERMS FOR DEATH

Official expressions stated that soldiers 'fell' (known from the sixteenth century), 'made the supreme sacrifice', were 'killed in action' (KIA) and 'gave their lives'; 'died of wounds' (DoW) was much more to the point.

WORDS AT WAR

For many of the combatants on the Western Front (apart from the French, fighting on their own soil), the war was the first time they had been in a foreign country. Of all the aspects of being abroad, the language difference was the most noticeable; foreign words, encountered at home in the conversation or shop signs of immigrants, were suddenly everywhere, and were enthusiastically tried out, altered and adopted. Everywhere that British soldiers came into contact with speakers of other languages, in the Indian subcontinent, Africa and the Middle East, they had taken up words for food, clothing, and artefacts. Several of these words, already in use among NCOs, were heard in France and Belgium for the first time by soldiers from Inverness, Rotherham or Barnstaple. Life as a prisoner of war also inevitably meant picking up some German expressions, though meaning changes and refusals to use German words were equally part of the experience. *Achtung* was resolutely rendered as 'Ack-Dum' (A and D in signalese), while *ersatz*, literally 'replacement', came to mean 'cheap substitute'.

The front was a linguistic melting point, mixing the dialects of different regions and classes of the UK, but also bringing words from languages as diverse as Russian, French, Urdu, Bengali, Arabic, Greek and Hindi, into common use among British soldiers.

AUSTRALIAN SLANG

Australians were noted for their inventiveness with words, 'stoush' for a 'fight' being developed into 'reinstoushments', and *bon* developing into 'bonsterina' and 'bontosher'. There was a noted disregard for sentimentality in Australian slang, as well as a fierce wit, as seen in these examples.

Abdominal and **gutzer** – a belly-down plane crash (from swimming)

Anzac soup – shell-hole water polluted by a corpse

A Belgium – a fatal wound

Breadwinner – rifle

Christen the squirt – first use of a particular bayonet to kill an enemy soldier

Chuck it up – surrender (hands raised; also 'chuck one up' – meaning to salute)

Deep thinker – a soldier enlisting late, compared to the 'Tourists', or '6/- a day tourists', the 1st Division, who supposedly thought that enlisting gave them a chance to travel, not expecting to fight; and the 'Dinkums', the 2nd Division, who were 'genuinely fighting for Australia'.

Domino – to kill

Fanny Durack or **Annette Kellerman** – the leaning statue of the Virgin on the Basilica at Albert in Belgium (Fanny Durack was Australian diving and swimming champion 1910–18, Annette Kellermann a champion diver)

Flybog – jam

Fresh faces in Hell – the comment after a successful attack on a German position

Gasometer – gas mask

Junker – superior officer (from the German term for nobility)

Methusilier – troops too old for combat duties

Nail-scissors – symbol of crossed swords denoting rank of general

Noah's doves, olive branches – troops on the way to Europe at the time the Armistice was signed

Round feet – trench-foot, which caused the feet to swell

Send her down, Steve/Hughie – please carry on raining (to postpone a parade), but also a comment on the rain generally

W.H. Downing, *Digger Dialects*, 1919 & *Glossary of Slang and Peculiar Terms in Use in the A.I.F.*, 1921–24

NORTH AMERICAN SLANG

From Canada and later the USA, words were quickly recognised by British soldiers and sometimes absorbed into their own speech. Canadian slang gave British English the familiar 'swipe', for acquiring something by less than openhanded means, while the British 'thingumyjig' was the Canadian 'hooza-ma-kloo'. The familiar term for an American soldier, a 'doughboy', comes from the American Civil War, a nickname which, according to Eric Partridge, originated from the shape of buttons worn by the Regular Army, which were supposed to resemble a kind of biscuit called a 'doughboy' (though it is also alleged that the term originated from the dusty state of their uniforms in the Spanish-American War). American slang also brought 'cooler' and 'boob' for 'prison', 'clabber' for 'clobber', 'to bum something up', meaning 'to boast about', and 'I'm your meat', meaning 'I'm your man'.

AFRIKAANS

Though the Boer War, known then as the South African War (1898–1901), was the most recent war the British Army had been engaged in, hardly any words from Afrikaans or indigenous languages entered common usage through contact at the end of the nineteenth century. One possible example is 'pozzy', meaning 'jam', which was in use by 1884, though jam was not a Regular Army food by then; 'pozzy' was an indigenous South African word for 'preserves'. From the *Glossary of Slang and Peculiar Terms in Use in the A.I.F.*, the term 'slanter', from the Afrikaans *schlenter*, meaning 'false play, deceit', was common among Australian and presumably South African troops.

HINDI AND URDU

A large number of words entered army lingo during the nineteenth century from the army stationed in India; many of these words remained easily identifiable. The most famous of all is 'Blighty', derived from *bilati*, meaning 'foreign', which, when applied by Indians to Britons, came to be perceived by Indian Army servicemen as the term 'British'. From the same root as *bilati* was the Arabic *wilayati*, meaning 'governmental' (the Arabic *wiliyat* meant 'government'). The famous 'Hobson Jobson' *Anglo-Indian Dictionary* states that *biliyati* or *wilyati* 'is applied to a variety of exotic articles'.

Khaki was another term that had been in military use in the British Army for some time by 1914; derived from the Persian Urdu word *khak*, meaning 'dust', it was known from about 1870.

> *January 26th, 1915. Talking of slang, the Tommies' name for England is 'Blighty'. This puzzled me for a bit, till I remembered one of Kipling's stories in which 'Belait' occurs as a Hindustanee word for Europe. I suppose they brought it from India.*
> (A Soldiers Diary of the Great War, *1929*)

OTHER WORDS FROM HINDI INCLUDE:

Boberje, bomerjee, and other variants – adapted from the Hindi word *bawarchi*, meaning 'cook'

Bondook, bandook, bundook – for 'rifle' was Indian Army slang from the nineteenth century, from the similar-sounding Hindi word; it was possibly reinforced by awareness of the similar Swahili word *bunduki*

Chokey – from *chauki* ('a shed', becoming 'a watch-house or lock-up'), old slang for 'a prison'

Cushy – 'pleasant' or 'comfortable', from *khush* ('pleasure'). 'Cushy was widely used: cushy billets (comfortable), cushy trenches (in quiet sectors), 'All Very Cushy', the nickname for the Army Veterinary Corps.

Dixie or dixey – the large ration cookpot, was adopted in India from the Hindi *degchi*

Hookem – in the phrase 'That's the Hookem', meaning 'That's the rules' (*Hukam* was Hindi for 'order')

Kutcha – Hindi *kachcha*, meaning 'crude or unfinished' became 'kutcha', meaning 'unsubstantial, temporary', the opposite of 'pucka', of longstanding Indian Army use, where a Kutcha Major was a brevet major, while a Pucka Major was a regimental major. The jam-tin bomb was described by F.C. Hitchcock (*Stand To*, 1936) as 'a very "kutcha" show'. In Mesopotamia a 'kutcha' was a mule

Muckin – Butter, from Hindi *makhan*

Pawnee – water
Puttee – from the Hindi *patti*, 'a bandage', adopted in the 1880s
Roti (often 'rooty') – bread
Wallah – from *wala*, meaning 'belonging to', which gave a whole range of applications. In use during 1914–18 were 'Lewis-gun wallah', 'amen-wallah' (priest), and 'staff-wallah'; generally 'wallah' tended to be used less by ORs than by officers

---

As a protest against men sent into the Army being placed by the authorities in what were described as 'cushy jobs' the Gravesend Local Tribunal went on strike seven weeks ago.

The Times, *4 September 1917*

ARABIC

British involvement in Egypt brought a lot of Arabic words into army slang:

Backshish or buckshee – reinforced by its rhyme, meant 'free', but also 'fake'. It was used at least as early as 1915

Buckshee, meaning free or gratuitous, is, I suppose, the same as 'baksheesh.
(A Soldier's Diary of the Great War, *1929*)

Bint – meaning 'girl', from the Arabic word for 'daughter', which had been used in English since the mid-nineteenth century. To 'go binting' meant to go on leave to Cairo to get a girl
Burgoo or burgue – 'oatmeal porridge', was used in the navy, from the Arabic *burghul*. The term was mostly obsolete by 1897, but survived in the Regular Army and, according to Eric Partridge, 'had a very vigorous life in 1914–18'

Calm Laylas – the name given to the Egyptian Labour Corps, from the song 'Kam Layla, Kam Yom', translated roughly as 'How many nights, how many days'

Iggri – quickly

Imshi – 'go' or 'scram'

Mafeesh – from the Arabic for 'there is nothing', had originated as the reply to 'backshish', a request for money, but during the war became a term for 'dead'

Maleesh – from the Arabic *ma alay-s*, meaning 'it doesn't matter', widely used on the Eastern Mediterranean fronts

Mungaree – a word used by Egyptians, apparently thinking it meant 'food' ('I'm hungry', spoken on seeing food); it was adopted back into English as a slang word for 'food'. The word 'paltan' had functioned in the same way, as a local pronunciation of 'battalion', being adopted as slang by British troops

BACSHICHE?

'Bacshiche';
postcard from
c. 1917.

YIDDISH

'Clobber', which grew from meaning just 'clothes' to 'equipment' by the end of the war, came from Yiddish (for a long time many of the urban poor had bought secondhand clothes from Jewish vendors). The term 'shemozzle' was also in use for 'a disturbance', from the Yiddish *shlemazl* meaning 'misfortune'. An article in the *Manchester Guardian*, 23 July 1918, pointed out that thieves' slang, some of it from Yiddish, had entered army slang, giving the example 'snider', a counterfeiter, from *schneider*. Through its inclusion in the song *Belgium Put the Kibosh on the Kaiser*, the word 'kibosh' or 'kybosh' became firmly associated with the conflict. Known from the 1830s, this word's origin is contested, but it may have come from the Yiddish *kabas* or *kabbasten*, meaning 'to suppress'.

RUSSIAN

Contact was frequent between Britain and her ally Russia throughout the war. Regular though scattered contact with Russian troops brought a few words into army slang; 'Spassiba', 'thanks', was adopted early on. There was a noted increase after 1918 when British troops were stationed in Russia during the campaign of 1918–20.

Russian words and phrases picked up most likely at this time include:
Barishnya – woman
Dobra and **niet dobra** – close approximations to the Russian for 'good' and 'no good'
Pozhalstya – please
Starie chelevek – old man (i.e. 'C.O.')
Xaroshie – very good
Yah ne panemiyu – I don't understand
Zdrast – good health

FLEMISH

Given the large number of British troops stationed on Belgian soil, in an area where Flemish was the local language, very few Flemish words made their way into English. Partly, this was because of the difficulty in understanding and pronouncing Flemish. The rapidity with which Flemish place names were anglicised through the process of folk-etymology, making the unrecognisable or unpronounceable term recognisable and pronounceable, is an indication of how British soldiers dealt with this: Ploegsteert became Plugstreet, Wytshaete became White Sheet and Dikkebus became Dickybus.

Apart from the difficulty in understanding Flemish, there was also a possible perception that it was close to German, and indeed one ideological stance taken during the war by the German authorities was that they were 'protecting their Flemish brothers from French oppression', and that German soldiers should speak Flemish to the occupied Belgians rather than French (*German Soldier Newspapers of the First World War*, R.L. Nelson).

However, a large number of words in use in the army had their roots in Flemish or the closely related Dutch (Flemish is often referred to as a Belgian dialect of Dutch), in some cases dating back to military contact in the sixteenth centuries when English troops were involved in wars in the then Spanish Netherlands. These words include: 'bantam', from Java via Dutch colonial trade; 'furlough', from the Dutch *verlof*, first adopted in the 1630s; 'gas', the word invented by the Dutch chemist J.B. Van Helmont in 1652; 'knapsack', in use by soldiers from the 1640s; 'tattoo', from Dutch words indicating that the tavern taps were to be closed; 'wagon', adopted in the sixteenth century as a term for a military vehicle; and more generally 'loiter', 'kink' and 'splinter'. 'Piots' for 'soldiers', the Flemish equivalent of Tommies, was used rarely, but was picked up by the British press at the beginning of the war when public interest in the Belgian Army was at its height.

Flemish-speaking refugees (i.e. the majority of the quarter of a million Belgian refugees who arrived in Britain) caused the refugee committees and government departments some difficulties: many of the refugees were educated to only an elementary level, few officials of the Local Government Board (responsible for co-ordinating the settlement of refugees) spoke Flemish, and, as the Report of the Central Register of Belgian Refugees put it, there was a 'Shakespearean tendency of the Flemish peasant to spell his surname differently on any occasion that arose for spelling it'. The *Ilford Recorder*, 16 October 1914, wrote that 'the task of succour is a difficult one. The victims are of another race, speaking an alien language, and in other ways differentiated from our own.' Nevertheless, there was some attempt to grapple with the Flemish language, with an Ilford barber offering free haircuts to Belgian refugees in a notice written both in English and Flemish.

FRENCH

Words were adopted from French in a number of different ways – through contact with French troops, officials, trade with locals, through billeting and estaminets, brothels and shops, through place names and transport terms, and through the survival and revival of schoolboy French. 'In the British Army Zone a sort of bastard neutral language is springing up, neither French nor English, but odds and ends and leavings of the same' (*A Soldier's Diary of the Great War*, 1929). As an example of this movement of terms, the *Manchester Guardian* on 20 April 1915 noted that the term 'émbusqués' was used by the French to describe those who tried to avoid work or duty at the front – literally meaning 'ambushing' or 'in a bush', the term was translated as 'waiting' rather than 'lying in wait'; somehow the sound of this was anglicised as 'umbrella men'. For the French, the equivalent English term, 'doing a Cuthbert', must have been equally mystifying.

No compree: Tommy's French.

Vague attempts at French pronunciation:

Apree Ler Gare Finee – (based on experience), never
Couchay – coucher (sleep)
Compree – compris (understood)
Cum-sah – comme ça (like that)
Finny – fini (finished)
Hissy – Ici (here)
Sava – Ça va (OK)
Say-pah – je ne sais pas (I don't know)
Shamun dafar – chemin de fer (railway)
Vanblanc anglays – 'English white wine' (whisky)
Van blang – vin blanc
Vent a tair – ventre à terre (at great speed)

Jokey Anglicisations

Aunt Mary Ann / Sanfaryan / Tabby an – ça ne fait rien (it doesn't matter)
Beans – bon/bien (good/well)
Buckoo – beaucoups (lots)
Cat-sow – quatre sous (four sous)
Come on tally plonk? – comment allez vous? (how are you?)
Delloo – de l'eau (water)
Gas gong – garçon (boy)
Hencore – encore (repeat)
Japan / Dupang – du pain (bread)
Mercy blow through / mercy manure – merci beaucoup (thanks)
Mungy – manger (eat)
Nitchivoo / Napoo / Narpoo – il n'y a plus (there's none left)
No bon – non bon – pas bon (no good)
Onk – franc
Party – partir (leave)
Plinkety Plonk / Point Blank – vin blanc
Selvooplonk – s'il vous plait (please)

Tooter the sweeter – tout de suite (as soon as possible)
Trez beans – trez bon/bien (very good/well)
Von blink – vin blanc (so 'von blinked' meant 'drunk')

> My company commander ... strove to pacify me by telling me that
> England was a 'no bon' just now – Devil a drink could a man get at a
> reasonable hour, and all the nicest girls were nursing.
> (Cinque Ports Gazette, *May 1916*)

German use of French

Graff and Bormann's *Schwere Brocken, 1000 Worte Front-Deutsch*
(1925) and Karl Bergmann's *Wie der Feldgraue Spricht* (1916) demon-
strate that German trench-slang developed its own versions of French
– *Parlewuh* (*parlez-vouz*, a French person), *Ohlala* and *Wulewuh*
(*voulez-vous*) (also a French person), *naplü* ('narpoo'), and *Tulemong*
(*tout le monde*, the French, particularly used in French attacks).

'Napoo'

Probably the French term most used by the British Army, 'napoo' or
'narpoo' had a wide range of applications to do with 'finished', 'none
left', 'dead' and 'empty'. According to Ernest Weekley it was also used
to close a discussion in indefinite fashion, as in the *Pall Mall Gazette*
February 1917 pushing for 'not the napoo victory ensuing from neutral pressure and semi-starvation, but the full decisive military victory.'
For the Germans a *naplü* was a beer, and a *naplüchen* ('a little *naplü*')
was a cognac, both clearly in short supply.

> October 3rd, 1915. The Jocks' French is sometimes very funny. The expression
> 'n'a plus' (short for 'il n'y a plus'), used by the little shopkeepers to
> mean they are out of stock in some article, is rendered in the soldiers'
> letters (which I have to censor) as 'na-poo' or 'napu.'
> (A Soldier's Diary of the Great War, *1929*)

Old Major Hubbard went to the cupboard
Of souvenirs he'd quite a few
But a Mills bomb in there went off with a glare
And now the old Major's napoo
(*F.T. Nettleingham,* More Tommy's Tunes, *1918*)

About 15 minutes from the finish the Warwick forwards scored twice
through well-placed shots. And so we had to 'napoo'.
(*Report of a football match in the* Cinque Ports Gazette,
magazine of the 5th Royal Sussex Regiment, May 1916)

This year – to use a common language – motor touring
in France to the south of Paris is *narpoo*.

The Times, *25 March 1919*

AFTERWORD

'Daddy, what did YOU do in the Great War?' The staring face with its mouth tight shut stares out from the recruiting poster, but might equally serve for the soldier who returned home after three or more years of experience that beggared description. The man or woman who 'never spoke about the war' is one of the great motifs of the war and its aftermath, one of the major cultural symbols of the horror, the stoicism, the inexplicability of it. And as the culture of the war then and since has been to such an extent a verbal culture, this notable absence of words needs to be considered. To what extent was the silence engendered by the soldiers, to what extent was there pressure on them to remain silent, and to what extent was there a passive drift into leaving part of the experience behind? A number of ideas and proposals have been put forward which may be considered briefly, all of them contextualising and giving some meaning to this phenomenon.

One context concerns the social aspect of the body in the 1910s and 1920s. A growing coyness with regard to bodily functions had developed through the nineteenth century, with the improvements in public health and domestic sanitation leading to greater privacy. By the end of the war, the soldier's relationship to his body at the front was vastly different from that relationship at home, with totally different expectations of decorum and decency. Many soldiers coming from a kind of home where the choice between the words 'toilet' and 'lavatory' acted as a marker of class, returned from the war where a latrine was a bucket in a recess in the trench wall, and the job of 'sanitary-man' was envied as it took men away from the fire trench. The hiatus between the physical contexts of trench and home was unavoidable.

A culture of control over written communication had developed during the war, the civilian army finding their letters censored for the first time, and the press knowing that information was being withheld. The various updates of the Defence of the Realm Act (DORA) left people unsure of what they could or could not say, as dissent was prosecuted, and the 1916 wording made a criminal offence out of 'any expression of opposition to, or criticism of, the war in any art form'. In this environment, with press positively encouraging the prosecution of the war, together with such phenomena as the Order of the White Feather, there was considerable pressure not to express negative feelings. Even the 'Are we downhearted?' exchange, whether eliciting 'yes' or 'no', implied acknowledgement of the positive as the default position. Talking of war experiences which would cause people to doubt the worth of pursuing the war, and leave them feeling that the costs were too high, was not an easy course; a pragmatic response was that of silence. That silent pragmatism had a very clear model in the trenches; the story of the dead soldier's leg sticking out of the side of the trench being used as a hook for equipment is found repeatedly. Soldiers at the front groused but did not mutiny; at the Somme and in other battles they kept on walking towards the machine guns, leaning forward as if walking into a rainstorm.

Another proposal is that soldiers just did not know how to talk about what they had experienced. The absence of slang terms for major injuries – the slicing away of parts of the body by shrapnel – or even codes similar to those used in communiqués implies that these could only be expressed in clinical or literary terms, or not at all. Around ten years after the war, a spate of books appeared which explored the 'pornography' of war, but at the time of the war this was avoided; compare 'a Mills bomb would blow seven men to rags' from Charles Edmonds' *A Subaltern's War* (1929) with 'concerning their actual killing exploits the men were absurdly reticent' from *Troddles in the Trenches* by R. Andom, printed for *Newne's Trench Library* (1919). But for many people trying to describe the smells, sounds and sights of the front there were only words that described degrees of badness; it was 'beyond description' (H.H. Cooper), 'utterly undescribable' (Paul Nash), 'terrible' (Gunner Leonard Ounsworth), 'the stench and the flies were simply appalling' (Lt M. Cleeve).

A repeated motif in trench papers is the idea of the front as 'home', where the soldier belongs; Blighty is difficult, 'no bon', not what it should be. For Robert Graves 'home was awful because you were with people who didn't understand what this was all about'. Despite previous entries in Cpl J. Bemner's diary saying 'off I go on leave', 'have a grand time' and 'still enjoying myself', when he returns he is 'not quite over my leave yet', and three days later, 'I am beginning to feel all right again after leave' (6 August 1915). A poem, 'On Leave', in the *Depot*

Review No.5, begins:

> I wanter get back from the war news
> I wanter get back to the Hun;
> I wanter retreat from the chaps in the street
> Oo know how the war should be won ...

Erich Maria Remarque summarised this view in *All Quiet on the Western Front* (1929): 'I do not belong here any more, it is a foreign world.' Silence maintained that space, the front as home; it could be talked about with other soldiers, who would fill in the gaps of the indescribable with their own knowledge, but those who had not been there could not.

Cultural mores of the time praised reticence. Sangfroid was employed and no doubt felt at all levels – 'nothing makes you feel madder than being fired at when doing a job that has to be done slowly and carefully, such as insulating the wire after baring the cable and joining the ends. A man who has been fouled at footer has the same feeling', wrote C.W. Langley in *Battery Flashes* (1916). What seems now to be a crippling refusal to face emotional reality was indeed the reality of the time; holding one's nerve could be reflected back as bravery, increasing self-esteem and status. Rudyard Kipling, devastated in private by the death of his son at the front, mentioned his name in passing in one sentence in his two-volume *The Irish Guards in the Great War* (1923). Arnold Bennett supposedly felt his war experiences too deeply to be able to write about them, presumably feeling that dignified reticence was more important than the risk of embarrassing himself by too much emotion. Charles Edmonds wrote in *An Essay on Militarism* (1929) 'about these sensations [boredom and comradeship] soldiers have been tongue-tied ... the typical soldier has held his tongue, vaguely disliking the character that has been thrust on him.' In the face of difficulty, silence was the expected and praiseworthy position.

For those whose experiences were a cause of distress in forms ranging from shell shock to grief at the loss of friends or brothers, the 'talking cure' was barely an option. Those who declared themselves unable to cope were more likely to be treated as malingerers than victims, and with the exception of doctors such as W.H. Rivers and Arthur Brock at Craiglockhart, there were few who explored the verbal expression of trauma. For shell shock victims, treatment up to

1917 had involved being forbidden to talk about the war. In the case of one officer treated by W.H. Rivers at Craiglockhart, 'he said at once that it was obvious to him that memories such as those he had brought with him from the war could never be forgotten. Nevertheless, since he had been told by everyone that it was his duty to forget them he had done his utmost in this direction.' This view proposed essentially that silence was a way to settle the mind, that undesirable memories could be replaced by pleasant open-air activities. An advertisement in the *Pall Mall Gazette*, 8 May 1919, read: 'So bury all those unpleasant memories in Dora's waiting grave (no flowers by unanimous vote) and get your Austin Reed straw hat to signalise the event.'

Henri Barbusse's *Under Fire* was published in 1916 and quickly translated into English. It was very widely read on both sides of the front, and became an exemplar of writing about the physical side of the war; a 1917 reviewer in the *Manchester Guardian* wrote that Barbusse's world 'is that of which we only hear in the whispers that from time to time ruffle the smooth agreement by which the "horrors of war" are taken for granted but ... mercifully concealed.' But the majority of the novels and poems which verbally explored the 'pornography' of the body's destruction were not published until some years after 1918: the translation of Erich Remarque's *All Quiet On The Western Front* (1929), Robert Graves' *Goodbye To All That* (1929), Charles Edmonds' *A Subaltern's War* (1929), Helen Z. Smith's *Not So Quiet...* (1930), Frederic Manning's *Her Privates We* (1930) and Siegfried Sassoon's *Memoirs of an Infantry Officer* (1930) – in fact over sixty books on the war were published in these two years. T.S. Hope's *The Winding Road Unfolds* (1937) is one of the most graphic, as war-related books continued to be published through the 1930s. For Graves, *Goodbye To All That* was, as the title states, an attempt to set down his memories in a 'formal goodbye': 'once this has been settled in my mind and written down and published it need never be thought about again.' The implications of this are that the interim silence was as much about 'holding on' as 'holding in'. The ten-year gap before the rush of publications of war memoirs with details of trench fighting was a deliberate silence, with writers and publishers no doubt waiting until the time was right, but then broken with a tumult of descriptions of violent death.

The extent of grief following the war was a disincentive to speaking about it. With every family affected by the death of immediate or close relatives, any spoken reminiscences would potentially cause distress. In *Not So Quiet ...*, Helen Z. Smith describes the traditional attitude towards soldiers as sentimentalising them during the war, and starving them afterwards. While many ex-servicemen and women did face poverty and unemployment after 1918, any talk about the war would only emphasise the absence of loved ones. Those who noted that their fathers 'did not speak about the war' often observed the lapses into silence, the 'thousand-yard stare' or 'a vacant look', all of them characterised by something to do with absence. Common to all these experiences is an absence or a silence, and it is seen also in the major war memorials: the empty tomb of the Cenotaph, the absent name of the Unknown Warrior, the open space in the centre of the major architectural memorials in France and Belgium, at Vimy, Thiepval and the Menin Gate; and most of all in the two minutes' silence. The 'empty space in the centre' became the defining motif of memorialising the war, and the absence of words is at the centre of this.

There is one final proposal, largely implicit in most of the others, that the people who were not there just did not want to hear. While relatives often needed details of time and place in order to make meaning out of their loss, did they want to know that the loved one's body had been blown apart or lain rotting unburied for days? For those who had been outraged by the atrocity stories in 1914 and picked up fragments of horror stories over the following four years, was there any desire to hear more? W.H. Rivers at Craiglockhart Hospital for victims of shell shock was clearly aware that two conflicting positions were apparent, both socially and operating within the mind of the soldier. There was the 'natural tendency to repress, being in my experience almost universally fostered by their relatives and friends', but at the same time he noted: 'Nothing annoys a nervous patient more than the continual inquiries of his relatives and friends about his experiences of the front, not only because it awakens painful memories, but also because of the obvious futility of most of the questions and the hopelessness of bringing the realities home to his hearers' (*The Repression of War Experience*, W.H. Rivers, presented to the Royal School of Medicine, 4 December 1917). For John Brophy, writing in 1965, 'for the men who survived it, it became in retrospect an experience to be thrust out of memory most of the time, an experience impossible for the mind to digest, and, for many, tolerable only when some of the less distressing events were selected for recall and dressed up with sentimental emotions.' For the core of the experience, there were no words.